THE POSSESSION AT LOUDUN

MICHEL DE CERTEAU

THE POSSESSION
AT LOUDUN

Translated by Michael B. Smith

With a Foreword by Stephen Greenblatt

THE UNIVERSITY OF CHICAGO PRESS

Chicago & London

At the time of his death in 1986, Michel de Certeau was a director of studies at the École des hautes études en sciences sociales, Paris. He was author of eighteen books in French, three of which have appeared in English translation as *The Practice of Everyday Life, The Writing of History,* and *The Mystic Fable, Volume 1,* the last of which is published by The University of Chicago Press.

The University of Chicago Press, Chicago 60637
The University of Chicago Press, Ltd., London
© 1996, 2000 by The University of Chicago
All rights reserved. Published 2000
Printed in the United States of America
09 08 07 06 05 04 03 02 01 00   5 4 3 2 1

ISBN (cloth): 0-226-10034-0
ISBN (paper): 0-226-10035-9

Originally published as *La Possession de Loudun,* © Julliard, 1970; Gallimard/Julliard, 1990.

Library of Congress Cataloging-in-Publication Data

Certeau, Michel de.
    [Possession de Loudun. English]
    The possession at Loudun / Michel de Certeau ; translated by Michael B. Smith ; with a foreword by Stephen Greenblatt.
        p.   cm.
    Includes bibliographical references and index.
    ISBN 0-226-10034-0 (alk. paper) — ISBN 0-226-10035-9 (pbk. : alk. paper)
    1. Demoniac possession—France—Loudun—History—17th century.   2. Couvent des Ursulines (Loudun, France)—History—17th century.   3. Grandier, Urbain, 1590–1634.   4. Loudun (France)—Church history—17th century.   I. Title.
BF1517.F5 C4713   2000
133.4′26′094463—dc21

                                                                        99-088078

∼ Contents ∼

List of Illustrations   vii

Foreword *by Stephen Greenblatt*   ix

Translator's Acknowledgments   xiii

History Is Never Sure   1

1   How a Possession Is Born   11

2   The Magic Circle   23

3   The Discourse of Possession   35

4   The Accused: Urbain Grandier   52

5   Politics in Loudun: Laubardemont   65

6   Beginning the Judicial Inquiry   77

7   The Theater of the Possessed   85

8   The Medical Eye   109

9   A Teratology of Truth   122
          I. THE IMAGINATION   122
          II. THE LIAR   138

10   The Judgment of the Sorcerer   152

11   The Execution: Legend and History   171

12   After Death, Literature   181

13   The Time of Spirituality: Father Surin   199

14   The Triumph of Jeanne des Anges   213

Figures of the Other   227

Primary Sources and Bibliography   229

Notes   231

Index   245

∼ Illustrations ∼

Figures

1   The City of Loudun in the Seventeenth Century   28

2   Physicians in Loudun   112

3   Catholic Resistance against Loudun   153

4   Printed Material on Loudun (1633–39)   188

Plates *(following page 108)*

1–3   Christoph Haitzmann's dead father as the devil (1677–78)

4   Anon., frontispiece to *Livre des spectres,* by Pierre Le Loyer (1586)

5   Jacques Callot, *Tentation de Saint Antoine*

6   Anon., frontispiece to *Saducismus Triumphatus,* by John Glanville (1691)

7–8   Galle and Collaert, episodes from the life of Saint Ignatius (1609)

9   Anon., from John Bulwer, *Chirologia* (1644)

10   Wyerx, *Allegory of the Names of Jesus*

11–12   Gr. de Manderer, the *est* and the *non est*

13   Théodore de Bry, microcosm of the body (1629)

14   Anton Wierx, *Lingua index cordis*

15 Anon., from Robert Fludd, *Utriusque cosmi* . . . (1629)

16 Anon., *Sortie du Diable de La Rochelle*

17 Anon., allegory on Louis XIII (1617)

18 Anon., Jeanne des Anges

19 Anon., Asmodaeus' letter (1634)

20 Anon., Urbain Grandier

21 Anon., the judges of Loudun

22 Anon., *Interrogatoire de maistre Urbain Grandier* . . . (1634)

23 Anon., Mgr. de La Rocheposay (1615)

24 Anon., Father Surin

25 Anon., view of Loudun (1609)

26 René Allain, portrait from life representing . . .
  Urbain Grandier (1634)

27 Jean de la Noüe, effigy of the condemnation . . .
  of Urbain Grandier (1634)

28 Still from Kawalerowicz's *Mère Jeanne des Anges* (1960)

~ Foreword ~

For months after the great drama of possession and exorcism was over—after Urbain Grandier, the handsome, libertine priest accused of being a sorcerer, had been tried, tortured, and burned at the stake; after the chief exorcist J.-J. Surin had himself been afflicted by demons; after the crowds of the faithful, the skeptical, and the merely curious had stopped flocking to Loudun—the principal demoniac, the Reverend Mother Jeanne des Anges, toured all of France in order to display her hand. On its surface the demons, as they departed from her body, were compelled to inscribe the names of the mighty forces that had triumphed over them: Jesus, Maria, François de Sales. The prioress's hand caused a sensation. In 1637, at Lyon, Nevers, Grenoble, Annecy, Tours, Paris, and other cities in the realm, thousands flocked to bear witness to the miracle. From four in the morning until ten at night, with the aid of torches, the hand was on display, and special viewing arrangements were made in some places to accommodate the frenzied popular interest: "They put me in a low room," Jeanne des Anges recalled, "in which there was a window at a man's height that opened onto the courtyard of the house. I was seated, my arm on a pillow, and my hand was extended out the window, to be seen by the people. People of the first quality could not enter that room because the ways leading to it were blocked by the populace."

But, of course, people of the first quality did get their chance to pay homage to a hand miraculously "sculpted by the devil." Princes of the church and of the state, the nobility and high-ranking gentry, Queen Anne of Austria, Cardinal Richelieu, and King Louis XIII, all examined and wondered at the beautifully wrought letters. The wily, infinitely cynical Richelieu, looking at the hand attentively, declared, "Now this is admirable"; the king, with "joy on his face," said in a loud voice, "My belief is strengthened." So it went, and so it evidently continued even after the first wave of excitement had spent itself. For years later the prioress, now back in her convent, was still showing her hand. Then, in 1645, a visitor to Loudun, Mr. Balthasar de Monconys, did something unexpected: "With the tip of my fingernail, with a light touch I removed the leg of the *M* [of the word MARIA] which surprised her greatly. . . . I was satisfied with that and took my leave of her."

"I was satisfied with that": it is a tribute to Michel de Certeau, who gives this and still more devastating evidence of miserable fraud, that he is not so easily satisfied. *The Possession at Loudun* tells a deeper and remarkably resonant story that includes fraud and its willing victim, credulity, but ventures into abnormal psychology, epistemology, politics, medicine, mysticism, and theology. To be sure, the possessed nuns of Loudun are not news to English-speaking readers: there is Aldous Huxley's well-known book on the subject, *The Devils of Loudun,* and an important scholarly discussion in D. P. Walker's *Unclean Spirits,* along with Ken Russell's popular movie *The Devils.* But Certeau grasps what is at stake better than anyone who has written on the case. He understands in intimate detail not only its political and psychological dimensions, but also its place in the larger histories of spiritual torment and visionary hysteria. He is also the scholar who has delved most deeply into the part played by the amazing mystic-exorcist-demoniac Surin, a figure who continued to fascinate Certeau throughout his career.

The Possession at Loudun is an account of remarkably vivid individuals: Urbain Grandier, who had the misfortune of being too softly seductive and who went to his hideous death with astonishing fortitude; the Jesuit exorcist Surin, who whispered Latin discourses into the ear of the possessed nun only to succumb himself to demonic possession; Jeanne des Anges, who analyzed brilliantly her own psychological complicity in the blasphemy and grotesque writhing to which she spectacularly fell victim. These and many others, the saintly and the scurrilous, the expert witnesses and the gawking tourists, are brought before us on Certeau's stage, where they speak their own words. In the seventeenth century many of them were literally brought onto the stage that had been constructed in order to display to the public the edifying spectacle of the war between God and Satan. But, as the book deftly shows, it is a story not just of individuals but also of institutions: the Ursulines, the Jesuits, the hierarchies of the Catholic Church, the royal court, law courts, academies, medical schools. The whole complex, interlocking structure of French society in this period was touched, lightly but decisively, by the writhings of a group of young cloistered women in a small provincial town. And linked to these individuals and these institutions are obscure but momentous changes that Certeau brilliantly evokes: a glacial shift in the relation between the sacred and the profane; a last, perversely theatrical manifestation of a certain form of ancient faith; a closing of the borders between the natural and the fantastic; a murderous rearguard action against an epistemological transformation.

The Possession at Loudun is also a brilliant and innovative book in its form. It is, as the French edition puts it, "présentée" by Certeau. The book first appeared in a series called Collection Archive, under the general editorship of Pierre Nora and Jacques Revel. The volumes in this series set out to publish the "archive" of documents, many of them not reprinted since their first appearance, of famous cases or historiographical problems. At the same time, unlike many such editions of documents, this one does not simply present the materials in their "raw" form. On the contrary, with the erudition and subtlety for which he was justly famous, Certeau commented on, explicated, and tied together the documentary materials. On the page, his own voice was distinguished typographically from the others so that the nature of the documents themselves and the scholar's relation to these documents became part of the meaning of the story.

There is an underlying passion and pathos in this book, glimpsed most clearly perhaps in the author's richly ambivalent relation to Surin, but suffusing his entire account of the traumatic, grotesque events. Committed to justice, decency, and the unvarnished truth, Certeau has no interest in remystifying a shameful episode. On the contrary, he ruthlessly uncovers the tangle of bad faith, ignorant fanaticism, and conspiratorial lies—but he makes us feel the full force of what was at stake and what was in the process of being forever lost.

Although he was a complex thinker and often a difficult writer, Michel de Certeau wrote books and essays that have gradually come to be admired for their penetrating intelligence, meditative power, moral urgency, and originality. Here, because of the task he set for himself, his unique weaving together of Christian mysticism, strenuous political and sociological analysis, psychoanalysis, and scrupulous attentiveness to the voice of the Other is clearer and more easily grasped than anywhere else in his works. *The Possession at Loudun* is his most accessible book and one of his most wonderful.

STEPHEN GREENBLATT

∾ Translator's Acknowledgments ∾

I would like to thank Berry College for providing a haven for the accomplishment of this translation; Luce Girard, who checked the entire manuscript against the original and made many corrections and astute suggestions; Alisa Ray of Berry College's Faculty Research and Sponsored Programs; my former student Sam Crowe, for help with final manuscript preparation; medievalist and editor Lys Ann Shore; and Martha Reynolds of the Berry College Memorial Library. My wife Helen, as always, has sustained my efforts with her constant encouragement.

~ History Is Never Sure ~

Normally, strange things circulate discreetly below our streets. But a crisis will suffice for them to rise up, as if swollen by flood waters, pushing aside manhole covers, invading the cellars, then spreading through the towns. It always comes as a surprise when the nocturnal erupts into broad daylight. What it reveals is an underground existence, an inner resistance that has never been broken. This lurking force infiltrates the lines of tension within the society it threatens. Suddenly it magnifies them; using the means, the circuitry already in place, but reemploying them in the service of an anxiety that comes from afar, unanticipated. It breaks through barriers, flooding the social channels and opening new pathways that, once the flow of its passage has subsided, will leave behind a different landscape and a different order.

Is this the outbreak of something new, or the repetition of a past? The historian never knows which. For mythologies reappear, providing the eruption of strangeness with forms of expression prepared in advance, as it were, for that sudden inundation. These languages of social anxiety seem to reject both the limits of a present and the real conditions of its future. Like scars that mark for a new illness the spot of an earlier one, they designate in advance the signs and location of a flight (or return?) of time. Whence there arises that quality of time immemorial associated with the irregularities of history, as if they harked back to a beginning without a past, the dark recesses of an insecurity, a latent "singularity," revealed in the continuous plurality of events. But how valid is this impression, too quick to relate the facts to an atemporal neutrality? Can we so easily exile panic from history—make it into something outside or below history, or history's law?

A Diabolical Crisis

In the past, these strange movements have often taken the form of the diabolical. In societies that either are not, or have ceased to be, religious, they assume other faces. But the great resurgences of sorceries and possessions, such as the one that invaded Europe at the end of the sixteenth and the beginning of the seventeenth century, mark serious fault lines within a religious civilization, perhaps the last that could be expressed by means of the religious apparatus—the last rifts before a new beginning. They appear to signal an end that cannot yet be spoken—hence their eschatological character. They also betray an uncertainty before the future, the very expression of which becomes an object of panic and repression. They bear witness to a gap that they attempt to fill with the means (still religious) at hand. Entire groups are no longer sure about "obvious facts" that, though not susceptible of proof, were previously taken for granted by a social order and an organization of values. To what will people turn to escape these intolerably shifting sands? How can firm ground be found to replace those certainties now undermined by suspicion, those no longer credible resources and situations henceforth devoid of meaning? Deviltries are at once symptoms and transitional solutions.

The "diabolical" crisis has a double significance: it reveals the imbalance of a culture, and it accelerates the process of its mutation. It is not merely an object of historical curiosity. It is the confrontation (one among others, though more visible than others) of a society with the certainties it is losing and those it is attempting to acquire. All stability rests on unstable balances that are disturbed by every intervention intended to reinforce them. In specific social systems, witchcraft and possession make manifest—but in a wild, spectacular way—a sudden widening of a rift. These fault lines, ever in proportion to the culture in which they occur, take on different traits elsewhere. But in any case, history is never sure.

Loudun: A Theater

As W. Mühlmann has remarked, there are "times rich in demons."[1] That is the case of the sixteenth and the first half of the seventeenth century. The possession of Loudun is situated almost at the end of a long epidemic, and during the very years (1632–40) when reason took a brisk step forward with the publication of Descartes' *Discourse on Method* (1637). By then, deviltry had already taken on more subtle forms. It was a public forum in which tendencies of all kinds emerged, confronting one another with word and gesture. Possession became a great public trial: a confrontation between science and religion, a debate on what is certain and what uncertain, on reason, the supernatural, authority. This debate was orchestrated by an entire erudite literature and the popular press. It was a "theater" that attracted the curious from all of France and practically all of Europe, a circus "for the satisfaction of these gentlemen," according to the wording of many official transcripts of the day.

The show was staged in Loudun for almost ten years, and soon provided a center for edification, apologetics, pilgrimages, and pious or philanthropic associations. The diabolical was becoming commonplace. It was gradually becoming profitable. It was reintroduced in the language of a society, while at the same time continuing to perturb that society. In this story, the diabolical played the role set out for it by the rules of the already traditional *commedia dell'arte*. An evolution took place. The Devil, violent at first, was slowly becoming civilized. He would lead disputations. He was discussed. He would end up repeating himself monotonously. The horror was transformed into a spectacle, the spectacle into a sermon. True, there was still weeping and wailing during the exorcisms that continued to be carried out after the execution of "the sorcerer," Urbain Grandier, but that did not prevent the serving of snacks to the spectators who filled the churches.

Possession and Sorcery

In order to understand that evolution and this fragment of a particular history, we must first set it within a larger framework.

Possession is not the same thing as *sorcery*. The two phenomena are distinct, and they alternate with one another, even though many early treatises associate the two, and even mix them up. Sorcery (epidemics of sorcerers and sorceresses) comes first. It extends from the last quarter of the sixteenth century (1570, Denmark; 1575–90, Lorraine) to the first third of the seventeenth century (1625, Alsace; 1632, Würzburg; 1630 in Bamberg), with prolongations until 1663 in Massachusetts, 1650 in Neisse (Saxony), and 1685 in Meiningen (Saxony). It raged in France (Brittany, Franche-Comté, Lorraine, Alsace, Savoie, Poitou, Béarn, and so on), Germany (Bavaria, Prussia, Saxony), Switzerland, England, and the Netherlands, but not, it seems, in Spain or Italy (except in the northern and mountainous region of Como). During the period Lucien Febvre considered that of the great "psychological revolution," between

1590 and 1620,[2] sorcery seems to delineate two Europes: the northern, in which it abounds, and the southern, in which it is rare. One last trait, but one that is of great importance: sorcery is predominantly a rural phenomenon. Even if the courts involved carry out the major trials in the city, they are obliged to delegate commissioners and judges in the country (such as Boguet, de Lancre, Nicolas Remy, and so on).

A different species of the same genus comes after sorcery, existing side by side with it for a while, then superseding it: possession. It first appears, tentatively, in isolated female cases, such as those of Nicole Aubry, Jeanne Féry, and in particular Marthe Brossier (1599). Its model is established with the trial of Gaufridy in Aix-en-Provence (1609–11), immediately orchestrated by the book that was to circulate everywhere and define the new series: *Histoire admirable de la possession et conversion d'une pénitente . . .* , by Father Sébastien Michaelis (Paris, 1612). Other "possessions" would follow—Loudun especially (1632–40), Louviers (1642–47), Auxonne (1658–63), and so on. Each one invents on the basis of the initial schema, attracts its clientele, and propagates its own literature.

This species is no longer rural, but urban. It no longer takes the wild, massive, and bloody form of primitive sorcery. It focuses on a few star performers only. It reveals personal relations and psychologies (involving individuals or micro-groups). The social milieu it involves is higher and more homogeneous, the characters are of a more "middle" level, and there is less social difference between the judges and the accused, who henceforth understand one another and move within the same kind of discourse. The former binary structure (judges–sorcerers) becomes ternary, and it is the third term, the possessed women, that receives an increasing share of public attention: in other words, the women have become victims, and are no longer guilty. As for the sorcerers, they are frequently priests, physicians, or well-educated people, sometimes considered to be "libertine"; thus, they contravene in a new way the traditional or popular image of the curé, the chaplain, or the physician. With these new "sorcerers," it is still a secret lore that is considered threatening and treated as magic, but a modern lore, creating a different form of distance from the group.

Deviltry moves from violence directed against the magicians to a pitying curiosity for its victims. It is located in the convents, and no longer on the moors and in remote villages. It becomes less vengeful and punitive, but more apologetic and preachy, and changes from a "war" on the sorcerers to a spectacle that has about it something of the circus and something of the popular mission—even though the "show" continues

to require an execution. The "possession" thus constitutes a next step
in relation to sorcery. But it will lead in turn to the political trials of
women poisoners.

These two moments of deviltry constitute a single stage in a larger
ongoing evolution. On the one hand, the "diabolical" phenomenon will
embrace more cultural forms, expressing itself in literature and folklore,
and dissolving into popular astrology and "pastorals" in which many anti-
establishment themes survive. On the other hand, although it will ex-
pand, it will be transformed as it becomes politicized; the resistance of
the common folk will manifest itself in a panoply of new languages, from
riots to peddler pamphlets, though it will continue to be marginal.

The Marriage of Heaven and Hell

Whatever the case of these evolving phenomena, we must also emphasize
the instances of synchronic cohesion. One of these latter concerns religious history in particular. There is a connection in a great many cases,
as if by some strangely prearranged meeting, between the possessed or
the "possessionists" (those convinced of the reality of the possession)
and the communities of religious. On the map of mid-seventeenth-
century France, the cases of possession and the most "devout" (in the
most positive sense of the term) groups are often found in the same
places: Nancy, Évreux, and so forth. During its wild years, Loudun was
also a school of spirituality. At the center of that demonological fair,
for three years, Jean-Joseph Surin, one of the greatest mystics of the
seventeenth century, was present. He was at once the Don Quixote and
the Hölderlin of that "extraordinary adventure." The Devil's theaters are
also centers for the mystics.

This is no mere coincidence. A cultural transformation seems to mar-
ginalize all the expressions of the sacred, from the most suspect to the
purest. They are pushed to the same position in society—on its outer
limits. Similarly, shaken ecclesiastical institutions let in through their
cracks, and also exude, certain religious symptoms—a mixture, so to
speak, of the most archaic and the most radical elements (Surin noted
this). These symptoms are then suspected and frequently accused together of constituting one and the same social and doctrinal "heresy."

More fundamentally, Alfred Jarry is correct in saying about Loudun
that "possession by the Holy Spirit and by the devil are notably symmetri-
cal."[3] Both "possessions" present an analogous structure. In the modality
of contrary solutions, they respond to a problem of meaning, but stated
in terms of the formidable and constraining alternative—God or the

Devil—that isolates the quest for the absolute from social mediations. Mysticism and possession often form in the same pockets in a society whose language thickens, loses its spiritual porosity, and becomes impermeable to the divine. In such a case, the relation to a "beyond" vacillates between the immediacy of a diabolical seizure and the immediacy of a divine illumination. Jeanne des Anges herself, the most famous of the possessed, would appear afterward, during the last twenty-five years of her life, in the persona of a "mystic" visionary.

Metamorphoses of History

From this perspective there is a complicity and, to borrow a phrase from William Blake, a "marriage of heaven and hell." This is a characteristic trait of possession, which coincides with one of the themes of baroque art—metamorphosis. The instability of the characters, the reversals of experience, the uncertainty of limits indicate the mutation of a mental universe. Like the grotto in Florence in which Bernardo Buontalenti sculpted human bodies still indefinite in the primitive mud, which lets them emerge or pulls them back into it[4] (it is unclear which), so Loudun—tucked away in a French province, on the border between Catholic and Protestant convictions that oppose and relativize each other—constitutes a world poised between what is disappearing and what is beginning. Complex, at once savage and subtle, it is a place of instability. It may be defined as a point of passage. Here we find the anguish and ambition that are inseparable from society's shifting sands. Deep shifts are evident, revealed by the "metamorphoses of the Devil," dear to Henri Lefebvre.[5]

These metamorphoses—which can be deciphered through the series of episodes that constitutes, over almost a decade, the war of Loudun—extend into the successive interpretations given to the events. From the *libelli* of 1633 to the opera by Penderecki (*The Devils of Loudun,* 1969), an entire literature is devoted to them. It includes Alexandre Dumas, Alfred de Vigny, Jules Michelet, Aldous Huxley, and others. In different cultural spaces, the old debates serve new causes. Other wars transform the history of Loudun into the legend of a present. Yesterday's antagonists, mobilized by the participants in more recent conflicts, offer the latter a means of entering into a dialogue with their own devils. In part, historians perform the service to society of putting the vocabulary of a past at its disposal. The figures of former times become the eponymous heroes of a present.

The bibliography of Loudun is the history of this recycling. The theater of yesteryear is enlisted in new trials that assign to Urbain Grandier a whole series of roles. The "sorcerer" of yore is metamorphosed into a victim of Catholicism, a "precursor of free thinking,"[6] a prophet of the scientistic spirit, or a herald of the gospel of progress. His "adversaries" are promoted to similar but opposite destinies: Jeanne des Anges reappears as a martyr of persecuted Christianity; Surin, as a witness to a universal "magnetism" or to the "primordial fact"; the exorcists or Laubardemont as zealous servants of a "social" or political "order." . . . There is a history of the history of Loudun.

Visit Loudun

Even today you can visit Loudun, now diminished by two-thirds of its former inhabitants, shrunken down upon itself, its little streets clutching too many absences, too many phantoms. You will be instructed to follow, from the *palais de justice* to the church of Sainte-Croix, the "stations" staggered along the Hero's final journey, as if the town had rearranged its architecture into a way of the cross. Isolated spots reconstitute, thanks to the voice and gestures of the guide, the unfolding of a lost history: the room in which the death sentence was pronounced; the place where he fell the first time; the street-corner where "a monk" struck Grandier with a staff; the porch of the church of Saint-Pierre, in front of which the condemned man had to confess his misdeeds publicly, but was helped by Father Grillau, a good soul; and last of all, the square of Marché Sainte-Croix, for that is where, before the priest René Bernier, a good, repentant malefactor, and beneath the gaze of Louis Trincant, the persecutor insolently installed at his window, the Curé perished in the flames lit by his exorcists themselves. In the form of a walking tour, the quest for the past has taken the shape of a legend, and the itinerary has become a kind of initiation.

But what historical research does not set out from a *legend*? In providing itself with sources or criteria of information and interpretation, it defines in advance *what is to be read* in a given past. From this point of view, history moves together with the historian. It follows the flow of time. It is never sure.

A Book Divided

How could history be sure? History books begin with a present. They are constructed on the basis of two series of data: on the one hand, the "ideas" we have about a past, ideas that are still conveyed by old material, but along pathways blazed by a new mentality; on the other hand, documents and "archives," remains saved by chance, frozen in collections that attach meanings to them that are also new. Between the two, a difference makes it possible to disclose a historical distance, the way observation from two distant points made possible Le Verrier's *invention* of a planet as yet unknown.

It is within that "interspace" that this book on Loudun was formed. It is cracked from top to bottom, revealing the combination, or the relation, that makes history possible. Divided between commentary and archival sources, it refers to a reality that once had a living unity, and *no longer is*. It is, in short, broken by an absence. Its form is in proportion to what it tells: a past. That is why each of its halves says what is missing from the other, rather than its truth.

Archives of the Possession

The "sources" of the half made up of archives are considerable, and are given elsewhere.[7] Contrary to the way things were in the time of sorceries, the possessed have the floor. Henceforth, the accused and the victims do not come only from the illiterate and close-mouthed countryside, as if condemned to ranting protests that today can only be heard through the reports or analytical grids of notables or judges.[8] With the possessions, the Devil speaks. He writes. If I dare say so, he publishes, but because his clients belong to higher social strata. That is why we have hundreds of letters and writings of the possessed of Loudun—particularly writings (which abound, but are for the most part unpublished in the case of the last two) by Urbain Grandier, Jeanne des Anges, and Father Surin. We can hear what is happening on the other side of the barricade.

Furthermore, with possessions, proceedings no longer take place in camera; they are no longer dispatched in short order by traveling tribunals that move to the bad parts of the provinces. They are public, theatrical, interminable. Hence the massive files of minutes punctiliously written and signed day after day for months and years. Eyewitnesses have also left their accounts. These include not only the judges, the exorcists, and the local, diocesan, and national notables, but also the visitors: the curious of all kinds, socialites on holiday, scholars hot on the trail, collectors of the extraordinary, apologists interested in an extra argument, controversialists bent on refuting an objection, and especially the usual public at this sort of spectacle, pilgrims of strangeness for reasons their written accounts only allow us to guess. They converge on Loudun from Angers, Bordeaux, Lyons, Paris, but also from Scotland, Italy, the Netherlands, and elsewhere.

The archives also give us access to the mines of a more secret and more official history: reports addressed to Richelieu or Louis XIII; correspondence of the father general of the Jesuits (in Rome) with Paris, Bordeaux, and Loudun; letters from Laubardemont; medical testimony; theological consultations; warnings from administrations in Paris or Poitou; and so forth.

All these manuscripts (which have had to be assembled like the scattered pieces of a puzzle) represent the rest of the iceberg, what lies below the water's surface. They restore the hidden depths to what was "given to the public" from the start. Still, the extent of contemporary publication was already quite considerable. It took the form of tracts, *histoires extraordinaires, véritables relations* (true accounts), and leaflets that publishers would reissue from town to town, often in the same year, for their regional publics: Angers, Lyons, Paris, Poitiers, Rouen. These "pieces" are to be situated between devotional booklets and the first newspapers.[9] They are still propaganda, but tend progressively in the direction of the news item. Though scattered to the four winds since then, and not listed in the inventories after the death of the individuals or booksellers, they seem to have had a wide distribution. In any case, as far back as 1634, the *Mercure françois,* used by Richelieu and Father Joseph[10] as a means to direct and correct public opinion, gave almost forty pages to the official version of the possession.[11]

Thus strangeness is deeply rooted in the substance of a society. It is connected by too many sociocultural ties to be isolated from it. To attempt to extract it would mean drawing along with it all the soil to which it is attached in so many ways. Perhaps it reveals an overall change that, once again, consists in exorcising or marginalizing the first symptoms of a crisis that progressively gives rise to a new order.

But first we must try to understand.

~ 1 ~

How a Possession Is Born

In 1632 the city of Loudun was sorely tried by the plague: in the space of a few months (May–September), 3,700 deaths out of a population of approximately 14,000.[1] It was a tragic repetition of the plague of 1603. From the moment it broke out, the physicians, like everyone else who could do so, withdrew to their country houses. Such was the case of François Fourneau, Jean Fouquet, René Maunoury, and others. They would not return until later, as interpreters and witnesses of what took place among the Ursuline nuns.

The Plague: A Physics of Evil

That rather dishonorable withdrawal is nonetheless understandable if we bear in mind contemporary views on the nature of the scourge. The witness of a plague in Avignon writes: "On September 6th, the scourge of God called the plague descended in this city upon the house of a cobbler . . . God help us! Amen."[2] No treatment, and therefore no doctor, could overcome it. It was an evil without explanation or particular causes. It would emerge from within the body of a society and could not fail to spread through it. Epidemic by nature, it fell within the province of a sort of physics of the social and the divine. There was just *nothing to be done* about the plague. (The same was said about syphilis at the time.) People waited for it to run its course and end. The chastisement had to do its work. All one could do was to close the gates to the city and flee with covered head. According to many treatises on the plague (from Laurent Joubert in 1581, or Claude Fabri in 1568, to Antoine Mizault in 1623), and the many warnings issued to the citizenry to "protect yourself from the plague in suspicious weather," one might just

manage, within a city "possessed" by "the infection of the air," to surround oneself with a different atmosphere, by the use of aloe, terebinth,
wine rose, rose-cakes, and similar odorous drugs, producing with their
new aromas an enclave of a different air.

> It is also good to always wear perfume on one's gloves, shirt, and
> handkerchiefs, and in one's hair and beard. To wear a fragrant
> apple around one's neck, or a rosary, and to handle and smell
> them frequently. . . .
> The rich should often use perfumes in their houses, the
> best they can find.
> The poor should store up the leaves and branches of laurel,
> rosemary, juniper or cade, and cypress, and should make a prac-
> tice of burning them as often as possible in the middle of the
> main room and bedroom, especially mornings and evenings.[3]

The frequency of plagues in the region during the preceding two centuries had made death omnipresent[4]—and with it, "the fear and terror
of imminent death"—but it was an inevitable, irresistible death, "falling"
from heaven in the manner of the incomprehensible and the meaning-
less.

The trace left by the 1632 plague would be a mark. Loudun had been
struck by a theological evil of which the possession would then offer a
better defined version, and also an "explanation," since the evil would
be attributed to a cause (extraordinary, diabolical) distinct from human
nature.

In 1632 the city was already seeking exorcists for the plague. Prégent
Bonnereau, a physician from Mirebeau, was called but declined the responsibility, and finally Guillaume Grémian was called.[5] Sanitats were set
up in which the victims of the plague were isolated. In reality, each group
withdrew and obeyed the law of reciprocal shutting away. The physicians
and property owners fled to the fields. The nuns locked themselves away
behind their walls, and the convents closed themselves off in the same
way as the sanitats had, discontinuing parlor communication. Among
the Ursuline nuns, there were no plague cases. According to all reports,
Urbain Grandier, the parish priest of Saint-Pierre, was courageous and
generous; he administered the last sacraments to the sick and gave
money to the poor.

A City Broken

There is no doubt that the plague traumatized the city, as was the case
in many other places in France and Europe. "Rocking urban society, it

upset the mental and intellectual structures, causing first, through terror, mystic élan and mortifications, and later, beneath the obstinate silence of heaven, blasphemy and Saturnalia."[6] Where should one turn?
Doubts spread. No doubt the effect of the plague was added to that of
the Wars of Religion, which had bloodied Loudun's streets fifty years
earlier. The adversaries in that conflict both claimed the truth for their
side. They tore God limb from limb. Their opposition created a third
position, a common reference, in the form of a political status quo in
which the "solution" of the future could be discerned. But it was also a
period of latency, during which yesterday's enemies, forced to accept
one another, stored up their resentments or drifted toward skepticism.
Regardless of personal positions, the battle for truth remained indecisive, and the suspense threatened the convictions of both religions.

The plague, first attributed to God's wrath or to a social and astrologi-
cal physics, prompted certain men to struggle against uncleanliness or
malnutrition. From the sixteenth century on, in the municipalities, laypersons, magistrates, and physicians founded civil sanitary institutions
and began looking for cures. In those individuals, *work* compensated for
God's silence. At the same time, the society was becoming fragmented.
To prevent contagion, public assembly was forbidden. These restrictions,
necessitated by the conditions of urban life, caused the outward signs
of religious unanimity to disappear—public liturgical celebrations in
particular. The solidarity of work stands in contrast to the withdrawal of
religious believers, buried away in their respective trenches opposite
each other, unable to see ahead or above, with no other assurance than
the cohesion of small, closed groups. Such were the Ursulines in their
convent.

Phantoms

Did the "possession" take up where the plague, which had affected Loudun for five months, left off? One fact is noteworthy. The first phantom-
like "apparitions" took place in the convent at the same time as the last
plague cases in the city are mentioned—at the end of September 1632.
During the night between the twenty-first and the twenty-second, the
prioress (Jeanne des Anges), the sub-prioress (Sister de Colombiers),
and Sister Marthe de Sainte-Monique (who had just completed a retreat) saw in the darkness the shadow of Prior Moussaut, the nuns' confessor, who had died some weeks earlier. On the twenty-third there was
the incident of the black ball moving across the refectory. On the twenty-
seventh there was a man, seen only from the back. The phantom, at

first nocturnal, became diurnal and was losing its initial appearance, still anchored in memory. It was turning toward anonymity, as if unsure of its identity, until adopting first the silhouette and then, on October 7, the haunting figure of a parish priest who was quite alive: Urbain Grandier himself.

The Procession of the Clerics

The actors of the drama arrived in succession at the convent that had been shaken by the cries and writhing bodies of the nuns since the beginning of October 1632. The clergy were the first to visit Jeanne des Anges. Their rapid entrance has something processional about it.

First, the lesser clergy: the canon Jean Mignon, the convent's new chaplain; Antonin de la Charité (the prior of Loudun), Eusèbe de Saint-Michel, Eloi de Saint-Pierre, Calixte de Saint-Nicholas, Pierre Thomas de Saint-Charles, Philippe de Saint-Joseph, Eugène de Saint-René (the prior of Poitiers), all Carmelites—the most anxious to encounter the extraordinary. Pierre Barré, the curé of Saint-Jacques in Chinon, a "bachelor from the faculty of theology of Paris," was called to the rescue, as a specialist in exorcisms. He came immediately with a group of parishioners, and took charge of things from October 12 on. Then came the following: François Grillau, the warden of the Cordeliers; Uriel, the warden of the Capuchins; Elisée de Chinon, another Capuchin; Pierre Rangier, the curé of Notre-Dame-de Veniers, a village near Loudun, through which information spread to neighboring rural areas; and Mathurin Rousseau, a canon of Sainte-Croix—a notable already esteemed the affair worth the trip—and so on. Ten, twelve, fourteen priests took part in the first exorcisms. And their numbers would increase. Would people say there weren't enough priests staying home to preach? Ah, but for them it was a "ministry," not "curiosity." They could be mobilized. With all their backlogs of controversies, they responded to the summons of the event they immediately designated as a *possession*.

Yet in the town people were already saying all this was nothing but "imposture."[7] In the prioress's quarters the war of the sacred had begun.

The Possession Takes Hold

The first minutes present the beginning of the case before it became publicized. The boarding pupils of the *pensionnat* run by the Ursulines were still there, caught up in a pandemonium in which priests circulated. This beginning wavers between being a morally uplifting tale and deviltry. It is the brief, faltering moment in which the possession "takes hold."

It will take only a few days for the ambiguity to be dispelled, for the devil to be adjudged responsible for the "strange" facts, and for exorcisms to be considered "expedient" (on October 1). Consequently a *sorcerer* is designated (October 5–11). The diabolical, a neuter singular noun, soon becomes diversified into a plural. The proper names of demons (Astarte, Zabulon, and so forth) correspond to possessed nuns, who take on the voices and faces of roles long set by tradition. The characters assume their places very rapidly. In three weeks, the stage is set for the play that will elaborate the initial schema.

The First Minutes

The earliest report, dated October 7, reveals more about the little group that drew it up than they intended.

> In the name of the Holy and Supremely Adorable Trinity, the Father, the Son, and the Holy Ghost, we, Pierre Barré, a priest bachelor from the Faculty of Paris, canon of the church of Chinon and charged with the governance of the parish of said place, Jean Mignon, priest, canon of the church of Loudun and ordinary confessor of the religious ladies of Saint-Ursule of said place, Eusèbe de Saint-Michel and Pierre Thomas de Saint-Charles, a preaching father and a religious Carmelite of the convent of the aforementioned Loudun, being assembled in the monastery of said religious ladies, at their command and upon their plea, they let us know that, since the night between the twenty-first and the twenty-second of last September [1632], they had been obsessed, until this third day of this month [of October], by evil spirits.
>
> One of which, at night, appeared, from one o'clock till four, to Sister Marthe, in the form of a man of the Church, cloaked in a large coat and soutane, holding in his hand a book covered with white parchment; and holding it open, showed her two pictures, and after having conversed with her somewhat of said book, attempted to force her to take it. The which she refused, saying that she would never receive a book save from her mother superior, and the said specter fell silent and remained awhile weeping at the foot of her bed. At last the said girl being terrified, and the said specter beginning to tell her he was in great pain, that he could not pray to God, that she should pray for him, she, assuming it was perhaps the soul of someone in purgatory, said she would tell her superior about it. And upon which,

being unable to suffer the presence of said specter any longer, she called a girl boarder who was in another bed close to hers. They both got up, and at the same moment she saw nothing further, except that, after having knelt for an hour, she heard a voice next to her lamenting. When the four o'clock bells rang, no more was heard in that place.

But in the lodgings of the professed nuns, the same specter appeared to both the mother prioress and the sub-prioress, saying to the one: "Have prayers be said to God for me"; and to the other: "Continue praying to God for me."

As also they did inform us that on the twenty-fourth of said month, during the hour from six to seven of the evening, in the refectory, there appeared another specter in the form of a globe, all black, that went and threw said Sister Marthe violently to the ground, and said prioress onto a chair, taking each one by the shoulders; and at the same time two other nuns felt their legs struck, where red contusions the size of testons [a small coin worth 19 sous] remained for eight days.

Furthermore, they told us that for the entire rest of the month there had not been one night without great agitation, damage and terror. And even when they did not see anything, they often heard voices calling out to one another. Some were punched with fists, some slapped, some felt themselves being prompted to immoderate and involuntary laughter.

"Three Thorns from a Hawthorn"

Then they told us that on the first day of this month, at about ten o'clock in the evening, said prioress reclining with the candle lit, and having seven or eight of her sisters around her to help her in particular because of the attacks she was having, she felt a hand, though seeing nothing, which, closing her hand, left in it three thorns of a hawthorn, which were placed the following day in the hands of one of us to determine what should be done with them. And two days later it was decided that the prioress should burn them herself. Which she did, in the presence of the father warden of the Capuchins of this city.

But since said prioress, and other nuns, since the receiving of said thorns, had felt strange changes in their bodies and spirits, such that at times they would lose all judgment and be vexed with great convulsions that seemed to be brought about by ex-

traordinary causes, said thorns were thought to be an evil spell
to cause them to be possessed; and, in fact, on this third day of
this month, having seen strange vexations and agitation in the
body of said prioress, Sister Louise de Jésus, and Sister Claire
de Saint-Jean, we have judged it a true possession, and deemed
it expedient to proceed with them by exorcisms of the Holy
Church. We nevertheless delayed until the fifth of this month,
until we had seen the continuation of said vexations and agitation to such a degree that seven or eight people were incapable
of stopping them, which vexations grew more frequent after the
holy communion they took.

During the first exorcism of said day, the fifth of the month,
the evil spirits having been commanded in Latin to say their
names, they said nothing, two or three times, but "Enemies of
God." And during the litanies, upon the words: *"Sancte Joannes
Baptista, ora pro eis"* ["Saint John the Baptist, pray for them"],[8]
the prioress's demon, panting, blurted out: "Ha-ha! John the
Baptist." And as the exorcism was being recited over said prioress, [the demon] said thrice while assaulting her: *"Sacerdos"*
["priest"]. And he repeated it as the words in the exorcism were
pronounced.

The Enemy of God

During the second exorcism, which was performed in the afternoon of said day over said prioress, the devil, instructed in Latin
to state his name, answered in French, screaming and bellowing:
"Ha-ha, did not tell you."

And after further insistence, he repeated: "Enemy of God."

And as the exorcism proceeded, he shouted: "You are pressing me hard, give me at least three more weeks. There have only
been two weeks."

And shortly thereafter: "Ha-ha, the wicked one! He had intended to damn the whole community for me."

During the third exorcism, the prioress was greatly be-
reaved of sense and reason. The devil, ordered to say his name,
twice answered: "Enemy of God." Then, pressed not to conceal
it, he said: "I told it to you." Questioned as to how he had been
introduced, he said: "Pact."

And, further pressed, said: "I burn," shouting continually.
Then, commanded to say who the author of the pact was, he
said:

"Sacerdos."

"Quis sacerdos?" ["Which priest?"]

"Petrus" ["Peter"], he responded.

"Dignitas?" ["Rank?"]

"Curé."

Having been commanded to come out, after much violence, vexation, howling, gnashing of teeth, of which two back
ones were broken, he finally left said prioress in great peace,
and she declared that she was cured of a strong suffering of
spirit and great beating of the heart, and thought she was perfectly cured. She remained in that repose all night, sleeping
peacefully, more so than she had done since the first apparition.

The following morning said prioress and the other exorcised nuns showed a great repugnance at holy communion, and
when they were ordered to get ready for it, the devils began
their vexation, agitation, and benumbing, but finally, under
continual pressing, they let them confess.

When communion had been brought to said prioress, the
torture and loss of the faculty of judgment began, and the devil,
pressed to allow her to bless and adore God, said: "He is accursed."

And thrice: "I deny God."

Pressed at last he let her praise God. And when she was
brought to say, "My God, take possession of my soul and my
body," the devil thrice took her by the throat, when she tried
to say "my body," causing her to shout, grind her teeth, and stick
out her tongue. Forced at last to obey, she received the holy
sacrament that the spirit had several times attempted to make
come out of her mouth by causing her to vomit.

When holy communion was brought to Sister Louise de Jésus, it took more than half an hour to receive it, she being so
agitated that six to seven people could not restrain her. She
could not worship God; but finally she opened her mouth afterward and communed peacefully.

"A Priest Put Me Here"

She was exorcised in Latin immediately afterward; then the vexation
worsening, the devils were interrogated.

"Quomodo inductus?" ["How were you introduced?"]

He said several times: "Character."

Pressed: *"Sub quo symbolo"* ["Under what sign?"], he said: "It is thorny."

Asked: *"Ubi positus?"* ["Where were you placed?"]

"I do not know. You know enough about it."

Then he said: "O strength of [sacerdotal] character; it is all-powerful. A priest put me here, a priest will not dislodge me."

Sister Claire, having been exorcised with like violence, laughed continually, and twice said his name was Zabulon.[9]

On October 11 the net drew tighter. Urbain Grandier was designated by name as a sorcerer. The accusation was extremely grave: it combined all crimes into one. This is shown, for example, in the royal letter of August 12, 1632, granting the intendant of Limousin, Haute and Basse Marche, and Auvergne the mission of curbing "homicides, murders, rebellions against the justice system, evil spells, poisonings, and sorceries" that have been or will be perpetrated in said provinces.[10] *Sorcery* is a word that, in its indeterminacy, designates and synthesizes everything threatening.

Here are the minutes "taken in the monastery of the daughters of Saint-Ursule," on October 11, "between seven and eight o'clock P.M.," and signed: "Mignon; Fr. Antoine de la Charité, Prior of the Carmelites of Loudun; Fr. Eusèbe de Saint-Michel, Carmelite."

Roses

When we came to the exorcism that commands the devil to say his name, pressed again and again with great fury, he finally said thrice that his name was Astaroth. When commanded to say: *"Quomodo domo ingressus fuisset?"* ["How did you get into the house?"], he said: *"Per pactum Pastoris ecclesiae S. Petri."* ["By a pact of the pastor of the church of St. Peter's."]

As we were continuing with the prayers, the devil, with a terrifying shout, said twice in French: "Oh wicked priest!"

Asked: *"Quis sacerdos?"* ["Which priest?"], he answered twice: "Urbanista."

"Et jussus quinquies ut diceret clare et distincte quisnam ille presbyter?" ["And you are commanded for the fifth time to say clearly and distinctly who this priest is."] He answered, shouting loud and long, and with a hissing sound: "Urbain Grandier."

Pressed to say: *"Qualis esset ille Urbanus?"* ["Who is this Urbain?"], he said: *"Curatus S. Petri."* ["The curé of St. Peter's."]

"Cujus S. Petri?" ["Of which St. Peter's?"]

He said twice: "Du Marché."

Urged again and again to say: "*Sub quo novo pacto remissus fuerit?*" ["According to what new pact were you sent?"], he said: "*Flores.*" ["Flowers."]

"*Qui flores?*" "What kind of flowers?"]

"*Rosarum.*" ["Of roses."]

And all these answers were given in response to so many threats that it was easy to see the devil was strongly coerced. And even the pronouncing of his name in commanding him to answer was so vexing to him that he cried out once with a howl: "Ah, why did I tell you?"

The last pressure applied to him that evening was to say:

"*Quare ingressus fuisset in monasterium puellarum Deo Sacramentum?*" ["Why did you enter a convent of girls, consecrated to God?"]

He said: "*Animositas.*" ["Hatred."][11]

The Notables

Then a second wave rose to the prioress's quarters and settled into the convent—that of the notables. On the twelfth, a nobleman, M. Paul Grouard, the provost judge; another nobleman, M. Louis Moussault, the king's prosecutor; and M. René Maunoury, a surgeon. On the thirteenth, we have in addition: Messieurs Daniel Rogier[12] and Gaspard Joubert, Huguenots, we are told, and doctors of medicine, and also M. René Adam, apothecary. Concerning these three men, the minutes mention that they wept when they saw the rowdy Jeanne refuse communion with her surprising contortions.

> They testified aloud that such vexations were beyond human powers and could not be the effect of any natural malady.[13]

But what is *natural?* Therein lies the whole problem.

There is also the *bailiff,* the ordinary and presidial magistrate of Loudun. Guillaume de Cerisay, squire, lord of La Guérinière, is a "bailiff of the long robe," which means that he performs the executive functions of a bailiff (a civil servant of the short robe, or the sword), but also dispenses justice. He thus combines two roles that since the edict of 1561 were normally distinct. He is not only the most important of the notables, but the chief magistrate of Loudun. He is accompanied by the *lieutenant civil* (Louis Chauvet) and his brother Charles, an assessor; the *lieutenant criminel* (René Hervé); the king's prosecutor (Moussault); the *lieutenant* of the provostship (Paul Aubry); the assistants to the clerk of the court, Pierre Thibault and especially Urbain Dupont, always pen in hand. Other physicians are brought in: Mathieu Fanton and Charles Auger (from Loudun), Vincent de Fos (from Chatellerault), Alphonse Cosnier (from Fontevrault), François Brion (from Thouars), and so forth.[14] In short, an entire provincial "society" is reconstituted on the terrain determined for it by the possession: around the bewitched, it sets in motion a parlor game in which the values are the ante and the demon only the dummy.

The gentlemen have not yet arrived. Perhaps they do not wish compromise themselves too much. Furthermore, they live on their own lands, which are more distant. But they will not be long in coming, and with their arrival the spreading of news of the event will cross yet another threshold.

The Rules of the Game

The order of stage entrances appears to be determined by rank even more than by distance. To the unbiased observer it would seem to be regulated by an etiquette of ascending social categories. At the very least, it reflects the spatial and hierarchical organization of the city. It reactivates it, it does not shake it up. In this rendez-vous with the extraordinary, the rules of the social game function with the same haughty precision—perhaps all the more so as their *raison d'être* is put in question. On October 25 a witness, M. Dugrès, "a man of honor and good family," brings "his condition" and "his merit" to bear, in requesting that the bailiff recognize his right to enter the bedroom and "approach the bed of said Prioress."

This was just the beginning. The rumor was spreading that Urbain Grandier, the curé of Saint-Pierre du Marché, was named by the "possessed" as the one who had cast the evil spell of which they were supposedly the victims. And so began—in a convent in which seventeen Ursuline nuns were peaceably reciting the service and conducting classes for the girls of the region—the affair that would draw thousands of curious spectators from all over Europe, the most famous of the possessions that during this period erupted through the surface of the country like a series of abscesses.

After the appearance of phantoms during the night of September 21–22, the events unfolded in keeping with a cycle that was determined by an abundant literature.

The Admirable History of the Possession by François Domptius (Paris:

Chastellain, 1613) is divided into acts: they spell out everything in advance, right down to the thorn and the roses, furnishing a model in the form of a story. From the first act on, the scene is set:

> On the seventh and eighth of December, as the same exorcisms continued twice a day, the demons, upon questioning, answered that three of them were in Louise's body, being there by means of an evil spell, and that the first of them was named Verrine, the next Gresil, and the last Sonneillon, and that all three were of the third order, to wit of the rank of the Thrones.[15]

The various types of contortions, the names of the main devils (there will be regional variants and personal inventions), their edifying declarations when they are "constrained" and become true "doctors, apothecaries, and surgeons" of souls: the schema is complete. But the Provence *Histoire* is explained and justified by the addition of a *Discours des esprits* [Discourse of Spirits] that had been written earlier by Father Sébastien Michaelis (Paris: Chastellain, 1612). In Loudun, that beautiful unity between story and theory, between the *histoire* and the *discours,* will be lost: the *histoire* becomes dramatized, psychologized, and disproportionately developed; the *discours* becomes fragmented and dissolves, leaving room for other considerations.

As early as October 12, 1632, Jean Mignon stressed the parallel with the affair that led Gaufridy to his death. That threat against Grandier was also a confession. Did not the reference to the Aix trial make it possible to recognize immediately, "by all the visible signs, the truth of said new possession"?[16] But without a doubt the archetype had served as a norm before serving as proof. It had been tacitly accepted for a long time. It is surprising, reading the minutes, to see the mechanism working so quickly and easily. That is because it has its tradition, and the inhabitants appear to have assumed set roles without difficulty.

~ 2 ~

The Magic Circle

A mobilization immediately takes place. It organizes the city. It also reveals the latent tensions within it—those that were thought to have been resolved and best forgotten, and those that were increasing and would find an outlet in the affair. There was no way to foresee that on Rue du Pasquin, where the Ursulines were lodged, certain nocturnal episodes would occur. But when those events took place, it is not surprising that they caused so great a stir in Loudun. Their effect was not due just to the idle tales and lively curiosity always present in small provincial towns. It was not solely the result of local quarrels, battles between clans, personal rivalries that, after having fermented privately, would surface in the guise of a public debate between God and the Devil.

The debate is more than a consequence. It creates a new situation. It divides. The complex fabric of everyday life is torn in two, though it was already weakened at precisely that spot by prior wear and mending. The possession rekindles former conflicts, but transposes them, offering them a different range of expression. While presupposing earlier rifts, it constitutes a different experience, with a new language. It reveals something that existed, but it also, and especially, permits— makes possible—something that did not exist before. The topography of Loudun imposes a geography on the battle, which will in turn modify that region's sociocultural terrain. Something happens that cannot be reduced to what was before. Thus what takes place becomes an event. It has its own rules, which displace previous divisions.

A Religious Frontier

Among these divisions, the most important was unquestionably the one
brought about by the Wars of Religion. Sixty years earlier, Huguenots
and Catholics had been massacring one another in the same places
where, in 1632, they were satisfied with disputation. Held by the Huguenots, besieged by the Catholic forces and occupied by them, the town
was then taken back, pillaged, and burned by the Huguenots. "[The
churches are] completely stripped of ornaments and of their images,
broken and burned since 1562 by the same Huguenots who shouted as
they caused this damage: Long live the Gospel! Mass is abolished."[1]

The people suffered more than the stones. Ten years later the Catholics took their revenge. They perpetrated the same destruction, but in
the name of the opposite creed. A series of massacres repeated the process, successively securing victory for the opposing "truth." Thus things
continued until the Edict of Nantes (1598) made Loudun a "safe place"
for the Protestants and guaranteed them the position they had acquired.
Loudun was an outpost, a frontier town, as it were, beyond the regions
in which Protestantism was dominant, farther to the south and the west.
It also became a location of national importance, when an attempt was
made to bolster the shaky agreement between the two parties through
the Treaty of Loudun (February 1616), after a conference in which the
prince de Condé and Huguenot leaders met with delegates of Marie de
Médicis.

The fact of the matter is that a shift was beginning to compromise the
status quo. The Huguenots still constituted a majority in the city, in
which a national synod (1619–20) and so many provincial synods were
held (1610, 1631, and so on), and were still powerful, being a majority
among the notables, and owners of the schools to which they sent their
children. Still, they already felt isolated in that outpost and worried over
the menacing news of the fall of La Rochelle in 1628. A declaration of
Louis XIII, made in Paris on December 15, 1628, hard upon the taking
of La Rochelle, recalls the fatherly love of the king and his will to obtain
peace and tranquility, but it leaves no room for doubt about his will to
put an end to all rebellion, or about the reversal that was taking place
in the equilibrium of forces.

> Having put this affair to deliberation in our Council, in the opin-
> ion of the latter and of our sure knowledge, full power, special
> grace, and royal authority, through these letters signed by our-
> selves we have enjoined all our subjects of the so-called Re-

formed Religion, of whatever quality and condition they may be—who from now on are engaged in rebellion and bearing arms or holding our towns and fortresses against our service and the obedience they owe us, and are connected with those who hold and occupy them, and who, in whatsoever manner, are in them—to lay down their arms, to return to their duty, and to make and submit declarations of this in good form, before our Courts of Parliaments or Presidial Seats under our obedience closest to their residences, within a fortnight after the publication of these present letters.[2]

The Catholics had long been accustomed to resistance, but henceforth they were defended by the power of the throne, and they advanced to magistrate positions. Called to missionary work by traveling preachers, they were reinforced in their efforts by religious orders, which had been settling in progressively since the beginning of the century. They restored the churches, built new convents, and emerged in city life by means of a whole system of spiritual affiliations: the Cordeliers opened their convent near the church of Saint-Mathurin; then the Jesuits opened their residence, alongside the church of Saint-Pierre-du-Marché in 1606; the Discalced Carmelites, who had begun rebuilding their convent in 1604, had the church of Saint-Pierre-du-Martray, and held their first general congregation there in 1614; the Capuchins arrived in 1616; the Daughters of the Calvary, in 1624; the Ursulines, in 1626. The situation was thus being reversed, by a process that was revealed and precipitated by the possession.

Two Political Policies

One indication of that evolution was the replacement of the Protestant Boisguérin by the Catholic Jean d'Armagnac, one of the first valets of the king, as governor of the town and castle of Loudun (by letters patent of December 18, 1617).

But another type of dividing line was involved here. Beyond religious differences, it grouped the defenders of local privileges against the pressures of central authority. Jean d'Armagnac was continuing the work of his Huguenot predecessor when he completed the restoration of the fortress (in 1626). But it had been given to him by Louis XIII (May 13, 1622). His behavior was thus quite wavering. More passionate than intelligent, more shifty than skillful, he would end up serving other causes than his own and getting bogged down in his own intrigues. At first he tried to preserve the donjon, in which he took up residence, despite the king's decisions about the castle (1623).[3] In November 1631 the baron de Laubardemont received a royal commission to raze the castle and outer walls and towers, as he had already done to the castle of Mirebeau (1629) and the citadel of Royan (1630). But in a missive from Louis XIII to the commissioner, the keep was spared—as a favor to the governor.

> It being important to my service and to the tranquility of my subjects of the province of Poitou that the demolition of the fortifications of my castle of Loudun be expedited promptly according to the orders you have received from me, I draw up this letter to you to tell you that immediately upon receipt of it you are to execute exactly the commission that has been assigned to you for that purpose, with the exception of the donjon of said castle, which I desire and intend to be preserved, and beyond which nothing will be demolished.[4]

The donjon, the object of subtle schemes, temporary indulgences, and thinly disguised betrayals, had become the political pawn of two policies. The taking up of positions, whether in confrontation or subterfuge, determined a new geography. A political struggle did not simply transpose groupings by religious parties, it redistributed forces and options in the name of criteria that were no longer directly beliefs. Some Catholics, Huguenots, or skeptics joined in defending local jurisdiction, or even regional independence. That was equally the case for the other side. From this perspective, the possession set the partisans of d'Armagnac in opposition to those of Richelieu. The central power, by its action, mobilized the former and frustrated the interests of the latter, regardless of their religious motivations. The beliefs of both parties were secularized and displaced by becoming invested or enlisted in a contest with stakes that were of a different nature.

Politics was the axis that was quietly replacing frames of reference that had become debatable, and therefore doubtful. It made positions that claimed to be religious ones ambiguous. Catholics and Protestants continued to defend their respective groups, either by centralization, or in opposition to it. But in so doing, perhaps they bear witness to the fact that those groupings were no longer the essential ones. Power was ceasing to be religious. The power of decision, with respect to the truths or Churches in confrontation with one another, was slipping away from them. Henceforth right would be defined in terms of the State.

The Birth of a Language

Well before the possession began, there began to take shape the phenomenon that prevents us from either classifying it exclusively within
religious history or interpreting it solely as a political affair. The ambiguity, in this case, reveals an evolution, and speeds it up. One of the definitions of possession is to be that unstable moment, to symbolize that moment in a language that gives it an expression at once archaic and new,
and, in the chemical sense of the term, thus to "precipitate" a process
in which positions are staked out.

Father Tranquille, the most intransigent of the exorcists, the most
wildly convinced of the diabolical presence, best expresses in his naiveté
the power that was to emerge triumphant from the crisis brought on
by the uncertain frames of reference, and that was to replace the power
of the prior Catholic hierarchies. Possession, he writes, has shown "that
the demons can only be driven out by the power of the scepter and that
the crosier would not suffice to break this dragon's head."[5]

If the possession gave an outlet to the conflicts of a divided city, if it
caused them to come out in broad daylight, it did so by transposing
them. In the closed domain of a diabolical discourse, anxiety, revenge,
and hatred are indeed given free rein, as the expression goes, but above
all they are displaced, enclosed in a language—again masked, subju-
gated to the constraints of another system of expression. That is the
important element: this new, diabolical terrain, carved into the surface
of the country, and which cannot be reduced to its antecedents.

A Prison

Something other takes place henceforth. Once in place, the "theater"
has its own laws; it transforms the problems and passions on which it
feeds. On the one hand, it rechannels urban resentments, diverting
them toward great, formidable issues: the Devil, God, the natural or supernatural world, and so forth. It forces those feelings to a confrontation
with the goals or frame of reference they lack. On the other hand, it
locks the most varied problems into an either-or that throws together
all the yeses on one side and all the noes on the other. One must be *for*
or *against*. Transposing the countless quarrels within a city, the unitary,
monotonous law of bipolar structure enlists them all in advance in a war
of the gods. It simplifies the choices. From the start, it posits a normative
code that reduces them to being either in Satan's camp or in God's.

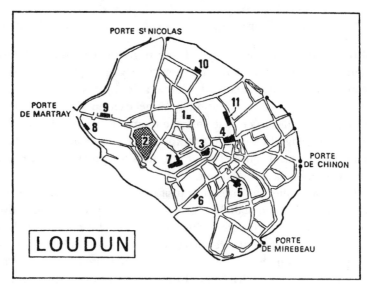

1. The city of Loudun in the seventeenth century

1 Tour Carrée
2 Grand Château
3 Palais (de justice)   7 Jesuits
4 Church of Saint-Pierre   8 Church of Saint-Pierre-du-Martray
5 Church of Saint-Croix   9 Carmelites
6 Ursulines   10 Capuchins
                                             11 Cordeliers

Although this language "frees" the passions, it is primarily a closed system or, as so many witnesses will say, a prison.

Framed upon a stage, the debate is organized into two camps, as in
that "Ballet" danced by the boarders of a Jesuit college in honor of the
taking of La Rochelle: *La Conquête du Char de la Gloire par le grand Théandre*
[The Conquest of the Chariot of Glory by the Great Théandre], according to the explanation of it given by Father Claude Menestrier, pits
the hero Théandre (Louis XIII), aided by the shepherd Caspis, his first
and principal minister, against the Charmes, which are Heresy and Rebellion.[6] The theophor, or God-bearer, of all the good causes confronts
the Rebel who symbolizes all the evils. But before this choreographed
drama, there is the violent one of the possession.

Victims or Accomplices?

The participants, who become more and more numerous, will be caught
up in the game. At the beginning, there is a minimal adherence—a
participation in any case, a "catching on"—to the dramaturgy that autho-

rizes saying everything, hearing everything, seeing everything, but in a diabolical, and therefore allegorical, language that hides everything. Everything is permitted, but because it is the discourse of another (of the devil): in reality, a discourse that is "other." But this game develops initial "intelligences," which it presupposes. It enfolds the participants in its logic.

No one has spoken better about that collusion between the complicity implied by a system in order for it to function and the constraint it exerts than has Jeanne des Anges when, in 1644, she wrote about her past state. To hear her for the first time explaining her own possession at the early stages is to perceive her sharp, coquettish lucidity, which always anticipates the expectations of her interlocutors. But she was not that lucid till much later, at a time when she, together with her "daughters," her "spiritual directors," and her devout clientèle, had entered another system, that of mysticism. She would not have spoken this way at the time about which she writes. Beyond her own psychology, and thanks to the insinuating perspicacity that is a sign of it, she has analyzed an aspect of collective possession. In their own way, the exorcists, the curious, and the public also performed the gesture that brought them to desire that abominable show, to wish for what they would condemn, to be themselves among the actors of what they reject as a scandalous object.

As we shall see, it was Surin who explained to Jeanne des Anges how she was an accomplice of the demons of whom she said she was a victim. But the prioress's prudent confession, honed sharp by the habit of the examination of conscience and a long familiarity with the finesses that make avowals into apologies, has the advantage of designating by what uncertain passages one is introduced into the constraining circle of magic.

A Diabolical Enjoyment

The devil would often beguile me by an enjoyable little feeling I had from the agitations and other extraordinary things he brought about in my body. I took an extreme pleasure in hearing it spoken of, and was pleased to appear more wrought up than the others, which gave great strength to these accursed spirits, for they take great pleasure in being able to amuse us with the sight of their operations, and in this way they gradually creep into souls and gain great advantage over them. For they act in such a way that their malice is not apprehended. On the contrary, they familiarize themselves with the human mind, and draw from it, by means of these enjoyable little feelings, a tacit consent to work within the minds of the creatures they possess, which is most prejudicial to them, for they thus impress within them whatever they please, and make them believe what they will, the more easily, the less the creatures see them as the enemies of their salvation. And if they are not very faithful to God and attentive to their conscience, they are in danger of committing great sins, and of falling into great errors. For after these accursed spirits have thus wormed their way into the will, they persuade the souls of a part of what they will; they sometimes give knowledge of their designs, and, afterward, troubling the imagination, cast one into great disorders. . . .

"I Was the Prime Cause of My Turmoil"

In most cases I saw quite clearly that I was the prime cause of my turmoil and that the demon only acted according to the openings I gave him.

When I spoke of that to my exorcists, they told me it was the demon who gave me those feelings in order to hide within me, or to cast me into a little despair at seeing myself in so much malignancy. I was not the more satisfied for that, for although I submitted to believing what they were telling me at the time, nevertheless my conscience, which was my judge, gave me no peace. Thus, all their assurances blinded me. I think the fact is that it was difficult for them to believe that I was so wicked, and that they believed the devils were giving me these scruples. . . .

To make myself better understood, I must give a few examples, both in important things and light matters, so that those who may read this will know how necessary it is that souls beleaguered by demons should hold firmly to God and greatly beware of themselves.

It so happened, to my great embarrassment, that during the first days when Father Lactance was given to me to be my director and exorcist, I disapproved of his way of conducting many small matters, although it was a very good way; but it was because I was wicked.

One day he undertook to have us all take communion at our grille.

At that time, since we were for the most part sorely afflicted with inner turmoil and great convulsions, for the reception of the Eucharist the priest would either come into our chancel or

have us go out to take communion in the church. I was angry
that he wanted to introduce a different practice. I began to murmur about it in my heart, and thought within myself that he
would do better to follow the way of the other priests.

As I dwelled negligently on that thought, it entered my
mind that, to humiliate that father, the demon would have committed some irreverence toward the Very Holy Sacrament. I was
so miserable that I did not resist that thought strongly enough.
When I went to take communion, the devil seized my head, and
after I had received the holy host and had half moistened it, the
devil threw it into the priest's face. I know perfectly well that I
did not perform that act freely, but I am very sure, to my great
embarrassment, that I gave the devil occasion to do it, and that
he would not have had this power had I not allied myself with
him.[7]

The Charm of the Musk Roses

But what is the proper locus of magic? There is nothing astonishing in
its being circumscribed by a "charm." It is marked by an evanescent sign:
an odor pervades the space, or rather "possesses" it. Those who are aware
of the importance of the olfactory sense in the seventeenth century will
not overlook this critical sign. Just as a mist shrouds the lands of legend,
or a golden halo hovers over saintly heads, so odor constitutes the terri-
tory of a time out of time, given over to the rigid and repressed laws of
olfaction, imagination, immediacy. For all the mad behavior of gesture
and speech, a magic circle is drawn about an odorous center: a bouquet
of musk roses.

This beginning is related by Father Du Pont, a most worthy gentleman,
a resident of Poitiers, a religious of Fontevrault, the brother or relative
of a Mlle Du Pont who had a country house a few miles from Loudun.
Always seated in the front row in the exorcism courts, curious, talkative,
he is the author of eight letters and a "relation" addressed to M. Hubert,
after three sessions of direct observation.

> On the very same day that Sister Agnès, an Ursuline novice, took
> her vows [October 11, 1632], she was possessed by the devil, as
> the Mother Prioress told me personally. The charm was a bou-
> quet of musk roses that were on a dormitory step. The Mother
> Prioress, having picked it up, smelled it, as did a few others after
> her, who all were immediately possessed. They began to cry out,
> calling Grandier, with whom they were so smitten that neither

the other nuns, nor any other persons could hold them back. They tried to go and find him, and to do so got up and ran on the convent roofs, climbed trees in their chemises, and remained perched at the very end of the branches. There, after frightful cries, they endured hail, frost, and rain, remaining four or five days without eating.[8]

Into this circle the whole town would enter, as another witness demonstrates a few weeks later.

I wish I had enough eloquence to depict the state of the nuns and their church during the time of the exorcism. Five girls could be seen, each one attended by two or three priests or religious: one girl, howling and shouting, rolling in the dust, grimacing and doing everything that can inspire horror; another talking, laughing, singing, raising her hand and voice to keep the tempo. . . . Added to all that, the common folk coming and going, running from one girl to another, some sighing, some making fun of them, amid very thick dust, overheated air, fuming and stinking with the smell of garlic, which is common to all who are from the region. I can see that it is an image of hell. That is why the firmest mind is affected by that storm, and the disorderliness of the place puts all thoughts in disorder; and if reason did not come to the rescue of the amazed senses to make it known that that church is a house of God, you would have said it was a prison of dread, terror, and torture.[9]

Minutes, diaries, and "accounts" furnish an entire gradation of odors, from the extraordinary smell of musk roses, of three thorns from the hawthorn, or of the marigolds and carnations found on October 20 in the library of the convent to that of garlic, which is also infernal, common to all who are of the region. It is probably a way of classifying, in a more subtle analysis, the diversity of experience. But taken as a whole, this vocabulary has its own meaning, which stems from a hierarchy of seeing and smelling.

The Magic of Smell

It is true that the spectacle of the possession, as in the theater of that era, transforms the whole town, surrounded by walls, into an "Enchanted Isle" in which the actors and the public are caught up in the same "illusion." It creates the space of a system described by d'Aubignac in his *Pratique du théâtre:* An "ingenious magic," he writes, "brings into view a

new heaven, a new earth, and an infinity of marvels we think are present."[10] Everything must take place as if it were not theater; everything
works thanks to the complicity maintained between an illusionist art and
a public delighted to be fooled. But seeing wavers between dream and
reality. The enchanted site lets doubt linger. An inner time resists the
ingenious composition of places. "At the same time," adds d'Aubignac,
"we are well aware that we are being fooled."

Cut up by objects that are represented but unstable, space only really
"possesses" minds by smell. Only then, and in the territorial sense of the
term, does it "occupy" witnesses and actors. Appearances are always at
a distance, hence suspect of a more and more subtle combination of
artifice and doubt. But they give occasion to another experience when
internal olfactory perception is added to them. There is a qualitative
leap. In this latter case, the internal space of the body participates in
the extension of things. Ultimately, smelling guarantees, judges, and precedes seeing.

Already in Montaigne's opinion odor bears itself to the nose, attaches
itself to the body, holds onto it, and sticks to it:

> He that complaineth against nature, that she hath not created
> man with a fit instrument, to carrie sweet smels fast-tied to his
> nose, is much to blame: for, they carrie themselves. As for me
> in particular, my mostachoes, which are verie thicke, serve me
> for that purpose. Let me but approach my gloves or my hand-
> kercher to them, their smell will sticke upon them a whole day.
> They manifest the place I come from. The close-smacking,
> sweetnesse-moving, love-alluring, and greedi-smirking kisses of
> youth, were heretofore wont to sticke on them many houres
> after. . . .
>
> Physicians might (in mine opinion) draw more use and
> good from odors, than they do. For, myself have often perceived,
> that according unto their strength and quality, they change and
> alter, and move my spirits, and work strange effects in me.[11]

He alludes to the maladies of the common folk that are "born of the
contagion of the air." Accordingly, certain odors are, as we have seen,
the best defense against the plague. They create a different space. In-
versely, Paul Zacchias, whose monumental work *Quaestiones medico-legales*
(Avignon, 1557) was still in the seventeenth century considered a classic,
writes at length of the dangers of the sense of smell, of the poisons whose
smell causes vertigo, headache, and suffocations. "We have a thousand
and one examples," he writes, "of living beings that have been infected

by olfaction alone. . . . We see many people every day who fall into a serious or very serious state because of good or bad odors, or who faint upon smelling certain things."[12]

Smell, according to him, can nourish, putrify, or kill. Is this efficacy of smell connected with the doctrine represented by Saint Thomas Aquinas, which posits as known the being with which one is permeated and saturated? That experience of contagion by smell reappears in the seventeenth century both in medical diagnosis and spiritual discernment. The doctor, upon entering the sick person's abode, sniffs the air and thus frequently discovers the illness. In innumerable stories from the convents, you can tell whether the object seen in a vision is authentic by the smell it gives off, or whether a deceased religious is a saint by the good odor surrounding her. Olfactory perception is a principle of discernment. Like a cook's palate, it judges reality and qualifies it.

Smell changes the surface of the things before you into a volume in which you are caught. The air you breathe is the index of the world into which you have been introduced—be it that of an illness, of grace, or of a spell. When you smell it, it means you are already in it, or more precisely, you are of it. In Loudun, harmful smells, deep breaths, and surprising respirations seem to anticipate (or summon) the visual designations that will clarify even further a change that has already been carried out and that one must express in a vocabulary of objects. A space is qualified by olfactory impressions before it can be described or gestured, before a series of spectacles come to show or gear down the original "magic." Like springtime, which is "in the air" before there is any visible sign of it, a strange air is already marking out the place for the Loudun story.

~ 3 ~

The Discourse of Possession

Ephemeral, thin as air, the locus born of a magic spell must be inscribed on solid ground. It has taken form in a setting. It is taking substance in a language. But in the end it will be affixed to a city, staked to a public square.

Two Bishops, Two Modes of Conduct

The possession, as we have seen, develops rapidly. On October eleventh Grandier was specifically denounced. On the twelfth the officers of justice intervened. On the twenty-second the parish priest appeals to the bishop of Poitiers, an amiable prelate, good-humored, a court gentleman and a man of taste. Henri de Chasteignier de La Rocheposay, the son of one of Henry III's ambassadors to Rome and of a mother who converted to Protestantism after the death of her husband, seemed to have two faces: that of the humanist, Scaliger's student, and that of an austere and strict reformer. It is true that Saint-Cyran, whom he had chosen as vicar general, had had to defend (1615) an ecclesiastic's right to take up arms in case of necessity, as his bishop had done against Condé. But unlike many of his colleagues, La Rocheposay is a resident. He is active in the Counter-Reformation, and after 1642 he will occupy an important place in the company of the Saint-Sacrement. He will not tolerate the misbehavior of the parish priest of Loudun. He needs that public and private order so he can abandon himself to the joys of an art lover, the subtle nuances of conversation, or erudite research. He was, according to Sully, a "phlegmatic." His majestic corpulence, that of a righteous man, harbors the freedom and the pleasures of the man of letters.

On November 24 he approves and officially authorizes the exorcisms. In December René de Morans and Basile, deans of the chapters of Thouars and Champigny, represent him in Loudun. Henceforth Marescot, the queen's chaplain, is also present. On the tenth Grandier addresses a request to the parliament of Paris.

On December 24 this tentative development is suspended by an intervention of the archbishop of Bordeaux. After having had the possessed examined and sounded out by a certain Mils, a physician and, we are told, a philosopher, Henri d'Escoubleau de Sourdis sends an order on dispositions to be taken. It is a text worthy of thoughtful consideration. It comes from a man who is open and impetuous, he too a reformer, but in the Gascon style, stomping booted into the convents to bring order. During the siege of La Rochelle, he was in charge of the artillery supplies and was the director of victualing. In 1636 he would participate in the Spanish War as head of the king's councils in the naval army under Sieur d'Harcourt and as director general of army matériel. A man of lively and restless spirit, he would be warned by Richelieu about "the hastiness of your wit and tongue." For reasons political (particularly his opposition to La Rocheposay), personal (he had two Ursuline nieces at Loudun), and religious (his piety has more bursts of enthusiasm than devotion), he is little inclined to believe in the reality of possession in the particular case of Loudun.

Knowing the Truth

First, he writes, the possessed woman will be isolated, then examined "by two or three [able] Catholic physicians"; she will be followed by them for several days, "and purged, if they see fit." After that, "attempts will be made, by threats, disciplines, if deemed appropriate, or other natural means, to know the truth." Last, they will consider

> whether they can detect any supernatural signs, such as responding to the thoughts of the three exorcists, thoughts that the exorcists have divulged to their companions secretly, and such as her divining several things that are going on at the very instant she is being spoken to, in some faraway place, or beyond what she may be expected to know; or that she should say eight or ten words, correct and well constructed, in several different languages; and that, bound hand and foot and lying on a mattress on the floor, where she has been left to rest with no one coming close to her, she should rise and float in the air for a considerable time.

Thus, a verification procedure is required; criteria are given. The archbishop proceeds nonetheless to furnish, from the assets of his abbey in Tourin, "all the sums" that will be required for the "transportation of the girls, to pay the physicians and the expenses of the exorcists and the women that have to be hired to care for the sick."[1]

This last point bears on the economic situation of the nuns, which was deteriorating rapidly. Many of the parents of the Ursulines, shocked at the news, ceased to pay the pensions they had pledged. The students began to leave. A manufacturer of furnishing trimmings that had been set up near Loudun offered only low wages, for a task the girls were no longer able to perform. In 1638 Jeanne des Anges would describe the downfall of her convent in terms all the more mournful for being addressed to the queen, from whom she hoped to obtain a subsidy.

> We fell into an extreme abandonment and a need of all things, most often without bread, and were obliged, to allay our hunger, to gather up what cabbages and other meager greens were left in our little garden, and to boil them with a bit of nut oil and salt, and to lunch and dine on that without bread. As those provisions were often lacking, we often had to forego lunch and dinner. Another hardship befell us—namely, that if we did have salt, oil, and greens, we had no one to cook them, for those of us who were sick and infected with devils gave so much work and trouble to those who were healthy that the latter didn't have time to take care of our paltry cooking, and the poor girls were faced day and night with such frightful sights that they had neither the head nor the heart to think of food and drink.[2]

Words and Things

With the Sourdis order, a first stage is completed, that of organization. Until that date, the display of the possession was being set up. It was only spread out over the surface of the neighborhood, the city, the environs. But bit by bit the pathways already traced out and the stories already enacted converged. All the materials there available took shape, to become *the discourse of possession*. A "discourse": in the first instance, a plurality of words, a diversity of elements come from elsewhere or a former time; but also a singularity, orienting these fragments of divers pasts, adjusting them to tally with the initial spell, and fashioning them into the language of the same ineffable something that had been given first in the form of a smell.

Thus a diversification takes place, which is at once the possibility of expression and the return of traditions now reinvested in a new phenomenon. It has the look of scholasticism. One classifies. Soon one will refine, go into subtleties. Already the kinds of possession are distinguished, along with the categories of devils, the types of gestures and contortions, and the various stages that one exorcism goes through. Witnesses and inquisitive souls begin to form subgroups; opinions polarize; tactics for "attacking the devil" become more diverse. But in all these guises, it is still the possession that people are talking about. Thus broken down into so many divisions and subdivisions, the primitive "flair" is transformed into verbal analysis. Very quickly, words replace smells.

On October 1, out of seventeen nuns, three are declared "possessed." In December there are nine of them, and eight are "obsessed," the other nuns being "healthy." This division reflects the differences observed among the Ursulines, but it classifies them according to a codification peculiar to demonological discourse, one that has been observed often:

> The main differences between obsession and possession consists in the fact that in obsession, the Demon acts solely on the obsessed persons, though in an extraordinary manner, such as appearing to them often and visibly, willy nilly, striking them, disturbing them, and stirring up passions and strange movements in them, and notably exceeding the reach of their natural complexions, or dispositions, or faculties; whereas in possession, the Demon takes advantage of the faculties and organs of a possessed person in such a way as to produce, not only in her, but by her, actions that that person could not bring about of herself, at least not in the circumstances in which she brings them about.[3]

Soon the former will be compared to a "blockaded city," and the second to a "besieged city." It will also be said that in one the demon acts as an "external" principle, and in the other as an "internal" one.

A Code

This first categorization is completed by a naming of the "possessing" demons. On October 13 Jeanne des Anges designates the seven who have taken up residence in her. Moreover, she specifies from the outset, by her contortions and successive masks, the leitmotifs and the "style" proper to each of them (for example, blasphemy, obscenity, or mockery). Hence their respective stage "entrances" can later be recognized by the nun's facial and verbal expressions.

—The name of the first one?
—Astaroth.
—The second?
—Zabulon.
—The third?
—Cham.
—The fourth?
—Nephtalon.
—The fifth?
—Achas.
—The sixth?
—Alix.
—The seventh?
—Uriel.[4]

That strange dialogue establishes a code. Proper names create points of reference and delimit regions within the neutral anonymity of the diabolical terrain. The naming might appear to be a deciphering, as if the goal were first to delineate, in that mass of gesticulations, the nocturnal forces moving the bodies from below, and then to give a verbal identity to those demons. In reality, the process is the opposite. Here, it is rather of the scientific type. The names of the demons superimpose a grid on the surface of the phenomena. The task of exorcism is to draw out of the "mixture" presented to it by the possessed the body proper, the pure element corresponding to the conceptual model.

Today we can say that that verbal imperialism does not provide the necessary conditions for a real verification. It leaves the possessed few possibilities of resistance, since they themselves "enter" into the system and conform to it. The coding always "works" because the functioning is purely tautological, since the operation takes place within a closed domain. For the exorcists, the difficulty resides not in securing a means of verification of the code, but in keeping "the girls" within the closure of the discourse.

The escape; and therein lies the danger. Sometimes the possessed "remain silent," and the contender must break that "pact of silence." At other times the nun "comes back to herself" but finds another means of flight. She says to the exorcist:

—Ah, Jesus, you're killing me.
—Mine God, mine heart hurts.
—Leave me alone, I beg of you. I can't take any more. . . .

> —Good God, what I have to take! I am all broken, I think
> I have a broken rib.[5]

With that pitiful misery, that relapse into consciousness, the possessed leaves the realm of the data of demonological experience. She must be brought back into the linguistic arena of the debate. Or, as is often done, they go to the next girl: In order to keep the discourse homogeneous, the terrain into which the outside has crept in is abandoned, and the work is resumed in a language demonologically "proper."

The Ruses of Possession

The memory of what preceded the possession, no less than the "coming back to oneself," is the permanent danger against which the laboratory constituted by the first definitions must be protected. A moment of consciousness makes a leak in the mechanism: the remembrance of what happened is an illicit resurgence. What makes the discourse of possession possible, what ultimately authorizes it, is that the nun must not remember what happened, that no personal element be permitted to compromise the automatic functioning of the diabolical grammar. That is how the network created by a code is maintained and developed. A pure text, a language without subject, an organization in which roles are devised and in which "proper" names are recited.

But the exorcist must constantly make sure that the nun who has escaped from the magic circle does not remember her exhausting contortions and does not understand the words she has spoken.

> And when she was returned unto herself, she said: "Jesus!" And said Barré having commanded her, in the name of the living God whom he presented to her, to say whether she remembered having spoken Latin, she said that she did not know what it was, had no remembrance of it, and did not believe she had spoken Latin or French, although she recalled having been moved to deny God, and not having suffered any pain.[6]

> And when it was all over, asked whether she had had a feeling of what had taken place, she said no, except that she felt greatly tired and broken. . . .

> The vexations having ceased, said prioress said to said Barré: "What are you asking me?" And having said to her that he spoke not to her but to the devil, she said: "I know not what you mean. I understand not a word of what you say."[7]

A question of language, then. But a closed language. It is reached through the unconsciousness, as in a dream. The devil's language is an *other* language, into which one does not enter by means of an apprenticeship. One must be "possessed" by these words, without understanding them.

Speaking without Understanding

In the course of the exorcisms, language is at once the terrain and the object of the battle. It first appears with the importance granted foreign languages. Latin, first and foremost, is the diabolical tongue. It is not a matter of indifference that the language of the Church should become a closed corpus, the text of the extraordinary. It is no longer, as in the past, the hallmark of a stable order, and the envelopment of the exceptional in the benediction from on high. And its primary effect is no longer to indicate that those who speak it without having learned it are in fact possessed. It is in the first instance a space, with this peculiarity that one can be in it unwittingly. The circumstance of Jeanne des Anges having in reality learned enough Latin in her breviary or at church service to venture forth, rather awkwardly at that, onto this foreign soil, is not the most important thing. We must inquire, rather, into the system that led her to mime knowledge one moment and ignorance the next, in order to satisfy the combination that possession required of her.

The paradox is that while she can speak without knowledge, others do know: the exorcist, and a portion of the public. The latter are observers, examiners, contenders. They are placed outside the diabolical, not by a foreign language, but by the fact of having learned it. The "supernatural" is on the side on which there is no work. That, too, has been laid down as a rule.

But according to the court transcript, the system was infiltrated from all sides: by the interventions of a curious public; by the trickery of the devil, who knows how to put on self-righteous airs to avoid embarrassing questions, or by the disarray of the exorcists. Barré, who claimed to be an expert, didn't know where to turn. He would get lost in the labyrinth of grammar, as the bailiff used to say. He would give commands in all directions. He would work to meet the (public's) demand.

The Devil's Tongue

The said Barré commanded, at the request of certain persons, to answer *Scotica lingua* [in Scottish]. Upon which the father warden of the Capuchins said it was not appropriate, given the fact that none of them understood the tongue. And it was answered to him that there was a man among them who understood it. He replied that the testimony of just one was not sufficient. To which demand the devil remained for a time without wishing to answer, and finally he said:

Nimia curiositas. [Too much curiosity.]

And as the exorcist pressed him to respond in the same tongue, he said:

Non volo Deus. [God does not will it.][8]

And upon the said Barré's having commanded him in Latin to answer with no mistake, she was no longer agitated. Which caused the said Barré to command the devil to return to the tongue of said mother superior, and he answered *Scotice* [in Scottish]. As the torments were recommencing, he said immediately:

Nimia curiositas.

And as said Barré continued to press him to answer in the same tongue, he said:

Non voluntatem Dei. [It is not the will of God.]

And upon being commanded to speak with no mistake, having been pressed again and again, he said for the last time:

Nimia curiositas.

Which caused said Barré, taking the floor, to say that it appeared that God did not want the devil to respond in that tongue, and that it would be a waste of time to press him further.

Meanwhile, said prioress being calmed and said Barré commanding the devil in Latin to answer what he asked, she responded:

"I know not what you say."

And some having said to her that the rumor was circulating that she knew how to speak Latin, she answered:

"I swear by the Holy Sacrament here before me that I never learned Latin."

And as the exorcisms continued, some said that if the devil answered in a foreign tongue, one would truly believe she was possessed. Whereupon said sir Bailiff bade said Barré command the devil to speak and to respond *lingua sacra* [in the sacred language]. Then the warden of the Capuchins, who was at the grille of the chapel, said that the Greek and Latin tongues were equally holy. Said bailiff said:

Hebraica.

And said Barré, having said that the hymn *Maria mater gra-*

tiae, etc., should be sung. The which song having been begun by the nuns, the torments of said prioress increased greatly, during which said Barré enjoined the devil by the power of God that he held in his hands to respond *lingua sacra:*

Quodnam esset pactum ingressus sui? [What was the pact of your entering?]

After several injunctions, he responded:

"Achad."

Those who understand the Hebraic tongue say that these two words, which are combined into one, mean *effusionem vel decursus aquarum* . . . [a flowing forth or running down of waters . . .]

And some having bade the said Barré to command the devil to respond *non uno verbo sed pluribus* [not with one word but several], said Barré, obeying them, commanded the devil to do it; and, to constrain him to speak, they began to sing the abovementioned hymn again. And at the same time the same torments and vexations recommenced strongly, during the which said Barré, commanding the devil in Latin to respond *pluribus verbis,* they heard this word being pronounced by the devil:

Eched.

And then some said:

"She means to deny God."

And the exorcist, holding the custodial up to her face, reiterated the commands to the devil to respond *lingua hebraica,* and to tell *pactum ingressus sui,* the devil lifted her into the air, without her touching her bed with her feet, though she twisted them, as well as her arms and hands, as before; the warden of the Cordeliers said he had passed his hand beneath her foot that was the lower and closer to the bed. And the devil, raising her arm, delivered a blow with all his strength to the rafter, as most of the people in attendance cried out: "Mercy on us!" With the devil not wanting to answer said Barré's interrogations nor his commands to speak in Hebrew, she falling frequently into the same torment and making indecent gestures and movements.[9]

"I Forgot My Name"

Fragile, unstable, contested, the words ascribed to the diabolical transcendence flew out of sight. They were compensated for by increased

exhibitionism. Soon they were to be replaced by the themes of preaching: the preaching devils would represent the last of diabolical discourse,
but a discourse nonetheless useful. Already, with the secondary and face-
tious malice to which Jeanne des Anges alluded in her autobiography,
the possessed women themselves would deny the exorcists those proper
words that they expected:

> When asked: *Quis es tu, mendax, pater mendacii? Quod est nomen
> tuum?* [Who are you, liar, father of lies? What is your name?]
> the demon said, after a long silence: "I forgot my name. I can't
> find it . . ."
>   And commanded once more to say his name, he said: "I
> lost my name in the wash."[10]

The intervention of royal justice will strike a blow against this linguistic
esoterism from which it will not recover. The devil will be either the
witnesses or the accused, and they will speak French like everybody else.

The Body Language

But from the outset the demon expresses himself in another language,
which in Loudun becomes much more essential: a body language. Grimaces, contortions, rolling of the eyes, and so forth, little by little constitute the devil's lexicon. A cutting-up takes place, circumscribing the supernatural, in this case satanic, thanks to corporeal points of reference.
The physicians will at first be content with adopting these points of reference, qualifying them as natural, to define certain of their illnesses.

In a sense, it is also something outside the common language, like
Latin and Hebrew. It is part of the larger tendency that contrasts the
received intellectuality with the inventory of a new world, "baroque," if
you will: that of the senses, of shivers and perspiration, of the changing
surfaces of the skin and the contradictory movements of gesture. This
geography plays, in literature and lived experience, the same role as that
of the unknown continents described by the explorers. The maps of the
body of the "theaters" of America are similarly set in contrast to the
traditional cosmologies or "geographies." A field of knowledge is born
of practice, which is contested, exploratory, though itself codified as well.

In Loudun, this discourse of the body takes on an obsessive character.
The slightest physiological changes of the possessed women are followed
with acute attention. Both the exorcists and the curious seem to have a
physician's eye even before he arrives on the scene. Description, in ful-
filling this role, makes use of a linguistic apparatus that is already rich,

and has just attained religious status in the literature of the latest "spiritu-
als." It constitutes, with the "movements" of the heart, the lungs, the
stomach, or the digestion, a vocabulary that substitutes for the medieval
dictionary of spirituality. Its origins can be seen with the passage, at the
end of the sixteenth century, from mystics[11] to medicine. For example,
the *Imitation of Jesus Christ,* that spiritual meditation on the return to the
heart, introduced and guided Van Helmont to his medical conceptions
of the biological "center" of the human organism.[12]

Henceforth the evolution becomes more marked. The visible body
becomes, in practice, the very legibility of history. Words no longer say
the truths that would be behind it, or that it would make manifest. They
describe that surface on which meanings are phenomena: they relate
the eye's passage over that surface, which is indefinitely rich in observable facts even before being observed. Here, a species of gaze precedes
the technique to which it will give rise. The observable is determined
before the observation.

In Loudun, the minutes of the possessions do not feature a possessing
subject, the devil, or lost subjects, the possessed women. As the report is
fragmented into names and roles, it obliterates the reference to beings,
replacing them with a series of different, and combined, stories: those
of the pulse, the digestion, the mouth, the tongue, or the legs. It is not
by accident that the conscious "I" of the possessed is eliminated. It has
to be. It is excluded in advance by the analysis that distributes the perceptible along the diabolical words of a diabolical topography that classifies
the "supernatural" domain into stories of organs. Thus it is possible to
move indifferently from one possessed woman to another, to follow—
as is done elsewhere (or as will be done later) for melancholy, the foot,
the sexual organs, or pollen—episodes that correspond to a scientific
and inhuman "unit." The religious women are alienated by this public
way of looking at them, far more than by the devil. The only things that
exist—and that make them exist—are the metamorphoses of deglutition, the modalities of ingestion, the spreading, twisting together, or
elevations of legs, sudden jumps in pulse rate, variations in perspiration,
and so forth.

God—the Flesh

What was sensibly admirable was that [the devil] having commanded in Latin to let her [Jeanne des Anges] join her hands,
one could observe a forced obedience, and the hands were
joined in trembling. And the Holy Sacrament having been re-

ceived in her mouth, he wanted, by puffing and roaring like a
lion, to expel it. Commanded to do no irreverence, it was seen
to cease, and the Holy Sacrament to go down into the stomach.
The rising spasms of vomiting could be seen, and, having been
forbidden to do it, he yielded.[13]

The spectator does not tire of seeing these bodily emotions.

And [the devil] having been commanded to say the name of
the third [of his companions], [the possessed woman] writhed
more vigorously, bearing down with her head, sticking out her
tongue with indecent movements, blowing and spitting, and rising up very high.[14]

Indecency fascinates the gaze. The eye examines in detail. The touch
verifies.

The body of the sister lying on her stomach and twisting her
arms back, there were great and violent contortions, as there
were also in her feet or hands, which, being tightly folded together and even the soles of both feet so joined that they seemed
glued and bound together with some strong ties, several persons
having tried as hard as they could to separate them.[15]

This discourse of the body only develops as religious discourse in the
name of what a "devil" dubs, with a stroke of genius, "God—the Flesh."[16]
Flesh, rather than "body," since the latter, fragmented by divisions that
do not take individuals into account, can no longer be a real unit. It is
no longer divided into celestial or terrestrial elements that make it up,
but into visible organs, members, and functions. But a flesh made God
by the very observation that privileges it. God no longer has the "body"
ancient cosmology gave him. He gets lost (devil or god?) in the neutral
space of a sacredness and a corporeal phenomenology. As for the possessed woman, she doesn't have a body either. The devil, it is said, prevents her from pronouncing the words: my body.[17] In the ideology, the
body belongs to the devil; in fact, it belongs to the public, who dissemi-
nate it in the form of objects displayed and distinguished from one another according to a different code from that of personal substantialities.

This discourse is often qualified as indecent in the minutes. The adjective doubtless designates a moral resurgence accompanying a new "curiosity." But in a second sense it defines very precisely what, through (and
under the cover of) the mythology of the devil, God is being made into.
He is no longer the subject that sustains the surface of things, and that

a hermeneutic deciphers through it; he is brought back to a surface of which he occupies only one spot; he is given there, immediate and exposed. The clothing that hid him has now become the flesh, naked, indecent, because there is nothing else for it to clothe.

Going One Better

The exorcists do not yet know it, but the physicians and visitors will teach them: in their own way they are unconscious, just like possessed women, who are required to speak a language that brackets the subject or the consciousness that speaks it. They practice what they do not know. But their ignorance has a different position from that of the possessed women. For the latter, consciousness is alongside possession, which is defined precisely by its exclusion. For the former, a distance is created between what their language is for themselves and what it is for a growing segment of the public—hence, between their interpretation and common usage.

In itemizing a physiological vocabulary, the exorcists believe they are defending a depth of hell or heaven, a diabolical interiority, a supernatural beyond. In doing so they make the outer world speak their own intentions. Straddling the logic of corporeal discourse, their interpretation welds together their spiritual interiority and a mystic interiority of things. They postulate the same thing within themselves and behind the corporeal phenomena. It is a tautological affirmation. But already their language no longer says that.

They realize this, though indirectly, when the public's reticence prompts them to a mystic one-upmanship. Lacking the means to defend their interpretation on its own ground, they can only throw themselves into the balance to tip the scales, calling down damnation upon themselves if what they say is untrue. The individual argument is the only one they have left. Through that challenge, they look for the miracle that would compensate for their weak arguments, for the lack of a common language. They challenge heaven, creating the danger in order to give the fact of their being spared the force of a proof.

Thus Barré, at the beginning of the exorcism of November 25, 1632:

> The said Barré, dressed in his priestly vestment, having the custodial in his hands and the body of Our Lord therein, pointed out to the whole audience that he knew that many persons were circulating the rumor that he and the religious women and the Carmelites who had assisted them were witches and magicians, and that everything they were doing was nothing but trickery

and imposture; that he prayed to God that, if thus were the case, not only himself but also all the said Carmelites and religious women, and the whole convent, be confounded and sink into hell. And kneeling, holding the custodial on his head, he repeated the same prayer. And then all the said Carmelites and religious women said in one voice: Amen. The same was also said and done by the prior of said Carmelites [Antonin de la Charité], also holding the custodial in his hands and placing it on his head, and all said religious and nuns responding as one: Amen.[18]

While impressive, this escalation nonetheless implies an alternative between two terms—heaven, hell—that are equally suspect; it remains internal to the system that is being challenged.

Loudun, an Open Town

As a matter of fact, the exorcists are soon deprived of the discourse of which they claimed to be the inventors and rightful owners. For a while, Mignon and Barré sufficed to do everything. They experienced their first debates with the devil as a heroic morn: solitude and intimacy protected the discoveries, whispered in Latin in the prioress's bedroom. They were the sole masters of the unknown tongue, discovered word by word, through many a threat and vexation, on the alien bodies that fascinated them and made fun of them by sticking their tongues out at them. And now they must share the treasure of those diabolical sentences with others. There is a rush for that gold that circulates, visible and captive, in the words and gestures of a few Ursulines. Already the whole city is involved in this possible beyond that is a here.

A legible vocabulary is presented by the exorcists as the sign of a mystic (that is, hidden) origin and endowed with inestimable value, since the fineness (of its metal) is supernatural. (Like the merchandise/money of the era, the words are held to give immediately what they represent.) But a language is a public institution. It belongs to everyone. No sooner have the words of the devil been "isolated" than they are taken away from their original holders, seized by the commerce of hundreds and soon thousands of different people. There is devaluation with respect to the initial valuation, which was maintained by a private circulation, in the prioress's own chamber. An unstable currency, whose exchange rate becomes increasingly unstable as the number of those using it grows.

The Powers

The first occupants of the terrain must give way to others. First, to non-local clerics, dispatched from Poitiers, Bordeaux, Paris, and so forth. But they also had to accept powers other than spiritual. The civil jurisdiction intervenes: Hervé, the *lieutenant criminel*, with close ties to Mignon, hence still "one of us"; then the bailiff, visibly irritated by this absurd conspiracy against his friend Grandier, whom he does not, however, defend with the utmost energy; his clerk; his assessors Aubry, Daniel Drouin, Thibault, Louis and Charles Chauvet, and so on.

The medical power is transported to the place as well. It is called there as a reinforcement, in the form of a few reliable physicians close to the exorcists. But regardless of whether that power certifies or denies the reality of the possession, the physician has a different point of view from that of the exorcists. Taking the prioress's head in his hands, Dr. Gabriel Coustier, a physician from La Cloistre, asserts aloud that "there are no pulsing arteries in her entire brain." Dr. Daniel Rogier notes the absence of perspiration after the convulsions. Alphonse Cosnier, a regular physician at Fontevrault, "remarks particularly all the accidents befalling several ladies," and taking place, he says, in "three days' time."[19] François Brion, a master surgeon in Thouars, makes similar observations.

Daniel Rogier and René Maunoury are among the first to sign an attestation, on October 18, 1632.

> We, the undersigned, Doctor of Medicine and Master Surgeon living in this city of Loudun, certify to whom it may concern that by order of the *lieutenant général criminel* of Loudun and the surrounding Loudunais township, communicated to us by Girard, the royal sergeant, we have come to the convent of the Ursulines of this city to see and examine the prioress of said ladies, and another named Sister Claire, whom we found lying in bed, sometimes having extortions and involuntary movements throughout their members, and particularly with yellow faces and eyes rolling upward and other very horrible movements, with stopping of the pulse during said rigors, which cause us to judge them to be neither voluntary, nor feigned, nor yet again morbid, because of the immediate return of strength, indicating after said violence no alteration in the subjects themselves.[20]

Among the doctors, regular physicians or master surgeons who will follow the two from Loudun, there will be many who are more subtle. The account of their visit will have a more learned tone. But already these men juxtapose the localization of a mystic language and the discourse of the body itself. Opposite the depth postulated with the abysmal value affecting certain words, they set the surface made up of the inventory of visible phenomena, such as nervous twitches, perspiration, a regular pulse rate, eyes rolled back in their sockets, and so forth. The diagnosis no longer pertains to the (supernatural) origin of isolated phrases, but to the relationship between the places successively "visited," palpated, observed, and explored by the physicians' eyes or hands.

On November 26, 1632, judges and observers Rogier, de Fos, Joubert, and Fanton requested a more thorough "visit."

> The bailiff and the king's men called us to the court of said convent, and ordered us verbally to say and declare unto them what we thought of said movements [of the possessed women].
>
> To which we all responded of a common accord that we could not with assurance and in good conscience, on the strength of one sole visit, ascertain for them the cause of such movements, unless they first permitted us to see said religious women more particularly, and that it please them to allow us, in order to have full and certain knowledge of them, to remain as a group for a few days and nights with said religious and with such magistrates and religious men as it should please said bailiff: and that it please them to order, so that we may all together judge the affair more fully, that they not be fed or medicated, if need be, except by our hands; that no one should speak to them unless it be out loud and in the presence of all, nor touch said nuns having said movements except it be ourselves, and in the presence of us all.[21]

A double seizure: both of the body they intend to reserve for themselves for a time at least, and of the full and certain knowledge they claim to draw from that examination. This taking possession is not the point of such and such an individual, but of them all together and "of a common accord." The power that is settling into place is that of a body: the body of the medical establishment.

A Public Square

The exorcists are the victims of their early successes. The space they have circumscribed is changed by those who enter it. It is altered by these entrances. The succession of places in which the affair is handled signifies, moreover, the stages of a progressive dispossession of the exorcists by a movement toward public places: from Jeanne's chamber we move to the Ursuline chapel, then to the parochial churches; later, the debate will be concluded in the city's public squares.

These topographical modifications, therefore, do not simply correspond to quantitative extension in the type of question asked and the solution to be found for it. The initial actors are dislodged from their original project, and from the meaning they attributed to it, by the indiscreet presences that fissure the mental cosmos of their "work." "You should not be here doing what you are doing": on October 25 the minutes note that injunction from a witness to one of his interlocutors. It will recur frequently. A face-to-face confrontation that is impossible to isolate translates into a displacement of the original place. Points of view and interpretations confront and destroy one another, and constitute the different terrain of another discussion.

The problem of Loudun can be formulated as follows: What is the "place" that will be the rendezvous of incompatible forms of reason? Is there a common language, and are there common points of reference, between projects affirming a "reality" in function of heterogeneous criteria? "What is *really* happening?" and "How can it be expressed?": These two different questions are really one, and they refer to the existence of a *locus communis*. The enigma of this story is the possibility of a discourse on possession. At the beginning, in the sacred enclave managed by the exorcists, the possession, considered certain, itself supplied a supernatural language. But once put into circulation, the words of the beyond are no longer anything but human words. They no longer circumscribe a place in hell, but argued over by human beings and successively mobilized by divergent intellectual systems, they refer to the place that is at once the object of the discussion and the principle of its imminent solution: a public square.

~ 4 ~

The Accused: Urbain Grandier

The discourse of possession turns on an absent figure whom it gradually renders more precise: the sorcerer. Contrary to what one might suppose, the theater at Loudun is not provoked by that formidable or fantastic figure. It is not determined by his approach or his visibility. It needs him in order to function. Thus, as it organizes itself for itself, developing and refining its procedures, it defines the silhouette, the name, the misdeeds of the "possessor," upon whom possession depends. First the exorcising procedures, the localization of a language, the rules of a diabolical crisis are perfected. But all that is only possible, according to the logic of the system, if there is a guilty party. What makes possible and what authorizes this language (and perhaps this is true of all language, though in other forms) is a death. It alone, ultimately, will authenticate the drama and make the theater into a "true discourse" *[discours véritable]*. That title, given to so many contemporary chapbooks on Loudun, orients them in the direction of an "end" that was the hidden postulate of the story. It takes a live burning at the stake to make the discourse true.

A hidden labor thus weaves the net to catch a sorcerer. Not without false starts. We saw that at the beginning the phantom had the traits of Moussaut, the deceased chaplain, before being replaced by the feared, hoped for, rejected chaplain: Urbain Grandier. And there is a reason, moreover, why the director of conscience who resists (Grandier) re-places the one who did not resist (Moussaut): it reflects the reaction, in their convents, of active women, themselves educators and directors, newly promoted, yet still subjected to the rigid authority of a sacred power and a masculine field of knowledge. In Nancy, ten years earlier (1622) but outside the cloister, in the urban life that was in the process of evolving, a physician was taken to be the one who had bewitched

Elisabeth de Ranfaing—a different field of knowledge, but one that still defined a *director*. A "feminist" rebellion targets, disguisedly, the traditional power, occupied by a new field of knowledge.

But who is this Urbain Grandier?

Conceited, Vain, Libertine?

"I am," Michelet would later write, "against the burners, but not in the least for the burned. It is ridiculous to make a martyr out of him out of hatred for Richelieu. He was conceited, vain and a libertine, who deserved, not the stake, but life in prison."[1]

A full-length portrait of Grandier has been passed down to us by the best of the contemporary historians of the affair, a long-time pastor in Loudun: Aubin. Aubin's style, like Grandier's, "always . . . well dressed, never walking except in long robes." It presents a rather powdered face. It speaks decorously: libertinage is referred to as gallantry, and cleverness becomes wit. But the measured language does, after all, convey an accurate overall picture, and epitomizes many documents.

The Fine Talker

He was tall and good-looking, with a mind both firm and subtle, always clean and well dressed, never walking except in long robes. That external politeness was accompanied by that of the mind. He expressed himself with great ease and elegance. He preached rather frequently. He acquitted himself of that function incomparably better than most monks who climb up to the pulpit. We have one of his funeral harangues on the death of the illustrious Scévole de Sainte-Marthe [1623], which is a very eloquent piece that shows the beauty of his genius. He was sweet and civil to his friends, but proud and haughty to his enemies. He was jealous of his rank and never relinquished his own interests, repelling affronts with such rigor that he turned people against him whom he could have won over by taking a different tack. Nevertheless he was exposed to many enemies. His haughtiness had made him a great number of them, and the extraordinary penchant he had for gallantry made him even more.[2]

Ismaël Bouillau gives his view of the man in whose proximity he lived for many years, in a letter addressed to Gassendi on September 7, 1634, after the execution of the curé. The writer is a Loudunais, a local witness, a man of learning, and the future curator, with the Dupuy brothers, of the library of Thou:

> He had great virtues, but accompanied by great vices, human vices nevertheless, and natural to man. He was learned, a good preacher, a fine talker, but he had a pride and vainglory that were so great that that vice made the majority of his parishioners into enemies, and his virtues brought him the envy of those who cannot appear virtuous unless the secular clergy are defamed among the people.[3]

A Career

Grandier was born in Bouère (in Mayenne), in a little house whose site is still pointed out, on the outskirts of the town.[4] His father, Pierre, and his mother, Jeanne Renée Estièvre, had six children: Urbain, François, and Jean, all priests (François was vicar of Saint-Pierre-du-Marché at the time of the possession); René, councilor at the court of Poitiers; and two daughters, one of whom married, while the other, Françoise, lived with her mother at the residence of the curé of Loudun.

Before obtaining the benefice of his Loudun cure, Urbain pursued a very ecclesiastical course. At age ten he went to Saintes, to his uncle, the canon Claude Grandier. Then he entered the Jesuit college of La Madeleine in Bordeaux. When he was twenty-five, he was ordained to the priesthood. Warmly recommended by the Bordeaux Jesuits to those of Poitiers, who held the cure of Saint-Pierre-du-Marché as a benefice of their college, he was accepted and took possession of the charge in 1617. He remained in that function until 1633.[5]

The Power of the Word

"He was a wonder to hear":[6] among a thousand and one others, a contemporary document indicates at once the nature of his success and the reason for his downfall. He has a power, that of the word. He seduces his public. The reasons for his success are no longer obvious to us. His most famous "piece," a funeral oration, belongs to a category much in favor at the time: accounts of admirable deaths. It has the fashionable marks of the genre. Published in Paris in 1629, the *Oraison funèbre de Scevole de Sainte-Marthe,* the funeral oration of the president and treasurer general of France in Poitiers, who died at the age of eighty-seven (1623), plays skillfully with life and death, to compose such pleasing contrasts as these:

A death in truth filled with lamentations, but a life far more fecund in consolations. For that man is not to be lamented whose extreme age far surpassed the ordinary term of man's life, who in addition raised his reputation above the most ambitious wishes, and who, by the constancy of his life in goodness and the circumstances of his death, has given us just grounds to desire, to hope and to believe that his soul lives happily in heaven while his body rests in the bosom of our common mother, in anticipation of the solemn day when, in accordance with the divine and infallible oracle, he will rejuvenate, no more to age, and be reborn, no more to die.[7]

In this way the curé charms many of the female parishioners, who are more easily charmed than they will say. With his rhetoric, he enflames them. After all, for these Loudunais women, what do a few passing fancies amount to, compared to good gold coin or a house down the street? Solid reality escapes words and amorous infatuation. Grandier's correspondence with the governer Jean II d'Armagnac and his wife, though cordial, full of information and attentions, gives that impression: their letters involve two distinct uses of the same language. Grandier is with his words, he enjoys them, is at home with them. The duke gives willingly of his advice and relates his interventions, but remains somehow distant from words: he uses them, but he lives and works elsewhere, on the terrain of his political and local maneuvers.[8]

The series of suits against the curé continue for ten years (1621–31). Beyond their immediate motives—quarrels of precedence, morals charges, and so forth—they serve as an allegory for the war of a provincial group against a fancy talker, a parvenu, a man who is not a native son and merely possesses the art of using words. That marks him as the stranger, the object of a resistance that does not declare itself for what it is. But he seems unable to grasp the significance of accusations that spell out that threat sotto voce, in the form of precedences he overturns or amorous liaisons, particularly unpardonable because of their notoriety. He takes pride in riding roughshod over the language of a little society that is all the more ferocious in defending its rites, its hierarchies and façades, because it nourishes so few illusions about the violence of its internal conflicts or the passions that infuse its institutions. Fundamentally, what people hold against this curé has less to do with practices than with words; it is less what he does than what he says about it, with arrogance. It is precisely his successes in oratorical sparring matches and legalistic quibbling that precipitate his loss. One segment of opinion applauds him, because this is theater. It will also applaud the theater in which he will play a man condemned to die.

Each time he falls into the trap hidden beneath the favor of the public, each time the brutal reality of his enemies tears him away from his proud eloquence, he is surprised and disarmed. But he thinks he can save the situation with more words. In December 1629, arrested on a morals charge and imprisoned in the tower of the bishopric of Poitiers, he writes to La Rocheposay in flowery terms: "Your selfsame hand can, an it please you, like Peleus's tongue, heal the wound it made."

In reality, he undoes himself, behind the language, itself pitiful, of conversion and despair. So this other letter to the bishop of Poitiers, written in prison:

> My enemies . . . desiring my undoing like a second Joseph, have occasioned my advancement to the kingdom of God. Hence the profit I've derived from their persecution has changed my hatred into love, and my appetite for vengeance into desire to serve them, which I would do better than ever should it please you to restore them to me, as I would desire to restore myself to them were I but out of here, where I have dwelt sufficiently for the healing of my soul and too long for the health of my body, which can no longer second my constancy, being weak by nature and further weakened by the inconveniences that here are great and so many they have left me naught intact save my spirit, which, honed keen upon my hardships, makes me the more miserable the further it fathoms my misfortune, I being besides in such a state that I would like to die did I not live in hopes of hearing soon from you that word of the Savior still rather powerless to resuscitate me ["Lazarus, come forth"], which would be all the sweeter to me as my prison is crueler than his tomb to him, in which he was at rest, tended needlessly by his sisters—and I am buried in my misery, without my friends being permitted to see or comfort me, nay, nor even gaze upon my prison.
>
> In which I find myself in a way more abandoned than that miserable one of the Gospel, who, from the midst of the eternal flames, had the freedom to speak to Lazarus and ask of him a drop of water to refresh himself. And I had not leave to go and see my own mother to ask of her or rather give her a drop of consolation, a trait of severity worthy of your pity and that would have been capable of killing me, had not God fortified me by

his grace, and greatly persuaded me that all this is happening
to humiliate me.

    For though I be innocent of that of which I stand accused,
being nonetheless in other respects too criminal before God,
He will, for my betterment, employ that false charge in the plan
He has to chastise my true iniquities.[9]

    That "affliction" announces the future. But it will be followed, as soon
as Grandier is released from prison, by a return to showy oratory and
witty wordplay.

A Quarrelsome Province

In 1621 a pulpit he refused to have moved in the church had already
caused public insults; Grandier lodged a complaint against the *lieutenant
criminel* Hervé.[10] That skirmish was followed by many others, brought
about by failure to respect precedences, modified processions, assaults
on the curé, and so forth. The entire lexicon of village quarrels. Then
several suits are brought against him for morals. Here the accusation
involves a more dangerous taboo. At the end of 1629 the affair "rises"
to the level of the *official*[11] of Poitiers; it is transferred to the parliament
of Paris, where the prosecutor general Bignon, on the basis of the ruling
concluding the deliberation of August 31, 1630, recalls the trial of the
curé of Beaugé, who was condemned to death "for spiritual incests and
sacrilegious impudicities." The ruling continues: "He [the prosecutor]
was of the opinion that in the proceedings there had been no abuse
because it was legitimate and the *official* turned the accused over to the
lay judge only *ex officio et non de necessitate* [by virtue of office and not of
necessity]."[12]

    The Grandier case passes from ecclesiastic to civil jurisdiction. This
circumstance is already frequent, but still conroversial: Laubardemont's
intervention will accentuate the laicization process. In 1630 the court of
Paris, following the lead of the prosecutor, "resolves to send the parties
before the *lieutenant criminel* of Poitiers to pronounce upon the instruc-
tion of the trial such as it had been conducted by the *official*, not excluding the hearing of new witnesses and proceeding to the aggravation of
letters of monition."[13]

    Instead of becoming a prisoner in Poitiers as the ruling requires,
Grandier returns to Loudun to prepare his defense. An imprudence, or
a provocation? His brother René, his attorney Sieur Estièvre, and Jean

d'Armagnac busy themselves on his behalf in Poitiers and in Paris. On December 14, 1630, the governer writes to the curé:

> For my part, I esteem that your case cannot fail to go well. Send me from time to time news of you and what you will do and to whom I shall yet have to write. If we go to Paris on Wednesday to remain there for good, as they say, I will have the criminal information excerpted and ruled out. Your brother [René] will tell you everything. Forget nothing of what you must do for your case, and go to Poitiers as soon as possible and say I am the cause of your not having gone sooner, because I wanted to take you there myself, as I am writing to M. de la Fresnaye to say to monsieur the king's prosecutor.[14]

Despite an arrest warrant (November 3, 1630), the trial dragged on until May 24, 1631, the date of the sentence that neither condemned nor absolved Grandier, but restricted itself to finding him not guilty "for the present."[15] It was a warning.

The Priest in Love

"He was accused," his compatriot Champion bluntly says, "of frequenting girls and women, and of enjoying some widows of rather good family." That reputation will drive the convents wild; it is well founded. In the little salons of Loudun, "he is a wonder to hear." He is the friend of the house and coveted interlocutor of the little literary and Catholic society assembled by Louis Trincant, the king's prosecutor at the royal courts of justice of Loudun, a deputy of the Tiers-État at the États Généraux of 1614. Trincant is an erudite historian, whose *Histoire généalogique de la maison de Savonnières en Anjou* would appear in 1638 in Poitiers (from Julien Thoreau, who published so many short Loudun treatises). Trincant is also a polemicist (as is clear from his *L'Anti-Anglois, ou responses aux prétextes dont les Anglois veulent couvrir l'injustice de leurs armes, avec une remonstrance à MM. de la Religion prétendue réformée de Loudun* dedicated to Richelieu, published by the same Julien Thoreau in 1628). The curé makes the conquest of his eldest daughter, Philippe. Whence a child, who is attributed to Marthe Le Pelletier. But the Loudunais are not so easily fooled.

Shortly afterward another, more surprising scandal sets the city astir. It takes place in the house of René de Brou, a councilor to the king, sieur de Ligueil, allied to all the "good families" of the region, and a close relative of the bailiff Guillaume de Cerisay. After the death of René and his wife Dorothée Genebaut (to whom the curé had often loaned money), the youngest of the three daughters, Madeleine, not yet married, was confided to the curé's spiritual direction. Unsociable, pious, tempted at one time by the convent, she became the mistress of her confessor.

Once again the fascination of the "spiritual director" makes itself felt, as if, losing his temporal power and his "civil jurisdiction," the priest were taking a different position and reinforcing a psychological authority. As this power ceases to define a sacred politics, it seems to be transferred toward personal ties—or determined by a political organization that no longer depends on him. Grandier, with his personal strengths and weaknesses, is but one sign among a thousand and one others of the evolution that fragments the old religious society and allots the ecclesiastics, on one hand, to societal roles and pressure groups and, on the other, to the spiritual conversation. In the second aspect, speech gradually ceases to be a public institution and becomes a private relationship. In his own way, Surin will also bear witness to this, when, after 1635, he replaces the spectacular exorcisms with spiritual communication with the possessed Jeanne des Anges.

The Treatise on Celibacy

In the union of Grandier with Madeleine de Brou, the sexual relation is prepared, mediated, justified by a theological doctrine. If we leave to one side the oratorical piece on the death of Scévole de Sainte-Marthe, the only developed text of the curé is situated at that articulation. It is to Madeleine, and for her, that Grandier wrote the *Traicté du coelibat par lequel il est prouvé qu'un ecclésiastique se peut marier, par des raisons et autorités claires et évidentes qui seront déduites succinctement et nuement, sans ornement de langage, afin que la vérité, paraissant toute nue et sans fard, soit mieux reçue* . . . [Treatise on Celibacy, by which it is proven that an ecclesiatic can marry, by clear and obvious reason and authorities that will be deduced succinctly and nakedly, without literary ornament, in order that the truth, appearing stripped bare and without make-up, may be better received . . .]. This theological discourse is a language of love. Here, passion speaks through a historical/scholastic argumentation that reorients the content of a tradition in order to make it serve the purposes of union. In so doing, it transforms the discourse into a baroque allegory of sentiment, into a strange clothing of "stark naked truth," which it at once states and hides. Elsewhere, contrariwise—and soon among the religious of Loudun—the description of ecstasies, of the sentiments of the soul, and of the "movements" of the body becomes the "mystic language," the language of "true" theology, or of the "new spirituality." These are two opposite aspects of the same change. A metamorphosis of religious language precedes and prepares the uses to which it is put with the most opposite intentions.

The treatise of the fine talker presents a very modern-sounding style of argumentation. Proof on the basis of history takes precedence over all others. Natural law passes its judgment on supernatural law. The logic, clear and urgent, is that of a lawyer pleading his case. It is the treatment of the question that is original, rather than the problem, which was often discussed in the sixteenth and seventeenth centuries.

The Law of Nature

In order to leave no suspicion in this matter, it must be shown that it was permitted by all kinds of laws for sacrificers to marry.

Now the law is nothing other than a rule, according to which man must prepare and conduct his actions. Its function is to teach this duty and oblige us to carry it out. There is a sovereign and eternal law, which is God himself, inasmuch as, by the infallible rule of his providence, He governs all creatures and conducts them to their end. From that eternal law all the laws are derived, to wit: the natural, the Mosaic—or written law—and evangelical law, which is the law of grace; which laws, since they come from a common source and are directed toward a common goal, which is to perfect man, are not in the least contrary to one another, nor do they destroy one another, but rather do they reach out a helping hand to one another, to serve their mutual attainment. Thus the law of grace perfects the written law and the latter assists the law of nature. Whence it follows that what one law ordains cannot be undone by the other. . . .

Natural law, therefore, is a mute doctor, a secret light, a participation in the eternal law, a ray that the increate sun has cast into our souls, which is called reason, which, causing us to know what is good and what is evil, inclines us to do the one and to flee the other. That law is inviolable, inasmuch as it is founded upon the immutable truth of things, and on reason, which is always one and like unto itself. That law is nature, of which all the other laws must be born, and animated by right reason; otherwise they are iniquitous. It produces a general precept that commands to do good and flee evil, which, well observed, alone suffices to make man happy. For he who does good and flees evil has nothing else to do to be perfect. But inasmuch as this natural precept was too general and enveloped, there was a need to particularize and develop it, which has been done by written law, which taught what was good and what evil. . . .

Marriage and Priesthood

I say that marriage is expressly ordained by the law of nature, inasmuch as without it, it would perish, and its main intention, which is not only to maintain the species, but also to multiply its individuals, would remain frustrated.

The first reason to prove this truth is drawn from that true maxim that God and nature never do anything in vain. That is why, having given to man and woman not only the desire and appetite of engendering their kind, but also the tools, instruments, or vessels proper to that effect, it follows that they can and should use them, for in vain would be that appetite of that power if it were not acted out and exercised.

And to show that that appetite is just and in conformity with reason, and not at all an effect of corrupted nature, it must be remarked that marriage has existed since the age of innocence and before sin. That reason is supported by a powerful authority, drawn from the history of the creation of the world, written in Genesis, where it is said that God, having created man, judged that it was not right to leave him alone and promptly gave him a woman to be his help and comfort, and commanded them to grow and multiply and replenish the earth, to love one another with a love so cordial and singular that it was enjoined upon the man to abandon father and mother to adhere to his dear other half.

You will tell me perhaps that is it not a question of knowing whether marriage be a good and holy thing, but of knowing if it be fitting to priests and sacrificers. To that, I answer that our first father was a priest, inasmuch as religion is as old as the reasonable creature, and that man was no sooner created than he was obliged to recognize and adore his Creator, offering Him sacrifice, which sacrifice is like unto the soul of religion, which cannot be without sacrifice. It follows therefrom that the first man sacrificed to his God, and thereby was a sacrificer, even though he was married. And after him, Cain, Abel, Abraham, Isaac, and Jacob were sacrificers and married. Whence it must be concluded that in the law of nature marriage was not incompatible with the priesthood.

As for the written law, it is clear to whosoever would look through the Old Testament that there was never mention of celibacy. On the contrary, marriage is held therein in such great honor that there was a curse on barren women. And as for the sacrificers, be it known that the whole people of Israel, which was the people chosen and well loved of God, was distributed in twelve lineages, of which only that of Levi was consecrated to the cult of God and held the sacerdotal dignity, which did not at all keep the Levites, who were the priests of the old law, from marrying. . . .

Each Man's Freedom

It remains to be justified that marriage be still allowed for priests under the law of grace, under which we live. I say allowed, inasmuch as it is neither commanded nor forbidden, and thus left to each man's freedom. On the subject of which it is to be considered that, in the law of nature and at the beginning of the world, marriage was absolutely necessary to people the earth. In the law of Moses, it was not absolutely necessary, but useful and honorable, and its opposite considered blameworthy. Under the evangelical law, which is the decline of the world, it is not necessary, nor as honorable as celibacy, which is its opposite, but it is allowed, and all are free to marry according to the need they have, or to keep their chastity for the greater glory of God. And indeed, if we read the new law which is in conformity with the New Testament, nowhere will we find that it is commanded or forbidden to marry or to stay a virgin. It is true that Saint Paul advises one, but without going against the other, in order to leave each person free to embrace the one or the other according to how he feels called. Marriage is exalted to the point of giving it the title of grand sacrament. Virginity is also praised therein, as a very noble virtue, even evangelical. God is glorified in both conditions, and both have their attractions, their laudatory qualities, and their praises of honor to make them be cherished according to the divers tastes and appetites and inclinations of persons. In short, to conclude with Saint Paul: those who marry do well; those who remain virgins do better. As for me, I am content to do well. Let those who can do the best. . . .

A Question of Preference

Let us now see how this sovereign and eternal priest governed himself when he laid the foundation of Christianity. He formed the college of the apostles of men married and virgin, such as were Saint Peter and Saint John, to show that both states should be received and admitted in the Church. . . .

But, you will tell me, it is said in the Gospel that the apostles left all to follow Jesus Christ, and consequently they left their wives, for he who says all excepts nothing. Here is the crux of the problem, and the passage upon which the law of celibacy was based. Which is why it must be seriously examined.

We remain in agreement that the apostles left all, even their wives, to follow the Savior, but this was not by obligation, but only suitability and convenience, for, the charge of apostle obliging them to travel to divers provinces to spread the Gospel, it would have been highly unsuitable and inconvenient to drag their wives and children with them. That is why they left them, not by duty, but out of convenience, preferring the service of God to their contentment. . . .

Upon which subject it is to be remarked that whenever Scripture commands to abandon something, which one is, moreover, obliged to love, that is to be understood not as an absolute abandonment, but in order of preference. To cling to one's wife does not mean one must absolutely abandon father and mother, for that is contrary to the law of nature, which, as we have said above, cannot be abolished by any other law. But it means that the husband must prefer his wife to his father and mother in the case in which he cannot assist all of them.

Grandier goes on in this vein. He goes back in time, goes through the Greeks, traverses the Middle Ages, quotes in that context the *Chroniques* of Carion and Jerome of Prague (a precious bit of information on his readings: Carion is the pseudonym of J. Nägelin, later revised by Melanchthon; Jerome, a disciple of John Huss). Lastly he approaches the question of the chastity vow (which, in his opinion, is binding only on religious),[16] and concludes as follows.

Ardent Desire

It is a thing no less cruel to keep a man from marrying than to deny him food and drink, inasmuch as he has no lesser inclination toward the one than the other. Indeed, the desire to marry is even much more ardent, the desire for it being sweeter and more ticklish, inasmuch as eating only sustains this brief life, but marriage makes man live again after his death in his children, who often by their prayers put in heaven the one who put them on earth.[17]

In a letter of October 14, 1634, Sieur Seguin, a physician at Tours, convinced of the possession, speaks to Sieur Quentin of this *Traicté*, which is well known in Loudun. His letter was immediately published in the *Mercure françois:*

> He [Grandier] confessed under question to a little handwritten book against the celibacy of priests, which gives suspicion that he was married. Note that it is addressed to his dearest concubine, whose name is suppressed throughout, in the title as well, and concludes with this distich and token:
>
> > Si ton gentil esprit prend bien cette science
> > Tu mettras en repos ta bonne conscience.[18]
>
> I cannot dissimulate from you that this treatise seemed to me very well done and consequent up till the conclusion, which is lame forsooth and discovers the venom. There is nothing therein that tends toward magic, and it seems rather one could induce the contrary, were there not elsewhere proofs sufficient.[19]

In fact, these proofs will be furnished only by the civil trial procedure. The discourse of possession spoke of the sorcerer: judiciary and political power will make him into a dead man.

~ 5 ~

Politics in Loudun: Laubardemont

Behind the stage on which the exorcists and the possessed play out their roles, other forces and other causes intervene. At first they appear in Loudun only in undergoing the distortions imposed by the discourse of possession. The diabolical thus becomes the metaphor of politics, which latter progressively determines the action. The conflicts stemming from the installation of a new public order begin by entering quasi-surreptitiously into this possession of extraneous origin. They use its vocabulary and its data; they will gradually organize it, reveal themselves in it, and make use of it, before dropping the mask and bequeathing it to piety and private curiosity.

The Appeal to the King

The arrival of the baron de Laubardemont in Loudun in September 1633 marks a turning point: the introduction of centralist politics. The baron has been commissioned by the king to demolish the castle. But that intervention was prepared by the adversaries' referral of their differences to royal authority. What each party lacks by way of assurance and power to overcome the enemy clan moves nearly all of them to appeal to the scepter or authority of the king. To the surprise of the local protagonists, these appeals (often simple verbal threats) will take on formidable weight. They open up a preliminary space for the intervention of the central power.

Thus, as early as December 12, 1632, Cerisay, the bailiff, Charvet, the *lieutenant civil,* and Chauvet, his assessor, underline, in a letter addressed to the bishop of Poitiers, that Sieur Barré, the exorcist of the Ursulines, had "said and done several things in defiance of the jurisdiction of the royal authority."[1] A rather vague and common protest. In becoming a reality, it will short-circuit all who call upon the royal authority, which will take them at their word. After having been for so long a manner of speaking, the bogeyman arrives in Loudun. It is Laubardemont.

The Gentlemen Destroyers

The *intendant* arrives in September 1633, charged with a mission having nothing to do with the possession, but rather with the demolition of the castle, this time including the donjon. In August he sends a copy of the royal letter he received to Mesmin de Silly, in Loudun:

> M. de Laubardemont,
>   Having learned of the diligence you brought to the demolition of the castle of Loudun, and in so doing to execute the command that you had received from me, I wished to draw up this letter to express my satisfaction with your service upon that occasion and, because the donjon still remains to be demolished, you will not fail, following the commission that has been sent you, to have it razed entirely without reserving any part thereof.
>   I have further learned that the portals of said city serve as a fortress and could be prejudicial to the tranquility of the inhabitants were persons of ill intent to gain control of them. Hence I desire that you open them from the inside in order that they may not be used to their disadvantage. Assured that you will carefully accomplish these things according to my will, I will make no further insistence, and pray that God, M. Laubardemont, keep watch over you.
>   Written at Montereau this 6th day of August, 1633
>   Louis Phélypeaux.[2]

The commission announced by the letter will reach Laubardemont a few days later. It supersedes the letters patent of May 13, 1632, in which Louis XIII, from Royan, made a gift to Sieur Jean d'Armagnac, one of his first *valets de chambre,* and to Sieur Michel Lucas, one of his secretaries, "in consideration of their services, of the domains, moats, and counterscarps of the great castle of Loudun, in case his majesty should resolve to have said great castle demolished as being useless, and except only the donjon to be kept for the surety of the town and the inhabitants of Loudun."[3]

One part of the material left from the demolition was to go to Michel Lucas, and the other to the governor.

A New Political Balance

In 1631–32 Jean d'Armagnac was plotting and planning to keep, along with the donjon that had become his residence, the functions of governor of Loudun. But he was deceiving himself when he rejoiced over the success of which he assured Grandier against their common adversaries, or over his ephemeral triumphs against the wreckers—"the Gentlemen destroyers," as he called them—or over the support he thought he would get from Laubardemont, who had recently been delegated by the king to attend his son's baptism (1630). "I am so pleased to see all those Gentlemen caught, and monsieur le baron (Laubardemont] who also rejoiced. My wife must be gloating before all who visit her."

Obliged to travel incessantly in the king's service, too far from Paris and Loudun, a victim of his own intrigues, he did not properly assess the importance of the changes that were taking place in the political personnel, nor the magnitude of the interests weighing against him. Sieur Lucas, secretary of the king's hand, had much more influence with Louis XIII; kept very well informed by his friends in Loudun, he now worked against his erstwhile co-beneficiary.

A Neighbor: Richelieu

Above all, Richelieu's seigneury of Richelieu (which was less than twenty kilometers from Loudun) had just been enlarged and made into a peerage-dukedom (August 1631), and it was his firm intention to consolidate its domain. He was approaching the height of his power, having become, as Mathieu de Morgues writes from Holland, "Cardinal, Prime Minister, Admiral, Constable, Chancellor, Keeper of the Seals, Superintendent of Finances, Grand Master of the Artillery, Secretary of State, Duke and Peer, Governor of thirty fortified towns, Abbot of as many abbeys, Captain of two hundred men-at-arms and as many cavalry men," obliged to subsume the rest of his titles with an "etc."[4]

By September 25, 1631, d'Armagnac was writing to Urbain Grandier: "I saw some of my friends in that city [Paris] who thought that M. de Laubardemont was already in Loudun, and who told me that I would certainly obtain full satisfaction, be it one way or be it another."

Certainly? That was saying too much, for he added: "[H]owever . . . it was thought that everything would be knocked down, even the city walls, destroying as much of the city and its jurisdiction as a councilor of the court is going to take over of it, for it is going to the establishment of the peerage-dukedom of the town of Richelieu."[5]

Being a realist (unlike d'Armagnac), Laubardemont didn't hurry. He took the time to see in which direction "the will of the king and of monseigneur the cardinal" was tending. He cultivated Michel Le Masle, the prior of Les Roches, first secretary to the cardinal, and, as we shall see, he was to maintain the best of relations with him. He also knows with what implacable fidelity, among so many affairs, Richelieu establishes the royal discipline, pursues his work of centralization, and pays special heed to anything that might serve as a place of refuge to the Protestants after the taking of La Rochelle (1628).

Laubardemont

A faithful henchman of the central power, "devoted to the State," as Richelieu will say, an agent assigned by the cardinal to specific and urgent tasks in a period of crisis, a *commissioner*—in the sense the word will take on during the French Revolution—he goes to Loudun to carry out an order. He must be the effective and mobile instrument of a political policy. But he has made his own calculations as well. He assesses both the power that is backing him and, once again, the bitterness of the conflicts in which he is intervening. It is at this point that Grandier receives a letter, the last, as it appears, that the governor of Loudun wrote to him (September 7). D'Armagnac becomes worried, but a little late. Since it is impossible for him to return to his city, he beseeches the curé to "have an eye to everything that takes place there." Alluding to the previous decisions of two supporters of the cardinal, Sieur Hervé and his father-in-law, Mesmin de Silly (a faithful correspondent of Laubardemont's in Loudun and less of a double agent than has been said),[6] the governor adds: "I am angry that this big brute of a *lieutenant criminel* and his father-in-law have sought and obtained the undeniable ruin of the city of Loudun."[7]

Laubardemont will stay in Loudun for only two months. He hears of nothing but magic and deviltry. He attends an exorcism. He gets information. He is doubly interested, because two of his sisters-in-law are among the Ursulines, and because he has already conducted investigations of witchcraft in Béarn, between 1625 and 1629, when he was a lay councilor of the Bordeaux parliament, and then president of inquests of the same parliament. But—and this was a cause of some surprise among the Loudunais, boiling over with excitement and curiosity—he kept his thoughts to himself:

He let no one know what he felt upon witnessing so strange a spectacle. Once he had returned to his house, he felt deeply touched with compassion for the deplorable state of these girls. In order to cover up his feelings, he received at his table Grandier's friends and Grandier himself, who came with the others.[8]

That same month Prince Louis de Bourbon, an illustrious spectator, makes a special trip to Loudun where he has not been since the conference of 1616 between Catholics and Huguenots. He is less discreet. Viewing the actions of the possessed women during an exorcism organized in his honor, his excellency, whose devotion is as excessive as it is late, is touched, moved to ecstasy, and he leaves the exorcists the testimony of his satisfaction.

The Affair of the "Cordonnière"

In the city whose present interrogates its past, an old story also resurfaces. Catherine Hammon, a Loudunaise of modest condition known as "la cordonnière" [the cobbler], pretty, crafty, chancy, had won the affection of Queen Marie de Médicis, who attached her to her personal service. She wheedled her way into the affairs of Loudun in the name of her mistress. She had been implicated, rightly or wrongly, in the publication of a violent pamphlet against Richelieu: *Lettre de la cordonnière de la reine-mère à M. de Baradas* (1627). In the lampoon supposedly addressed to François de Baradat, first gentleman of the king's chamber, who had been disgraced and turned out of the court in 1626, Charpentier, the cardinal's able secretary, stressed mainly the crime of *lèse-majesté:*

> One may say that the unbridled freedom of this century, having produced several of this sort, not one has yet appeared as bloody and pernicious as this. . . . These are slanders against the chief ministers of the State . . . and, what is worse, insults attacking and offending the person of the king, accusing him of irresponsibility, fickleness, and--and this is dreadful, in the face of his known virtue—of detestable impurity.[9]

Who was the author? He could not be identified. The text cast suspicion in the direction of Loudun, however. The "cordonnière" was believed to have written to Sieur Baradat: "I wish you wanted to come to our Loudunais. You'd get to know a lot more of them. I'll make a collection of them to send you the first chance I get."

Only the printer had been seized, one Jacques Rondin, Sieur de la

Hoguetière, a native of Bayeux. He was immediately brought before the grand court at the Châtelet, where despite his denials he was sentenced on May 27, 1627, "to be hanged and strangled," and finally was sent to the galleys at Rochefort.

Grandier a Pamphleteer?

The same year, however, a second lampoon appeared with the same title, less crude, more stinging, and carefully distinguishing the king, who was rather flattered, from his "bad counselors," who should be dismissed. Was Grandier, who had been closely associated with Catherine Hammon since 1617 (at that date she had visited Loudun, and the curé was arriving there), the author of this second pamphlet attributed to the "cordonnière"? It was so rumored. In any case, he was linked to that dangerous business, at the moment when Suzanne Hammon, Catherine's sister, one of the nonreligious possessed women, accused him of being a sorcerer. According to Ménage, the Capuchins whom Father Joseph, the "Éminence grise," had installed at Loudun took it upon themselves to report this to their protector—who moreover had plenty of other informers in the city of Théophraste Renaudot:

> The Capuchins of Loudun, in their design to take revenge on their enemy [Grandier], wrote to Paris to Father Joseph, their confrère, that Grandier was the author of a libel called *La Cordonnière de Loudun,* very offensive to both the person and the birth of the cardinal de Richelieu.[10]

More than one historian will share the conviction of the Capuchins— if indeed it was their conviction. Where in all this does legend end and history begin? This testimony of a curious contemporary observer is also indicative of the gossip that will target the Capuchins, but it is doubtless no less revelatory, à propos of the gossip disseminated by means of a pamphlet against the power, of the gossip surrounding and threatening Grandier. There is a multiplication of rumors. All these accusatory *histoires* envelop the city in a fog. What is true? What is false? Overcome by anguish in this disappearance of certainty and of distinctions, the Loudunais will yield to a security reflex: unable to discover where the truth lies, they will affirm one—but it won't be the same one for everybody.

The Letters Patent of November 30, 1632

It is the end of October: the donjon has been demolished. Laubardemont returns to Paris, with a stop at Chinon, to meet the exorcist Barré and gather new information from him. He sees Richelieu in Rueil, and Father Joseph. Michel Lucas is briefed. The king's council meets in Rueil, its participants including, besides the king and the cardinal, Chancellor Séguier, Superintendent Bouthillier de Chavigny, Secretary of State Phélypeaux, Father Joseph, and Laubardemont. Procedures were decided upon; letters patent were written and signed by Séguier on November 30:

> M. de Laubardemont, councilor to the king in his councils of State and privy, will proceed to Loudun and to other places as needful, and being there,
>
> investigate diligently said Grandier on all deeds of which he has been hitherto accused and other that will be brought against him, even touching the possession of the Ursuline religious of said Loudun and other persons that are also said to be possessed and tormented by demons by the evil spell of said Grandier,
>
> investigate all that has occurred since the beginning, both at the exorcisms and otherwise on the subject of said possession,
>
> collect and identify the minutes and other acts of the commissioners delegated thereto,
>
> attend the exorcisms that will take place and have minutes taken of it all, and otherwise proceed as is appropriate to bring proof and entire verification of said facts,
>
> and, on the entire matter, decree, investigate, conduct, and complete the trial of said Grandier and all the others who will be found to have been accomplices in said case up to, but to the exclusion of, definitive sentence—all opposition, appeals, and objections whatsoever notwithstanding, for which, and without prejudice to them, there will be no deferment, even, given the quality of the crimes, without regard to a dismissal that might be requested by said Grandier.
>
> His majesty mandating to all the governors and lieutenants general of the province, and to all bailiffs, seneschals, vice seneschals, provosts, their lieutenants, mayors and aldermen of cities, and other officers and subjects concerned, to give, for the execution of the above, all assistance and enforcement, help, and prisons should it prove necessary, may they be so required.

To examine all facts pertinent to the possession, to open an investigation of Grandier, Laubardemont has a full and entire competency, over

Loudun and anywhere else necessary, allowing him to override opposition, appeals, or demands for dismissal (although in principle these options remain permitted and usable), but not authorizing him to pass judgment on Grandier's guilt, or to pronounce the sentence himself.

To these letters patent are immediately added two orders signed by the king and Secretary of State Phélypeaux:

> to authorize said Sieur de Laubardemont to arrest and take prisoner said Grandier and his accomplices in a secured place, with similar mandates to all provosts of marshals, vice bailiffs, vice seneschals, their lieutenants and archers and other officers and subjects, to assist in the execution of said orders and to obey, in effecting them, the orders given them by said sieur, and to the governors and lieutenant governors to give whatever assistance and help shall be required of them.[11]

Lastly Louis XIII gives the commissioner a letter addressed to Msgr. de La Rocheposay, in which he recommends that the bishop take up the cause of the Ursulines—inasmuch, the king explains, as this affair comes under the authority of the Church. There is a certain humor here, since a lay investigation of the curé of Loudun is being ordered. Though not necessarily under the jurisdiction of ecclesiastic justice (the jurisprudence of the day is not unanimous, although by and large it tends to bypass ecclesiastic jurisdiction, even where priests are involved), this affair could have been handled by the bishop. But this marks a turning point.

Richelieu: To Make an Example

The decision is astonishing on Richelieu's part, less by its swiftness, severity, or "exceptional" character than by its object: "the possession" of girls "tormented by demons by the evil spell of said Grandier." Despite the usual precautions, it seems the die is cast. However superstitious or vindictive the cardinal may have been, he is acting rather in obedience to the "reason" he imposes with such rigor and coherence: the *raison d'État*. Amid far more serious preoccupations, tasks interspersed with so many struggles, perils, and deaths, this troublesome affair is treated according to a general rule. With the passage of time and in an obviously apologetic intent, Richelieu explains himself in his *Memoirs:*

> His majesty having, in his justice, given some remedy to the disorder that the malice of men had caused in his State, was obliged to again use his authority to strengthen the Church and help with remedies it was necessary to apply to the trouble the Evil

One had for some time stirred up in the Church, in the person of some Ursuline religious in the town of Loudun.

Since the year 1632 some Ursuline nuns in the town of Loudun having appeared possessed, the cardinal, returning from his journey to Guyenne, on advice he had received of it, sent some persons of ecclesiastical dignity and of piety that they should make him a true report of it. They learned, by the deposition of said religious, whom they heard severally, that at night, as they retired, some of them had heard their doors open, some persons to come up by their step, and then to enter their room with some dark light that caused some kind of horror.

All agreed they had seen in their rooms a man whom they depicted, not knowing him, such as was the curé of Saint-Pierre of Loudun, who spoke to them of impurity, and by several impious persuasions tried to win their consent. Then some of them found themselves tormented by these apparitions, and began to perform actions of women obsessed or possessed by the Evil One. Their confessors and some other wise and pious priests exorcised them. But after they had delivered them, the possession recommenced by new pacts in virtue of which the demons said they had returned.

But as in that matter there is much deception and often the simplicity that ordinarily accompanies piety causes to be believed things of this kind that are not true, the cardinal dared not make a certain judgment on the report made to him, inasmuch as there were many that defended said Grandier, who was a man of good appearance and sufficient erudition, though the bishop of Poitiers had, sometime earlier, condemned him and obliged him to abandon his benefice in a time he set for him, but having appealed his sentence to the archbishop of Bordeaux, he was dismissed absolved. But at last that affair became so public, and so many religious found themselves possessed, that the cardinal, unable to suffer more compaints that had been made to him from all sides, counseled the king to bring his authority and send there M. de Laubardemont, councilor in his Council of State, to investigate that affair so that the presence of said Grandier, who had credit in the country, could not keep the witnesses from setting down the truth, and have him led to the château of Angers.[12]

From the "dark light that caused some kind of horror" to the public "disorder" that the cardinal cannot "suffer," we have the evolution of the affair seen from Paris. Richelieu has no illusion about the "simplicity" that "ordinarily accompanies piety," and, at the very least, he remains hesitant about these religious women who *appear* possessed. But he does not tolerate a troublemaker who is perhaps also a pamphletist, in an era still close to the Ligues and the Wars of Religion. In order to defend at once the royal discipline, the respect for the central power, and the reform of the clergy, he intends to make an example.[13] Grandier is the price of a political policy. And he is seized by the royal justice as he appears on the surface of the official pages of history, caught in the net of Loudun rumor.

The Good Fortune to Succeed

Jean Martin, baron de Laubardemont, arrives in Loudun on December 8. In making his way down the frozen streets of the town to his lodgings in the Faubourg de Chinon, at the house of Paul Aubin, the son-in-law of Mesmin de Silly, he too enters the official pages of history, bent on success. Two years later, on August 28, 1636, he wrote to the cardinal:

> I have, Monseigneur, established good correspondences to obtain certain notice of everything that happens in the provinces of my department, in which I am loved and esteemed much more than I deserve. I have also always, Monseigneur, had the good fortune to succeed in all things that have been commanded to me, and I recognize that I am obliged, by your blessings and kindnesses, to employ my life, and all I have in the world, in your service, to which I have already devoted myself for a long time, with an inviolable affection.[14]

Unconditional and self-assured, a devotee of the king and the cardinal, but also ambitious, calculating, and harsh, Grandier's opponent in the trial that was beginning was a strange character. Mathieu Martin, his father, the treasurer general of France in the province of Guyenne, *audiencier* in the chancellery for the parliament of Bordeaux, had in 1607 acquired the castle and the mill of Sablon, near Coutras, with rights of high, middle, and low justice. Born in Bordeaux c. 1590, married in 1611 to Isabeau de Nort, in 1612 Jean Martin succeeds his father-in-law as lay councilor to the parliament of Bordeaux. In 1624, he gets the king to agree that the parish of Sablon and the village of Brautière be renamed Laubardemont. His career truly takes shape when, after having acquired the office of president of the first chamber of inquests of the parliament of Bordeaux (1627), he is called to direct the

commission charged with going to pursue judgment of the sorcerers of
Béarn: he is becoming a specialist. His success accelerates. The following
dates mark out its trajectory: 1629, first president of the court of aids of
Guyenne, in Agen; 1631–32, commissions for the destruction of the cas-
tles of Royan, Montereau, and then Loudun . . . In December 1635 he
will be made "*intendant* of justice, the police, and finance of the provinces of Touraine, Anjou, Mayenne, Loudunais and other surrounding
ones." Later, he will be charged with investigation on the doctrine of
Saint-Cyran (1639), commissioned to instruct the trial of Cinq-Mars in
Lyons (1642), called to take care of the possession of Louviers, and so
forth. As ordinary councilor to the king in his councils, he died in Paris
on May 22, 1653.[15]

The King's Saint Michael

"The good of the king's service and public utility"[16] are the same thing
for Laubardemont. The royal politics is his ethics. In his own way, the
physician Duncan will say as much in 1634, though Laubardemont does
not share the "simplicity" of the possessionists:

> In what concerns M. de Laubardemont, he is too judicious to
> desire his opinion of the possession to pass for law to others,
> and has sufficiently showed in several occurrences that he takes
> no offense against those who have other sentiments than he,
> and I am sure he demands no other praise than that of faithful-
> ness and diligence in the execution of his commission.[17]

That will be *to succeed.* But as his conscience as a man is in harmony
with his convictions and interest as a functionary, as the violence of conflicts give harshness and duplicity an air of moral courage and faithfulness, the commissioner also bears himself as a righter of wrongs. He
feels the crushing poverty of the people as unjust, and defends them
against the men of war or the tax collectors, called "partisans."

"The charges that the necessity of the age causes to be placed upon
the subjects of the king are very onerous," he will write again to Séguier.
"But, Monseigneur, the worst evil comes from the abuse committed by
those who are ordered to receive the results, as well as by the men of
war, whose violence cannot be depicted. Everywhere I hear clamors that
are capable of dismaying the most assured."[18]

A Crusade

Laubardemont's commission at Loudun begins to look like a vocation.
It becomes a crusade. And it is a chance, a "blessing" for Laubardemont,

that the king's order pits him against adversaries who are equally the foes of the central power and of God. In his private correspondence, he shows feelings of devotion for the angels, the Christ Child, the miracles, and so forth. His sincerity appears evident. His devotion furnishes him an affective margin that offsets the harshness of a struggle for success and combines a private piety and a public law. But a more personal principle unites these two halves of a life. The legacy of the wars and religious fervors of yesteryear is attributed to royal orders. Politics concil-iates devotion and arms itself with it. It annexes a religious tradition and religious feeling.

From this point of view, there is no longer any separation between the "temporal" and the "spiritual." As a layperson Laubardemont obtains from his political position an ecclesiatic investiture. He finds in the royal crusade a quasi-sacerdotal power. He acquires and gives himself a role of spiritual director in the name of that investing of religious authority in the civil authority. The passage from the religious to the "political," which is specific to this period, is lived by the commissioner as a coinci-dence. Hence errors in matters of dogma or of spirituality, just like oc-cult rebellions of the Devil, become for Laubardemont "royal cases, inas-much as that touches the State and the secular Magistrate can take cognizance of it."[19]

A promotion in status of the laity, the institution of a political policy, the mobilization of the sacred in the service of the State: such an end justifies the means. Laubardemont is thus established in a celestial "hier-archy," recovered and transposed in a *raison d'État,* while at the same time the clerics mobilize it in the service of a new theology of the priest-hood and the "ecclesiatic hierarchy." For years he will present himself with an undeniable seriousness as the spirtual protector and director of the Ursulines.

Thus he finds, with the Devil against the king, the great battle and justification of his career. As suggested by a Loudun flatterer in the piti-ful poem he will dedicate to him in 1634, Laubardemont wants to be, nay is, everywhere the archangel of the State and, sword in hand, the king's Saint Michael:

> Vous que le roi commet et donne
> Pour condamner en sa personne
> Les démons et les écraser
> Comme un second Michel archange . . .[20]

All opposition to power has the face of the demon. And here at last, before the archangel, the demon takes off his mask in Loudun.

~ 6 ~

Beginning the Judicial Inquiry

December 1633–April 1634

Laubardemont springs into action. He gathers the elements of the judicial inquiry. He has Grandier arrested at dawn on Sainte-Croix Square by archers [agents of the Judicial Police] sent from Angers under the command of Guillaume Aubin, sieur de la Grange, lieutenant of the Mounted Constabulary.

The Arrest

Aubin placed the royal seal on the rooms, wardrobes, and other places in the house, and charged Sieur Jean Poucquet, an archer in his majesty's Guards, to conduct him to the castle of Angers, with the help of the archers and the provosts of Loudun and Chinon.[1]

The premises of the curé were searched on December 7 and 9 and the following days (and even later, on January 1 and 31, 1634), in the presence of Grandier's mother, Jeanne Estièvre, by Laubardemont, Mesmin, Hervé, Bourgneuf, the prosecutor, and the king's advocate, Menuau. Among the papers seized were, according to the *Registres de la Commission:*

> 1. A certain writ in form of a treatise on celibacy, in the hand of Grandier, to prove that priests may marry.
> 2. Two leaves of verse and French rhymes, dirty and immodest.
> 3. Two copies of a letter from the bailiff of Loudun to the prosecutor general of Paris, to persuade him that the possession of the Ursuline religious was a fakery.

4. A response from the prosecutor general to the two preceding letters.

5. Several dispensations granted by the bishop of Poitiers to a large number of families of the parish of Saint-Pierre from attending service under said Grandier and from receiving from him the sacraments of the Church.

6. A discourse in the form of a remonstrance containing reasons, explanations, and arguments intended to prove that he had no part in the supposed possession at Loudun.[2]

This is followed by a series of inquiries, beginning on December 12, into grievances against the curé. The bishop of Poitiers adds his own, in a "monitory" that is read from the pulpit in the churches of the town. On the nineteenth, while another inquiry is being carried out, Jeanne Estièvre is able to get a letter to her son in Angers.

Jeanne Estièvre

Do not think for a moment that it was by lack of affection or goodwill that we have taken so long to get word to you or to send you anything, for it was because we couldn't find out how to do so till now. All our friends participate in your affliction and pray to God that he will make the truth be known, and your innocence appear. For your part, give yourself over to the will of God. We hope He will keep you and make the judiciary recognize you are in the right.

Send us news only on your present situation. We are sending you a shirt, a pair of underwear,[3] two pairs of socks, three pairs of house shoes, two falling bands, two pairs of cuffs, four handkerchiefs, two nightcaps, a sa . . .,[4] one pair of woolen stockings, your brushes, your slippers, small bandages, and . . . gold *pistoles* for your little expenses. If you need other things, send word. In the meanwhile we pray to God that he will give you courage. Your brother François and your sister send their greeting, and I as well, who will ever be

my son

your mother and good friend

Jeanne Estièvre[5]

A Mother's Indictment

On December 27 Jeanne Estièvre addresses a petition to Laubardemont:

To Msgr. de Laubardemont, councilor of the king in his Councils,

Jeanne Estièvre humbly beseeches, both in her own name and on behalf of messire Urbain Grandier, curé of Loudun, her son, presently being held prisoner in the castle of Angers, saying,

That for the past five or six years, some enemies of her said son have tried to take away his honor and life by false and slanderous accusations, from which to their confusion he was dismissed absolved.

That continuing their pernicious design, some of them used the power and direction they had over certain religious of Saint- Ursule, whom they said were possessed by demons, to verbally accuse her said son of magic, falsely unless I be mistaken, of which said Grandier lodged complaint and made an appeal to the court, and they went so far, Monseigneur, while you were in this town of Loudun to demolish the little château, as to engage you to seek and solicit yourself to commission to bring a suit against her son, as in fact you left this town with that resolve and spent a day in Chinon to communicate about it with Messire Pierre Baré, one of the chief instruments of plot and conspiracy. You then went to Paris to research and pursue said commission, as said supplicant will show at the proper time and place, even by your own writings.

That having, by misrepresentations argued and by surprise attack obtained said commission, and contrary to all orders of justice, you came to this town to have her said son taken prisoner.

That by your order, Sieur de Silly, his children, Master Pierre Menuau the king's advocate, and other chief enemies of her said son, with whom you had communicated before leaving and again since your arrival in this town, were present at his capture against the order.

That you slept and were treated several days, both before and after said capture, at the house of Sieur de Bourgneuf, son-in-law of Sieur de Silly and also equally his enemy.

That since then, you have been lodged in this said town at a different lodging than your usual one, in order to be among his enemies and to be able to confer more easily with them, as you do secretly every evening. That they usually stay with you until late at night.

That you have commissioned a young lawyer [Pierre Fournier] as king's prosecutor to work in this affair, on the nomination that had been made to you by said Maître P. Menuau, as he himself has boasted in several places.

That before having had any knowledge of the affair of her said son, you manifested a sentiment contrary to his innocence, showing you to have been prejudiced, and that prejudice that is in your mind of the inclination you have for said enemies also appeared in that you said to several persons and desired to have believed that the settlement of monseigneur the archbishop of Bordeaux, made to Richelieu on December 24, 1632, on the so-called possession of the Ursulines, had failed, and that you had caused the archbishop to recognize it, he being at your house, and on the view of the ritual of the curé of your parish that you had brought before him for that purpose. And nevertheless, to the contrary, said seigneur archbishop, in your presence and that of a great number of persons, being recently at the said castle of Richelieu, said the said settlement was canonical and on all points in conformity with the councils, and that no other could be legitimately made or practiced, which is a thing far different from what you reported to be the sentiments of said seigneur archbishop, by which dealings you aid and favor by all means possible to you the evil intentions of his said enemies.

Action against Laubardemont

In addition to which you are a relative, because of madame your wife, of monseigneur the bishop of Poitiers, which for very just considerations has withdrawn with respect of her said son and that she has heard that you are also related to some of said Ursuline religious.

For these reasons, Monseigneur, and for others still to be brought forth at the time and place, may it please you to withdraw your competency over the action and prosecution you are pursuing against her son, in which you would do well.[6]

The commissioner's response: he orders to "carry on regardless . . ., given said commission, and moreover having no knowledge of any true or legitimate reason to abstain." The fact is, the commission removed the case from all regular jurisdictions, including that of the parliament of Paris (to which Loudun is subordinate), and was valid "all opposition, appeals and challenges whatsoever notwithstanding." The depositions continue, therefore, and on December 28 it is "forbidden to all persons to intimidate the witnesses, and in case of failure to comply, permitted to said king's prosecutor to investigate it."[7]

On January 7 Jeanne Estièvre appeals this order by a document passed before the royal notary. On the sixth she had a police officer serve Laubardemont with the copy of the form and order issued on December 24, 1632, by the archbishop of Bordeaux for the exorcisms of the nuns. She also sends her son in Angers documents, advice, and orders relating to the future interrogation.

> Do not answer before M. de Laubardemont. He is being challenged. . . . Your friends hope to soon remove this impassioned commissioner. Above all, don't answer him. If he goes on to hear you, give him the reasons for impugnment brought by the above said petitions.[8]

On January 9 and 10 two new petitions are presented by François Grandier, the brother of the accused. Again on the tenth, an appeal for an *appointment* (a preparatory judgment ordering a written discussion for a complex matter that cannot be decided during the hearing) is made against Laubardemont. On the twelfth there is another appeal, with *prise à partie* (action taken against the judge).

Such Crooked Practices

On the seventeenth there is a new petition challenging the commissioner. Jeanne Estièvre does not lay down her arms. She has already conducted many similar battles. Moreover, her animus is directed even more strongly at the "chief enemies of her said son" than at Laubardemont. To her, apparently, the "true secret parties" and adversaries of Urbain are from Loudun, manipulating the commissioner and "pursuing [him] continually." For years she has defended herself, both herself and him, against the devils she could point to personally in her town. A resident of Loudun for the past seventeen years, a businesswoman, as proved by a long series of actions and proceedings, in the absence of a husband, of whom no document ever makes mention, she seems to have remained a stranger on these streets and before these families, of whose intrigues she is aware. In this hour of a graver danger, many "friendly" connections fall silent or melt away into the anonymity of a murmur.

In "protesting that she will lodge an appeal . . . before competent judges," she is relying on them in order to escape yet again from the circle of local hostilities. But does she see clearly what new power she is facing? The "supplicant" writes to Laubardemont:

That in the criminal proceeding you are conducting against her said son, she has learned and will verify before judges competent and not suspect

that you had dismissed several of the witnesses who spoke in his defense, without being willing to have their depositions written or redacted,

that in other depositions you have cut and removed what was said in defense of her said son, having committed to writing only what you esteemed to be incriminating of him,

that you have said and desired to be written down in his incrimination things of which the witnesses did not speak and that came from your volition alone,

that you have attempted to insinuate to and persuade one of your witnesses to testify to a capital crime in keeping with what you suggested to him, and to prompt him thereto, seeing he did not wish to do it, told him he would be cause of the death of four persons who had already testified to it, and to induce the so-called witnesses the more readily to testify what the enemies of her said son wished to invent and suppose, you attract them and customarily send them to the convent of Saint-Ursule where said enemies assemble and have conspired his downfall.

But since, foreseeing that such crooked practices with respect to various witnesses could eventually denounce your preceding and that there were already murmurings against them throughout the town, you found another expedient in order not to appear in such circumstances. To wit, with your agreement and connivance, two of the principal officers of this town, of those who continuously ply you, who are chief enemies of her said son and his true secret litigants, have the witnesses appear before them, and by gifts, promises, intimidation, and threats, try to influence them to the point of having a woman threatened with being sent to prison if she did not testify to what they wanted. Then said officers take the oath as if they were judges in that case, and after that, if they recognize they cannot induce the witness to consent to their pernicious design, they dismiss him without having him heard.[9]

The petition is again denied, unless Jeanne Estièvre appeals to the king. She appeals. Laubardemont continues with the case, "with interdiction to said Bertrand and to all other law officers and police sergeants to take similar action, either by virtue of said relief of appeal [of the right to repeat or renew the appeal] or otherwise, under pain of exemplary punishment." Notice of that order is served on January 15 to Gilles Poucquet.[10]

Grandier's Silence

Once the depositions are over in Loudun, the commissioner goes to Angers in the company of his clerk of court, Jacques Nozay, a lawyer from Loudun, Pierre Fournier, and a delegate from the bishop of Poitiers, the canon René de Morans. With the authorization of Msgr. Claude de Rueil, the bishop of Angers, he proceeds to the interrogation of Grandier, for eight consecutive days (4–11 February). In keeping with his mother's advice, the curé refuses to answer. He does, however, recognize the contracts, bonds, obligations, and other papers seized in his lodgings, among which were the *Traicté du coelibat* (but without admitting anything about its intended recipient). On the eleventh Laubardemont is on the road to Paris, from which he brings back the ruling from the Council of State, stipulating that

> without regard to the appeal lodged with the parliament and to the proceedings pursued in consequence thereof, that his majesty has nullified, it is ordered that Sieur de Laubardemont shall continue the trial by him begun against Grandier, all opposition, appeals, or challenges made or to be made notwithstanding, and without prejudice thereto; that to that end the king, as far as it be necessary, attributes to him again competence, and that to the exclusion of the parliament of Paris and any other judges, with interdiction to the parties to appeal it, under penalty of 500 *livres* of fine.[11]

The Return to Loudun

At his return, on April 9, Laubardemont's first decision is to have Grandier brought back to Loudun. He is locked up on the top floor of a private dwelling, in a room with boarded-up windows, the fireplace walled over, and the door guarded by Sergeant Bontemps—a name as fraught with irony as that of the exorcist Tranquille! But the imprisonment must be total, physical and mental, and let there be no leak in language itself: in his Angevin prison, the curé had composed a book of prayers and pious reflections, he confessed, took communion, chatted freely with Pierre Boucher, a canon at the collegiate church of Saint-

Pierre, who will assist him during the trial. To the walls are added eyes, ears, and mouths:

> For the last few weeks [Father Du Pont will write] there are two Capuchins in Grandier's room, who, by order of monseigneur our prelate [La Rocheposay] have not moved from there day or night, praying to God for him and saying mass in his room every day. I know not what that will bring about.[12]

The local prisons, at least, could not present cellular and psychiatric refinements better suited to forcing confessions.

A Son's Secret

Jeanne Estièvre intervenes once more. Her son answers:

> Mother mine,
>   I received your letter and all you sent me, except the woolen stockings. I bear my affliction with patience, and lament yours more than my own. I am very uncomfortable because I have no bed. Try to have mine brought to me, for if the body does not rest, the spirit succumbs. Lastly, send me a breviary, a Bible, a Saint Thomas for consolation, and, for the rest, do not be distressed. I hope God will bring my innocence to light.
>   I send my regards to my brother and sister and all our good friends.
>   I am, mother mine, your very good son at your service
>   Grandier[13]

The curé's solitude brings out the problem of his relationship with his mother more more clearly. In the absence of a father, of whom no one speaks, a woman seems to be, for Grandier, the law of nature. In prosperous times, Grandier can doubtless allow himself all women, as long as they pass or hide, because in his life there is but one. Doubtless, if he shows to the outer world, during his days of success, all the brilliance of eloquence, it is because, behind these words that scintillate and pass like women, he is the beneficiary, the victim, and the ephemeral rebel of a maternal dependency. Without knowing to what "idol," to what law, he is attached, he passes his time trying and refusing to break it. Between him and Jeanne Estièvre, there is his secret, the secret of his arrogance and his "misconduct," that of his "patience" in the face of his destiny as prisoner.

~ 7 ~

The Theater of the Possessed

Spring 1634

Thus the curé has been carefully circumscribed and set apart, like an object of the judiciary, which isolates him before eliminating him. In an analogous way, the possessed women are individually sequestered. They are distributed in compartments that are not yet those of a science, but already those of an urban topography. The judiciary classifies them. Laubardemont sees to it that Jeanne des Anges, Louise de Jésus, and Anne de Sainte-Agnès are placed in the house of Maître Jean de la Ville, an elected official and a private lawyer (he is also Michel Lucas's counselor); Claire de Sazilly and Catherine de la Présentation, at Canon Maurat's residence; Elisabeth de la Croix, Monique de Sainte-Marthe, Jeanne du Saint-Esprit, and Séraphique Archer, at Nicolas Moussaut's house, at the house of the widow Barot, who is Mignon's aunt, and so forth. Obviously the guardians chosen were selected for their reliability. A more specific characteristic here is the gesture (already scientific) of isolation. To separate and to give itself an object: these are, with respect to Grandier and the nuns, the two complementary aspects of the judicial inquiry.

The judiciary breaks the homogeneous whole constituted by the demonological discourse or by the magic circle of the convent. It set up in opposition to it a different "reason," its own, of an analytic sort. It carves out the objects that will be presented for examination by the physicians. Power precedes science, in establishing for the latter not its judgments, but a kind of epistemological unit upon which the doctors will be called upon to pass judgment.

The Exorcists

This intervention of the judiciary modifies the equilibrium of roles in the organization of the possession. Because the analytic and operational procedures are taken in hand by the commissioner, the exorcisms are shifted in the direction of spectacle. Their theatrical aspect is accentuated.

The place of the ritual celebrations offered to the crowd is also clarified. Moreover, the personnel assigned to these horrific and sacred "games" is increased and changed. Barré and Mignon leave. These seculars are replaced by religious, who are added to the Carmelites, already present. Four Capuchins are officially designated: Fathers Lactance (not to be confused with Recollect Gabriel Lactance), Tranquille (the warden, that is, superior of the Capuchins of La Rochelle), Protais, and Elizée. With the religious, the pressure of national or international groups on the local structures is increased. The predominance of exorcists from the large neighboring towns, who are preferred to "village" exorcists, is also fostered. Guilloteau, *théologal* of the bishop of Poitiers,[1] and Gabriel Lactance, a Recollect of the convent of Limoges, are on the new team. These two last choices represent a success for Msgr. de La Rocheposay (and, with him, for the partisans of the Counter-Reformation) over his more liberal and more "autonomist" neighbor, the archbishop of Bordeaux.

The Private and the Public

The exorcisms also receive their own status. They are administered according to a first principle that distinguishes between the private and the public: the former provided by the isolation and distribution of the possessed in private homes, the latter henceforth subject to civil regulations. Thus exorcisms have their own proper time and place. They are conducted simultaneously in the churches of Sainte-Croix and Saint-Pierre du Martray, and in the chapels of Notre-Dame du Château, of the Ursulines, and of the Carmelites. On the front of the main altar of the collegiate church of Sainte-Croix, generally reserved for the prioress, an *échafaut* (stage of planks on trestles) is erected, on which the action will unfold so as to be seen by the entire public. In the chapels of the church and on the stage and against the trestles, bunks were placed, made up of a simple mattress and a bolster at the head of the bed, so that the possessed women would not wound themselves during their convulsions.

Once or twice a day the women leave their private lodgings, and the moment they do so, they also abandon the peaceful life they lead there:

> It was an admirable thing [said an ecclesiastic from Tours] to
> see that . . . they never discontinued their observances nor broke

routine of the exercises of the community. Visit them privily when they have goodly intervals. You will see well-behaved, modest religious who do some needlework or spin before you, who take pleasure in hearing God spoken of, and in learning ways to serve Him well. They perform their examination of conscience, confess exactly, and take communion, when they are not agitated, with as much peace and repose of mind as if they were not possessed.[2]

A Spectacle

The convulsions are reserved for the general assembly. The demonic tragedy only reaches public religion. "Privily," as the ecclesiastic says, in private, it is a different spectacle that you will have before you. To pass from that devoutness when they are at home to the exhibitions for the crowd, the nuns make the trip through the streets of Loudun, in small groups. They bring with them, or go pick up at the sacristy, undergarments and ropes. When one of the "possessed" refuses to go to the church of the exorcisms, one of the priests commissioned by the authority comes to get her, and she follows obediently. Once they have entered, they are bound.

> Arriving to be exorcised, these girls are put on a bench, their heads laid on a pillow, their hands in handcuffs that are easily broken with the slightest effort and tied onto the benches with two straps, across the legs and the stomach. At first all this gives the impression of chaining up lions. But as soon as the demon appears, the girls are untied and left in complete freedom, so that they are bound as girls and set free as demons.[3]

And are not the lions set free in the amphitheater? It is the condition of the spectacle.

In the morning, when they arrive, "the girls" all take part in mass, sometimes without agitations; usually convulsions and contortions occur from the beginning of the service, or during mass, at the moment of the elevation or the communion, and the exorcisms are begun immediately.

Enter the Actresses

In the afternoon, there is the same entrance ceremony, described by the English writer Thomas Killigrew (the *voyageur*, as he is called, also passed through Loudun):

The priest having said some prayers at the altar, repaired to the grate of the nunnery; where, when he had rung the bell, the nuns appeared: He called forth one that was possessed, who entered the chapel with her companion only, a nun that was not possessed. They came, one at either hand of the friar, and so kneeled by him, and prayed at the altar for the space of half an hour, without any kind of action that expressed she was possessed: But these prayers being ended, she turned herself to the friar, who cast a string full of crosses about her neck, and there tied it with three knots: she kneeled still, and ceased not to pray till the strings were fastened; but then she stood up, and quitted her beads; and, after a reverence made to the altar, she went to the seat, like a couch, with one end made purposely for the exorcism, whereof there are divers in the chapel. The head of this stood to the altar. She went to it with so much humility, that you would have thought that patience could merit enough, without the prayers of the priest, to have chased out the Devil. When she came to it, she lay down on it, and helped the priest to bind her to it with two ropes, one about her waist, another about her thighs and legs. When she was bound, and saw the priest with a box wherein the sacrament was included, she sighed, and trembled with sense of the torture she was to suffer.[4]

Thus begins, with the situating of the nun, tied down, facing the sacrament as it approaches her, the battle awaited by the public. The gods of night and the god of day, equally invisible, must struggle here in the form of a collision between the humiliated woman and, brandished in the hands of its ministers, a *sun* (so is the monstrance designated, the center of which, the custodial, is sometimes separated). The victim, stripped of her religious insignia, bound hand and foot (but not too tightly, in order to make possible a time of convulsions) is temporarily abandoned to her demons, so that she may be offered to the victor, recognizable by the advancing golden weapon. On the stage, there are no longer any human beings; in this sense, nobody is there anymore—there are only roles.

For the actors on the stage, the goal is to force the demon to manifest himself as a vanquished rebel and to face the demons to show the wonders of Jesus Christ. This theater consists in unmasking the forces at work behind human appearances, in making masks in order to unmask. The representation effaces men and women. It must open onto the representation of what takes place beyond them, on a supernatural and inner world. The decor will thus be the curtain opening onto a different stage. That in itself is tragic for some, comic for others: it could well be that it is nothing but a representation, that the unveiling of supernatural realities is nothing but an artifice of an artifice, that the combination of successive decors and horizons is but a *trompe l'oeil.*

Young Women

Who are these possessed women? They are young women, as was often the case with the witches or possessed of the seventeenth century. Pierre de Lancre had made that observation in Béarn fifteen years earlier: "Tis a fairy tale to say all witches be old."[5]

In Loudun, they are for the most part Ursulines: a congregation founded very recently (1592–94), southern in its initial recruitment, fascinating to many girls, closer to the exaltation of beginnings than to the installation typical of orders whose origins have been woven into a rich legacy. As one of their early apologists puts it, these young damsels set out as "Amazons"[6] on spiritual crusades to regions abandoned by charity, education, and contemplation. In houses still not solidly established, often poor, barely players in the game of fiefdoms, customs, and local labyrinths, they find, along with courage, illusion and fear as well.

The Ursulines

There, possessions proliferate: in Aix-en Provence (1611–13), Pontoise, Faubourg Saint-Jacques (1621–22), Loudun, Auxonne, and so forth. Individual cases are numerous: Antoinette Micolon, at age seventeen, pursued by diabolical "voices," attempts to hang herself; Françoise de Bermond, a strong woman, is terrified by a "vision of hell" that makes the loneliness and darkness of night unbearable to her; in Toulouse, Jaquette de Maynié, obsessed by a similar vision and "an unbearable stench," is driven to despair by "a secret voice reproaching her for her atheism and idolatry"; in Bourges, Sister Pinette de Jésus sees the demon for entire nights "grimacing, outraging the image of the Virgin with a thousand indignities, and vomiting a hundred and one impostures . . ."; and so forth.[7] Indeed, there is nothing in all this that is distinctive to them. By hundreds, by thousands, analogous monsters and cases of anguish haunt the collective imagination of an era, and not just the imagination of other nuns. The chronicles of those years are full of them. Perhaps the demons and specters that also fill the pages of so many erudite treatises betray their secret when that violence enters the social language, when the nocturnal vision becomes a diurnal spectacle, when the pressure of doubt and blasphemy breaks through into the liturgy, when anguish finds a way out in possession and exorcism.

Whatever the case may be, there is a human response in the activity that divides, defines, localizes, and attempts to isolate these manifestations. The power that imposes its artifices and classifies phenomena is already that of a scientific discipline [*savoir*] that produces objects of knowledge, as opposed to the seeing that receives enigmas. It also has a therapeutic value.

A Diabolic Atlas: The Lists

This power is expressed not only through the organizing activity of the commissioner or, as we shall see, in the nosological distinctions of the physicians, but also in the counting and identifying of the posssessed women and their devils. Dispersed elements are gathered in the minutes. The result is a strange geography in which localization by families for persons is coupled with physiological localization for the devils. More precisely, three types of references—to the social body, to the Angelic Orders (from which the demons have fallen), and to the physical body— make up the coordinates thanks to which an identity is given to these women, who for the most part are already hidden and classified under a "religious name." The following table, drawn up from several "lists,"[8] answers this need to find and identify, by combining three hierarchical systems: social, demonological, and medical. In order to orient oneself in this nomenclature of the "real," it must be understood that, in the angelology of the times, beginning from the top, celestial beings are divided into Seraphim, Cherubim, Virtues, Powers, Principalities, Dominions, Thrones, Archangels, and Angels properly so called.

I. Religious
  A. Possessed
    1. *Jeanne des Anges,* superior, thirty years old
      Daughter of Louis de Belcier, baron de Cozes, and Charlotte de Goumard, of the house of Chilles; niece of Louis de Barbézieux, seigneur de Nogeret; grand-niece of Octave de Bellegarde, the archbishop of Sens; and so forth.
        Seven possessing demons:
        Léviathan, of the Seraphim, lodged in the middle of the forehead
        Aman, of the Powers
        Isacaron, of the Powers, lodged below the last rib of the right side
        Balam, of the Dominions, lodged in the second rib of the right side

Asmodaeus, of the Thrones;

Behemoth, of the Thrones, lodged in the stomach

2. *Louise de Jésus,* twenty-eight

Daughter of Louis de Barbezières, sieur de Nogeret, and Dame Douz-erant.

Two demons:

Caron, of the Virtues, loged in the middle of the forehead

Easas, or *Easar,* of the Dominions, lodged below the heart

3. *Jeanne du Saint-Esprit*

Sister of the preceding.

One demon:

Cerberus, of the Principalities, lodged above the heart

4. *Anne de Sainte-Agnès,* nineteen

Daughter of Jean, marquis de la Motte-Brassé, and Perronnelle de Cornu.

Four demons:

Asaph, of the Powers, lodged in the middle of the forehead

Asmodaeus, of the Thrones, lodged below the heart

Berith, of the Thrones, lodged in the opening of the stomach

Achaos, of the Archangels, lodged in the left temple

5. *Claire de Saint-Jean,* lay sister, thirty

Née de Sazilly, a relative of the cardinal de Richelieu.

Seven demons:

Pollution, of the Cherubim, lodged near the left shoulder

Elimy, of the Virtues

Sansfin, alias Grandier, of the Dominations, lodged in the second right rib

Nephtaly, of the Thrones, lodged in the right arm

Zabulon, of the Thrones, lodged in the middle of the forehead

Ennemi de la Vierge, lodged below the neck

Concupiscence, lodged in the right temple

6. *Elisabeth de la Croix,* twenty-two

Née Bastad.

Five demons:

Allumette d'impureté, of the Cherubim

Castorin, of the Dominations

Caph, of the Thrones

Agal, of the Archangels

Celse, of the Archangels

7. *Catherine de la Présentation,* thirty-three

Née Auffray.

Three demons:

Penault, of the Principalities

Caleph, of the Thrones

Daria, of the Archangels

8. *Marthe de Sainte-Monique,* twenty-five

Daughter of Serph, sieur du Magnoux, bourgeois of Loudun.

One demon: *Cédon,* of the Virtues

    9. *Séraphique,* a novice, seventeen or eighteen
       Possessed or obsessed by *Baruch*

(N.B.—The four last religious were not exorcised before December 1634.)

  B. Obsessed or "Maleficiated"

    10. *Gabrielle de l'Incarnation,* subprioress, thirty-five
       Daughter of Charles de Fougères de Colombiers and Françoise de
       Manon.
       Obsessed by three demons: *Baruch, Behemoth, Isacaron*
    11. *Angélique de Saint-François,* thirty-two
       Daughter of Jacques de Pouville, sieur de la Morinière, and Louise
       de Clairauvaux.
       Obsessed by one demon: *Cerberus*
    12. *Marie du Saint-Sacrement,* twenty-five
       Daughter of Mérit de Beauvalier, sieur de la Maillardière, and Marie
       de Rasilly.
       Obsessed by two demons: *Berith* and *Caleph*
    13. *Anne de Saint-Augustin,* thirty
       Daughter of the the late François de Marbef, sieur de Champoireau,
       and Jeanne Le Blanc.
    14. *Renée de Saint-Nicolas,* thirty-four
       Obsessed by one demon: *Hagar*
    15. *Marie de la Visitation,* thirty-six
    16. *Catherine de la Nativité,* novice, twenty-two
    17. *Marie de Saint-Gabriel,* novice, twenty

(N.B.—The proper names corresponding to the four last religious names are—
but in what order?—: Anne d'Escoubleau de Sourdis, obsessed by *Elimy;* her
sister, obsessed by the same demon; Marie Acher, obsessed by the demon *Fornication,* of the Angels; and Mademoiselle de Dampierre, Laubardemont's sister-in-
law and a relative of Jeanne des Anges.)

II. Secular

  A. Possessed

    18. *Isabelle* or *Elisabeth Blanchard,* eighteen or nineteen
       Six possessing demons:
       Maron, of the Cherubim, lodged beneath the left breast
       Perou, of the Cherubim, lodged beneath the heart
       Beëlzebub, of the Archangels, lodged beneath the left armpit
       Lion d'Enfer, of the Archangels, lodged under the navel
       Astaroth, of the Angels, lodged beneath the left armpit
       Charbon d'impureté [Coal of Impurity], of the Angels, lodged beneath
         the left hip
    19. *Françoise Fillastreau,* called la Benjamine, twenty-seven
       Four demons:
       Buffétison, of the Powers, lodged below the navel
       Souvillon, of the Thrones, lodged in the front part of the brain
       Caudacanis or *Queue de chien* [Dog's Tail], of the Archangels,
         lodged in the stomach
       Jabel, of the Archangels, who comes and goes in all parts of the
         body

20. *Léonce Fillastreau,* sister of the preceding, twenty-four
    Three demons:
    Esron, of the Thrones, lodged in the front part of the brain
    Lucien, of the Archangels
    Luther, of the Archangels
21. *Suzanne Hammon,* possessed by *Roth.* She is the sister of Catherine, the "cordonnière," whose ambition and success have been mentioned. (Suzanne undertakes a different career, demonological and not political.)
22. *Marie Beaulieu,* called du Temple
    One demon: *Cédon*
23. A young boarder, who remained at the convent.
24. *Mlle de Rasilly,* possessed, is exorcised in her family, outside of Loudun, in Omelles.
B. Obsessed or "Maleficiated"
25. *Marthe Thibault,* obsessed by the demon *Behemoth*
26. *Jeanne Pasquier,* obsessed by the demon *Lezear*
27. *Madeleine Béliard.*

Houses and Residences

Is this table hallucinatory or real? That is precisely the question asked during all these months. What is "real"? But a space that maintains its coherence throughout all its parts is posited by the lists in which, following their own peculiar taxonomy, "the names of the demons, their place of residence, and the name of the possessed"[9] are associated. The "girls" belong to "houses" in a hierarchy of families; in their bodies, "residences" belong to these fallen angels, whose hierarchy again is determined by their rank of birth. Between houses and residences, between social upgrading and diabolical grottoes, the lists posit series of "proportions," of which the body is the table. As demons are both possessors and properties, both signs of dependence and of rank, more of them— and posher ones—are associated with the superior, a relative of Richelieu, or the daughter of a marquis. The "residence" of the devils in the forehead, the stomach, or "below the navel," indicates not only their character (described at length, for there are the haughty, the choleric, the talkative, the obscene, and so forth), but also recondite correspondences between their celestial functions and the body's physiological ones. An entire network of relationships sustains the coherence of this *locus communis,* this common place.

Moving Tables

The elements of these tables are nonetheless in flux. In the course of the exorcisms, a change of posture organizes the body around another diabolic "residence." A modification of the gaze, in the possessed, marks the entrance onto the stage of another demon, hence the presence of another organization of hell and the sign of new psychological combinations. Moving tables, with which a cosmological landscape is metamorphosed. To follow these subtle combinations, a knowledge of the vocabulary does not suffice. It takes a sustained effort of attention and the habit of deciphering a language.

> Not only are there many different girls [writes Father Du Pont, long conversant with this language] but each one makes many different movements, all extraordinary, and quite often new. The change in the look of the face cannot be natural, for, since each one of them is possessed by several demons, sometimes the one who is pressed and abjured, to avoid the force of the exorcism, puts you off the scent, like hares do, sending another one in its place. But he cannot do it without your seeing it. For with the change of demon the face of the girl also changes looks, and seems like a different face. The eyes in particular seem to be a different color, and that so noticeably that not only the exorcist, but any other person nearby will recognize it very easily, as I have done and several others. What is also surprising and shows that the change comes from an inner cause of possession, is that while it lasts the possessed makes no grimace, but rather her face remaining in its natural state seems nonetheless completely different, by reason of the eyes, whose color and light are changed in an instant.[10]

A Proof: The Pact

Upon his arrival in Loudun on April 14 to preside over the public exorcisms, Msgr. de La Rocheposay declared peremptorily: "I have not come to find out whether the possession is true. I am already convinced of it."[11] Nonetheless, the functioning of the possession is not satisfactory, may it not displease the gentleman from Poitiers. "Signs" referring from certain elements to others in a closed system are insufficient. It is not an autonomous, self-contained system. An insecurity is revealed within it, by the internal requirement of external confirmation. There is a need for *proofs,* medial phenomena that, interpreted according to the space into which they are summoned and received, furnish at the same time a mooring on an alien externality, the world of "unbelieving" or "curious" observation, the reality one does not believe, but that is observed. Thus the exorcisms bring to light *pacts,* court exhibits, objects that will give more weight to a discourse consisting of gestures and spoken words: papers supposed to be the product of a contract with the devil, telltale leavings, objective signatures, visible remains. The fact is, these are not so much proofs that possession gives *of* itself as proofs given *to* itself. Rather than being an argument in favor of possession, they are its product.

By means of a sheet of paper written and signed by the demon, hence perceptible and tangible for all, the pact is an attempt to hold together the elements of a system that is collapsing. The relation between them is this pact, which functions like a metal clamp to retain the separating stones in a cracked wall. But the tie between the *here* and the *beyond* is secretly so doubtful that that object/trace must show, along with the tie, the possibility or the existence of the devil that is one of the ends tied— and that by the intermediary of what is seen by "unbelievers" and spectators uninitiated to the demonological language. The unbelievers are called upon to certify (to render certain), by their viewing of the document, the possessionists' internal interpretation. The equivocation consists in drawing from the witnesses who see the *visible* face of the phenomenon the justification of a *mystic* face; in making the perceived work in favor of the hidden meaning; in transforming the pact offered to the public into a pact with the public; in defending a certain language thanks to one element inscribed in two heterogeneous tables. That object becomes the decisive terrain for each interpretation, but it is the place defined by its very ambivalence. Thus, with this tiny symptom, we see the installation of a space of objectivity that is one of ambiguity, at the moment in which a common social interpretation is being torn apart.

The pact is therefore a document in this story. It is tangible and verifiable. It may take the form of body hairs, ashes, fingernail or hair clippings, orange seeds, blood, or *phlegm* ("a most volatile passive principle which exits by the slightest heat of fire in the form of clear, insipid water," says Richelet). In short, it is their leavings and "droppings" that the possessed designate as "pacts."

Technique of Production

How is this document obtained? How is it "produced"—a term signifying in the seventeenth century a bringing to light, and for us fabrication? This is what is explained by the minutes of one of the exorcisms (May 17, 1934) that, in April and May, had this quest as their objective. The Recollect Fathers and Msgr. de La Rocheposay operate in the church of Sainte-Croix, "filled with a very great number of all kinds of people." The "we" of the text refers to Laubardemont, who wrote the minutes.

Said Father [a Recollect] having taken said Sister des Anges and commanded Léviathan to appear, her face became mirthful and gracious in an extraordinary way.

Asked: *Quo profectus eras hodie mane?* [What had you done this morning?], said: "I had gone as far as to Picardy."

Having been commanded to go fetch his pact by him previously declared, said: "I care not a whit to do what you say. After that we would have no hold left. The others will have something to make fun of me about, just as I made fun of Asmodée."

Pressed to obey, the gracious expression that was on the face of said sister was changed into a most furious look and was agitated by very violent convulsions. And the exorcist, continuing still, pressed Léviathan to bring back the pact.

It was said by the mouth of said sister: "To whom do you think you are speaking?"

Questioned: *Quis es tu?* [Who are you?]

Answered "Behemoth."

Whereupon the exorcist made commandment unto Behemoth to withdraw and to Léviathan to rise up into the sister's head and to fully occupy her mouth and tongue to speak in her. And after a few violent convulsions that were made with great contortions in all parts of said sister's body, her face again became all mirthful, gracious in such a manner that it was recognized that Léviathan was occupying her head.

Which gave occasion to said exorcist to bind him in that part, as he did by order of said seigneur bishop, who—having said to said exorcist that, the better to constrain the demon to bring back said pact, he should remove the holy sacrament from the custodial and present it uncovered to said sister's mouth, and foreseeing that, in this manner, she would have more violent agitations—climbed to the stage where we were with said exorcists and religious, and, having sat down upon a little low chair, took hold of said sister's two arms. And Léviathan, being pressed with very great vehemence, as much by said seigneur bishop as by said father exorcist who held the holy sacrament near to said sister's mouth, there were produced in her such very great and very violent contortions, with most frightening cries during which the *Salve Regina* was sung thrice.

After which, the demon being still commanded and pressed to bring back the pact, it was said by the mouth of said sister in a hurried, precipitous voice, which seemed to come out of the depths of her chest:

"Seek there."

Asked: *Ubi est?* [Where is it?]

Said: "It is here."

Asked: *In quo loco?* [In what place?]

Said with the same hurried, precipitous voice: "Beneath the monsieur."

And since when said sister, being agitated and the demon speaking of said seigneur bishop or of us, did not for the most part designate either the one or the other except by the word "monsieur," was asked: *De quo domino loqueris?* [Of what monsieur are you speaking?]

And he responded through her, with the same precipitation: "Monsieur the bishop."

Bodily Waste

And then said seigneur bishop having risen from said low chair, went and found beneath his soutane and next to his left foot a piece of paper in which something appeared to be wrapped. And having been picked up and held by said seigneur bishop and trying to put it in our hand, said sister made, or the demon through her, all sorts of efforts to take it away from us. Since she was unable to do so, we put it and kept it in one of our pockets, while the *Te Deum laudamus* was sung in thanksgiving for so favorable a success.

After said seigneur bishop told us that Asmodée, a few days before leaving the body of sister des Anges, had told him, having approached him during the exorcism then being performed on said Sister Agnès, that the pact of Léviathan was spotted with blood on the top, and demanded that we see if that was so. In attempting to do which, we drew out from our pocket said piece of paper, which being unwrapped we found it contained and served as covering for another piece of paper, which was tainted on top with much blood. And as we tried to open that second envelope to see what it contained, we found that said second paper held strongly, as if it had been glued, because of which, and fearing to break it and drop something of what was enclosed therein, because of the great press and inconvenience that was caused to us by the onlookers who were around about us in a great crowd, we placed said second paper back in its envelope and gave it all to our court clerk to serve and weigh in the trial as it should.

And after the commandments that were made to the demons then agitating said sister to withdraw to their usual places of residence, said Sister des Anges told us, questioned about it under oath, that she had no memory of what had been said and done by her during said exorcism, having herself contributed nothing to it of her mind and her own will.

And as after the exorcism was done, we wished to withdraw, said sisters were again surprised by great agitations, which finally ceased by the commandments that both said bishop and said exorcists made to the demons to desist. After which we withdrew.[12]

This pact is found in the place of excretion. Like the blood that circulates within the body, it is charged with attesting to an inferiority beneath the world of appearances. It goes from the bishop's chair to the commissioner's pocket. Later it will be necessary, as in other cases, to discover on the sorcerer's body the wound/orifice through which this blood has come. Localizations abound after the object/proof. Each of these pieces is a *deus ex machina.*

"I Deny God"

There remain three texts of pacts written by Grandier to the Devil, one in Latin,[13] two in French, only the "copy" of which gets to the exorcists, the "original" being kept in hell. Here is the second of these *extracta ex inferis* [extracts from hell]:

> I deny God, Father, Son, and Holy Ghost, Mary and all the Saints, particularly Saint John the Baptist, the Church both Triumphant and Militant, all the sacraments, all the prayers prayed therein. I promise never to do good, to do all the evil I can, and would wish not at all to be a man, but that my nature be changed into a devil the better to serve thee, thou my lord and master Lucifer, and I promise thee that even if I be forced to do some good work, I will not do it in God's honor, but in scorning him and in thine honor and that of all the devils, and that I ever give myself to thee, and pray thee always to keep well the bond that I gave thee.
>
> Urb. Grandier[14]

Where is the desire to be "changed into a devil"? Where the subtle opposition between the objectivity of the good work and the evil intention that dwells within it? It is not difficult to say: the religious themselves.

The Wild World of Desire

But if the distinction between "intent" and "act" is traditional in spirituality, during this period it takes on a new and dangerous weight. It permits a spiritual discernment: faith is no longer identifiable with its works, though indissociable from them; the good intent cannot go without the good deed, though the former is not guaranteed by the latter. That instrument of differentiation between meaning and sign becomes, among many contemporary religious, a sword that dangerously cleaves the objective observance of the rules of religious life and the bad instincts it may cover up. Good acts and the observance of the rules become separated, as an appearance, from an inner reality that a keen attention discovers with horror and anxiety: the wild violence of desire.

The well-established practice of the examination of conscience, the requirement of a religious faith that was certain but subject to that examination, and the general discrediting of the institutions that could be invested with meaning and act as guarantors of conformity with the Christian spirit: these factors lead constantly to the locating of real experience behind the theater of the well-regulated religious life. The dark proliferation of unavowable intentions, is that not the reality? The quest for truth thus wavers between observance, which is perhaps but a decor (and what would those gentlemen, edified by the sight of the nuns busying themselves with the service or with needlework, know about it?), and the secret malice that is after all perhaps nothing but illusion and a disturbed imagination (but how can one be sure, and what confidence should be put in the advice of one who generally speaks of ineffable things he has been unable to understand?).

Many Ursulines, as we have seen, fall at this point into "despair," to which they are drawn by an experience that is certain but unstable, with doubts and urges intolerable in the language of faith. According to the received theological schemes, all they can do is attribute all this reality to the Devil, recognize him in the infernal shadow spreading out onto their inner landscape and dividing it.

But if such is the true story, that of the "interior," it must be expressed, confessed, reintroduced into the social language. To make a pact with the Devil or (which amounts almost to the same thing) to suppose it of someone else, but also to enter into the character of the demoniac, is this not at once, with the cultural material on hand, to allow what is ("I am a demon") to come to appear, and to allow a secret that is too burdensome ("I demand to be known for what I am") to come into communication? In this respect, the exhibitionism of the nuns allows them to attain a truth with respect to themselves and society.

The Profit of the Avowal

A profitable character, since it eliminates what it avows. The possessed are victims. An other—devil or sorcerer—is responsible. Thus they free themselves of the fault at the moment they confess it publicly in church, in the course of a spectacle that is still for them a liturgy. They get rid of it, since the threatening inner truth is located in "unconsciousness" (an elsewhere that they let slip and that is not them) and in an isolated part of their time. The intolerable secret occupies only a space that has been carefully circumscribed by a series of entrances and exits: entrances and exits of exorcism, entrances and exits from unconsciousness, entrances and exits of the devils. The rest of the time is good, by the very fact of the delimitation of a bad time. There remain only "good" nuns. What authorizes them to declare at last, under cover of the devil, "That's what I am," is precisely what permits them to protect themselves from it, to declare, "That is not what I am," to demand of the representative of the Church, "Tell me that isn't me."

From that point of view, the theater is a true exorcism. It is all the more necessary in that the religious are no longer those "sorcerers" who didn't know whether they were possessed and expected the judiciary to make the determination, like this condemned man, whose declaration is quoted by Jacques d'Autun:

> What grieves my spirit sorely is that I know not whether I be guilty or not. That is why I beseech you to tell me whether one can be a sorcerer unwittingly, for if that be possible, I may be of that miserable sect, though I know it not.

To that dependence on social judgment stands opposed, among the Ursulines, a capacity for personal self-judgment. They *know* that there is "sorcery" in them. Henceforth society becomes the means for ridding themselves of an occult deviancy, just as society takes advantage of the possessed women to expel its own anxiety in theatralizing it. A complicity between the actresses and their public reinforces the play of the exorcisms in multiplying its advantages. There is an aspect of social security to this theater.

The Plague of Atheism

Is the therapeutic an adequate response to the questions asked? Is it a response or a palliative? For the problem that becomes discernible through the minutes, in the tireless mention of blasphemy, the repetition of the denials of God, the monotonous constraint placed upon the possessed to confess God, is that of atheism. It is the focus of an entire literature of *Atheomachie,* of *Discours contre l'athéisme* or *contre les athées et libertins,* of *Atheomastix,* of *Atheismus triumphatus,* but also of political measures, of judicial sentences and social precautions against atheists. The "atheists" who first occupy the polemic are the "heretics" of every Church, the nonconformist believers and such. But soon the controversy centers on the existence of God. Around 1630 groups of "libertines," erudites, and skeptics wpring up; they will fade away around 1655 (approximately at the same time the possessions disappear, it should be noted), before coming back around 1680. "Atheism," which was never spoken of a hundred years earlier, becomes a recognized fact. It is not restricted to the learned. The cobbler Jean Boucher, a Franciscan, among countless others, denounces it everywhere.

> You will never see a curled moustache that doesn't continually toss your way his "why?": Why did God give the world laws . . . ? Why is fornication forbidden . . . ? Why is the Son of God incarnated?[15]

According to Mersenne, "Paris alone is afflicted with at least fifty thousand atheists. For many, the most dangerous are the so-called *men of virtue,* in reality *worse than the devils,* who have as their maxim that one should conduct oneself according to the religion of the country, but have a belief all one's own."[16] An exaggeration? Without a doubt. But the problem preys on people's minds, and especially those constantly battered by preachers. Father Surin points this out in one of his works devoted to Loudun, the *Science expérimentale:* "I say that, though the profession of atheism be no ordinary thing among Christians, it is nonetheless a temptation that arises rather naturally in the mind." By that he means "the one that suggests there is no God." He adds that the God proposed by the Church "though He be the object of the ordinary faith of most Christians, is not so believed as to prevent several from having opposition thereto, and sometimes violent temptations against faith, to which the good are often subject."[17]

"Temptation that arises rather naturally" and to which "the good are often subject": the spiritual literature of the times bears this out. After

the time of possession, Jeanne des Anges (leaving aside for the moment
her psychological structure) relates in her own way the anguish or the
rebellion the demons were charged with announcing:

Blasphemy

My mind was often filled with blasphemies, and sometimes I
would proffer them without being able to make any reflection
to keep me from it. I felt a continual aversion against God, and
I had no greater object of hatred than the sight of his goodness
and the readiness He has to pardon those who wish to convert.
My thought was often busy with seeking inventions to displease
Him, and cause others to displease Him.

Also, he gave me a very great aversion against my religious
profession, such that, sometimes when he occupied my head, I
would tear up all my veils, and those of my sisters that I could
get my hands on; I would trample them underfoot, I would eat
them while cursing the hour that I entered into religion. All
that was done with great violence.[18]

"Temptation," associated with the Devil, is accompanied by despair:
"I resolved in despair to be damned, and my salvation became indifferent
to me."[19]

Jeanne des Anges abandons herself to the logic of possession. She
finds a destiny in it. She is swept up by the interplay of speech, by a
fascination with the Devil, who is, as de Lancre said, a "prattling spirit,"
but also by the ritualization of a choreographic and verbal orgy in which
personal salvation disappears, along with moral constraints, in the intoxi-
cation of a common madness.

To Suffer for Reassurance

There is something else. Yves de Paris, with a hundred and one of his
contemporaries, announced in opposition to the skeptics "the desperate
torments and anxieties of these miserable souls."[20]

Doubt and blasphemy must be not only admitted, but punished. Exorcism provides the possessed with this punishment. They must pay for
the advantage of being reassured by undergoing this punishment. From
this point of view, they benefit from being victims. They are the accomplices of the chastisement that returns them to the religious "society"
and that must return that society to itself. The punishment can be extreme. By the hundreds, during these very years, women "sorcerers" demand to be burned or become the agents of their own death,[21] anticipat-

ing the last day of judgment or of reassurance, hurling themselves of their own accord toward that end that couples ultimate punishment and definitive salvation. Nay more, perhaps in order to say all it is necessary to die, and to "take one's own life" to find in words the communication they always promise without ever really delivering.

If there is still a tragedy of language in Loudun, it has been tempered by the fact of its having been put on stage. There remains a structural analogy. From these celebrations that are no longer celebrations but exhausting exercises, the nuns derive the privilege of being victims, subjected to the hard law of a purifying theater. But in becoming a tragicomedy, it only punishes and saves them halfway—and perhaps not at all. The possession presented itself as an escape from time and doubt, a confrontation between heaven and hell, a locus of the essential and of visibility. In fact, it is the repetition of an eschatological imaginary. In it, the supernatural reality is signified in the form of bodily waste; the actresses transformed into victims of dispair; the time of the action into time lost; and fiction into meritorious labor.

In the course of an exorcism in April, Jeanne says: "I am Jeanne the crazy woman. . . . Ursuline the crazy woman. My brain is lopsided. You would be better off leading me to Saint-Mathurin."

And to her exorcist, Father Lactance: "Oh, how I'll make you lose time."

And of herself: "You have to suffer. . . . We are good trumpet horses. We don't get startled by the noise."

The work of a horse, a beast of burden, in a war of attrition. For the infernal show goes on, a daily task, while the passers-by attracted by the publicity can move on, shaking their heads:

> After the first exorcisms [relates a Loudunais, Champion] there is a great rumor that spreads, not only in France, but throughout all Europe, and though the supposed demons have not given any other signs than some very ugly grimaces and disagreeable postures, it is cried out and published that they run the streets of Loudun, that girls can be seen transported to the church pinnacles flying through the air, and other fairy tales of the same ilk. To the point where the people come running from all directions to see that folly. The hostelries are not big enough to shelter the crowds that come. And what is admirable is that most of them stay there for a week or two, waiting from demon to demon to see wonders. And they go away no wiser than they came.[22]

That it is something other than the expected wonders does not mean it is not a grave display. Champion is playing the role of the corner gossip. Only later, ceasing to be serious, will the spectacle be no more than "curious."

The Amazons' Rebellion

From another point of view, the possession is equally a rebellion of women: women who are aggressive, provocative, exposing to the broad daylight of the exorcisms their desires and demands, beneath the mask of those devils that have many uses. They belong to a time of female regents, woman reformers, female mystic saints or pioneers in literature, a time when *Le Triomphe des dames* is sung and *La galerie des femmes fortes* is presented. They are educators, well educated, of good families, and of that young congregation of "Amazons" that knows the value of obedience but whose religious could often tell their curé a thing or two. Their chaplain, the prior Moussaut, is but a shadowy figure. Many others who traverse their history in life are scarcely more than phantoms. Not so Grandier.

> At that time [writes Jeanne] the priest I spoke of used demons to excite love in me for him. They would give me desires to see him and speak to him. Several of our sisters had these same feelings without communicating them to us. On the contrary, we would hide ourselves from one another as much as we could. . . .
>
> When I didn't see him, I burned with love for him, and when he presented himself to me [at night, in dreams] and wanted to seduce me, our good God gave me a great aversion to him. Thus all my feelings changed. I hated him more than the Devil.[23]

Face to face with the man. But also face to face with the priest. The possessed do not have, before the exorcists, the reverential docility of the witches of bygone years. They insult them, deride them, strike them, without sparing the bishop. The prioress makes fun of Father Lactance, the good Capuchin from Limoges: "Go carry your beggar's bag back to your Limoges. . . . Do you want me to give you a slap?"

The good man reddens with anger. The devil is not impressed: "Oh! You're getting on your high horse! Speak graciously."

Claire de Sazilly is no less sharp-tongued when, before the bishops of Nîmes and Chartres, Richelieu's secretary, Laubardemont, and a whole

distinguished company, the exorcists do their routine, repeated countless times, of whispering a few words among themselves and asking her
to reveal what they said—a public sign that she is indeed possessed. She
says to Father Elisée, a Carmelite who has seen a lot in his day: "You take
me for a Bohemian. Really, you are trying these gentlemen's patience.
What will they say to the king and to monsieur the cardinal."

And to Laubardemont: "And you, sir, you are caught. You have till
now fooled so many people, but now you've been exposed."

She kisses Father Elisée's companion, saying his little cheeks are good
to kiss, and approaching M. des Roches, the cardinal's first secretary,
she stops short: "You're too old." This is being nice, compared to the
blows that follow: "and then she gave us two big kicks," an exorcist's
account notes pitifully. The minutes of one such proceeding speaks of
the prioress "who, being agitated, soon afterward, she or the Devil
through her, gave a slap to said Father Gault. Because of which Father
Lactance, an exorcist, to chastise the devil, delivered five or six hard
slaps to the face of said Sister des Anges, who only laughed."[24]

They address one another informally,[25] they fight with one another,
they come out swollen: sometimes there are real domestic squabbles.

The Wild Hunters

The exorcists, for their part, metamorphose into "wild hunters,"[26] hunters of creatures, as the accounts say, and tamers of bodies. The dark
games and ritual struggles that take place before a rapt public simultaneously reveal and deny (by the very fact of being a representation) the
relations between sexuality and religion. It is a function of this language
to be a return of the repressed, the remnant of sexuality that scientific
discourse and religious discourse are in the process of eliminating.

Thus, on May 8, 1634, this struggle between the man and the woman:

> After which the exorcist [Father Lactance] constrained the devil
> [Jeanne des Anges] to adore the holy sacrament and had her
> put in all the posture he wanted, in such a way that all the assis-
> tants were as it were in rapt admiration, and even in that, by his
> word, he had that body put belly to the ground, head lifted high,
> arms and legs turned back, joined and intertwined, and had
> them partially release and join again in the same way.
>
> And as, returning to herself, the creature was commanded
> to chant the verse *Memento salutis* and was trying to pronounce
> *Maria mater gratiae*, there could be heard suddenly coming from
> her mouth a horrible voice saying: "I deny God. I curse her."

And then she bit her tongue, then her arm, in furious fashion, despite the exorcist's efforts to stop her.

Seeing which, Father Lactance threw the body of the possessed roughly to the ground, trampled it very violently beneath his bare feet, then, with one foot on her throat, repeated several times: *Super aspiden et basilicum ambulabis et conculcabis leonem et draconem.*[27]

Freud held seventeenth-century pathological tableaux to be easily interpretable, like openface mines.[28] This one would confirm his views. It is the mimed exegesis of a Psalm: "Thou shalt tread upon the asp and the basilisk / Thou shalt trample underfoot the lion and the dragon."[29]

The verse was traditionally attributed by the ligurgy to Mary, the new Eve triumphing over the Serpent that had been the tempter in the Garden of Eden. It is here pressed into service by the man struggling against the "diabolical" woman who denies her allegiance to the Faithful Mother, identifies with the "Father of Lies" and takes the place, in the closed arena of the stage, of the lion and the dragon.

"Thou Urbain Grandier"

From this struggle one can form an idea, with the recorded minutes of the confrontation between Urbain Grandier and nine religious and three seculars that took place in the church of Sainte-Croix on the afternoon of Friday, June 23, 1634. Among those present were Laubardemont; La Rocheposay; the secular and regular clergy; Sieurs Dreux (*lieutenant général* of Chinon), de la Barre, and de Brézé; M. Fournier (the king's prosecutor); and of course three physicians, Grolleau, Jacquet, and Brion. There was also a crowd of spectators drawn by the great days. Father Gabriel Lactance proposed that Grandier himself perform the exorcism of the possessed women. Hence the scene reported by no other than Laubardemont:

> Said Grandier having been requested to continue with the exorcism, when he asked the demons who had sent them in said bodies, all the said energumens, or the demons by their mouths, said:
> "Thou Urbain Grandier."
> The which saying that that was false and that he did not believe it to be within the power of any man or magician or any other to send the demons into any body, it was answered by the mouths of all the said energumens that he had sent them and

had been a magician for the last nine years, having been received by Asmodaeus in Béarn [the land of witchcraft, in Laubardemont's estimation], on a day similar to that one, the vigil of the Feast of Saint John. Which was particularly maintained before him by Asmodeus, speaking by the mouth of said Agnès, extraordinarily agitated.

And said Grandier, asking them whether they [the demons] would answer questions put to them in Greek, it was said by said energumens or the majority of them that he had given good order and expressly come to terms with them so that said demons by their mouths would speak no other language than French. And nonetheless it was said by some of them that if he wanted to put forth questions in the Greek language himself, they would answer. Which was particularly said by Sister Catherine; who beforehand declared to us that she had never learned to read or write, and said Sister Catherine presented herself for that trial with a marvelous assurance.

And by Verrine speaking in Sister Claire, and by Astaroth speaking in Isabelle, it was said that if the Church would allow them, they would forthwith show the magician's mark that he had on his body; also with great assurance, and that he had committed in that quality more evil than all the other magicians together. . . .

And then [Grandier], addressing himself to said seigneur the bishop, told him that he begged him, in the case that he were a magician and had sent the demons in said bodies, to command said demons to wring his neck forthwith; upon which it was said by all said energumens, with voices full of fury and rage:

"Ha! That would soon be done, if it were allowed us; but thou knowest well that neither the Church nor the judiciary will allow it."

As also both said seigneur the bishop and ourselves said that we neither could nor would give such permission, and quite to the contrary most express interdiction was made to the demons by said bishop to do anything to the person of Grandier and to us [Laubardemont]; he was told that having several times previously made the same proposal to us, we had declared to him as stated in the records thereof that such permission could not be granted and that he had to employ other means for his justification. And at this same time, so great and furious a tempest was stirred up by said energumens that all was but disorder, confusion, and fright, because of which we said to said seigneur bishop that that action must be ended as soon as possible. . . .

All the said energumens were shaken by the most violent, extraordinary, and frightful convulsions, contortions, movements, cries, clamors and blasphemies that one can imagine, it being impossible to describe or in any way represent them, unless by saying that it seemed to all present that they were seeing on that occasion all the fury of hell.

After which we had said Grandier removed and taken back to his prison.[30]

Between Fright and Laughter

After that face-to-face confrontation between the furies and the priest, during which they want to strip his body and wring his neck, should we say, like Elisabeth Blanchard to Father Du Pont: "Come now, Father, look here. You've never seen anything like it"? But eighty years earlier Joachim du Bellay sent his friend Remi Doulcin, a priest and a physician, impressions similar to those of many of the Loudunais onlookers:

> Doulcin, quand quelquefois je vois ces pauvres filles
> Qui ont le diable au corps, ou le semblent avoir,
> D'une horrible façon corps et têtes mouvoir,
> Et faire ce qu'on dit de ces vieilles sibylles;
>
> Quand je vois les plus forts se retrouver débiles,
> Voulant forcer en vain leur forcené pouvoir,
> Et quand même j'y vois perdre tout leur savoir
> Ceux qui sont en votre art tenus des plus habiles;
>
> Quand effroyablement écrier je les ois,
> Et quand le blanc des yeux renverser je les vois,
> Tout le poil me hérisse, et ne sais plus que dire.
>
> Mais quand je vois un moine avecque son Latin
> Leur tâter haut et bas le ventre et le tétin
> Cette frayeur se passe, et suis contraint de rire.[31]

Freudian Introduction

1–3. In the paintings in which the
Bavarian Christoph Haitzmann
(Vienna, winter of 1677–78) depicts
his fantasies, the dead father is metamorphosed into a devil with teats,
keeper of the written law that is substi-
tuted for that of the father.

Freud analyzes this case in *A Seventeenth-Century Demonological Neurosis*:
the Devil/God ambivalence; a pact
that substitutes a diabolical father for
the missing father; a combination of
submission to a new law and the benefit the neurotic derives from it.

Manuscript, Österreichische National
bibliotek, Vienna

Visions

4. Frontispiece of the *Livre des spectres* by Pierre Le Loyer (1586). Paris, Bibliothèque Nationale

5. *Temptation of Saint Anthony* by Jacques Callot. Source: Bulloz

Hair-raising visions adorn both landscape and learned literature. The imaginary is part of history. Like the architecture of Callot, the writing is haunted by the unstable vision that is mind in the spectator and object before him: a dangerous ambiguity between what the subject produces and what he perceives of the world.

6. Frontispiece of *Saducismus Triumphatus* by John Glanville (1691). Paris, Bibliothèque Nationale. Devils and angels enter the human world as the cosmology that placed them in a celestial hierarchy begins to crumble. Conversely, men become angels or devils. The boundaries blur.

7–8. Episodes from the life of Saint Ignatius, engravings by Galle and Collaert (Rome, 1609). Paris, Bibliothèque Nationale

Ignatius of Loyola is successively the demon's serf and master. But the Devil is man at night, when he dominates, and beast during the day, when he is driven out by the exorcism. A figure of power emerges: man.

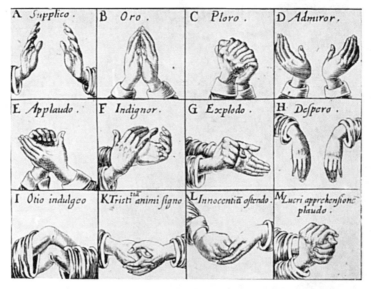

9. The hand, that object whose poses constitute a vocabulary. John Bulwer, *Chirologia* (1644). Paris, Bibiliothèque Nationale

10. Things are words. The litany of the name of Jesus becomes a dictionary of the visible. The dispersion of metaphors on the space of a picture betrays the absence of any religious "figure." Wyerx, *Allegory of the Various Names of Jesus*. Paris, Bibliothèque Nationale

11–12. Between lying and truth, between the est and the non est [the *is* and the *is* not], the battle becomes obsessive and baroque: an endless struggle around an open grave or a broken empire. "Each one thinks he is right, without seeing that each one limps," says the proverb. Gr. de Manderer. Paris, Bibliothèque Nationale

Legends of the Body

13. The microcosm body of the past is installed at the intersection of natural and supernatural hierarchies: body-king, child of the world. Robert Fludd, *Super-naturali ...* (Oppenheim, 1629); engraving by Théodore de Bry. Paris, Bibliothèque Nationale

14. The body of spirituality: a plurality of heads and hearts in an enigmatic relation. Even though the tongue is the manifestation of the inner movements, the head is deception in relation to the celestial, human, or bestial heads that cannot be seen. The tongue tells the secret of multiple, hidden faces. Engraving by Anton Wierx. Paris, Bibliothèque Nationale

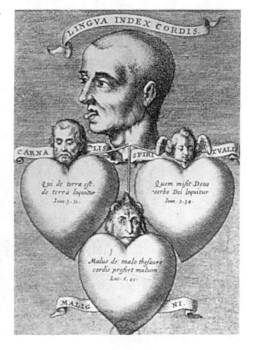

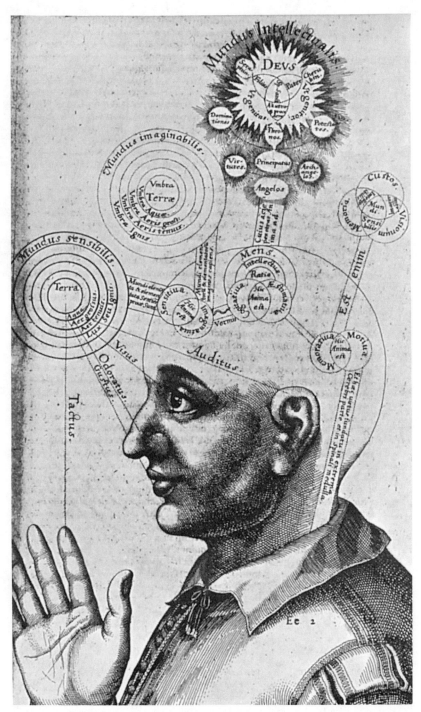

15. The cerebral body of medicine: the brain is the new cosmos. Earth and sky are articulated in the skull, a space and object of knowledge. Robert Fludd, *Utriusque cosmi...* (1629). Paris, Bibliothèque Nationale

The Hand and the Pact

16. The wars of religion make the adversary into the Devil. Repeating the first "exit" of the king dispossessed of La Rochelle, the theater of Loudun will present a series of analogous "exits." [The caption at the top of the figure reads, "Exit of the Devil from La Rochelle."] Paris, Bibliothèque Nationale

17. Against the dragon, a new God: the king of glory, at once the Saint George of yore and the sun of the state policy for tomorrow. *Allegory on Louis XIII* (1617). Paris, Bibliothèque Nationale

18. Jeanne des Anges in the popular iconography: the possessed woman, successively the Devil's grotto and God's tabernacle; the woman-object, with that long sacred hand she will offer to the cult. Paris, Bibliothèque Nationale

19. The devil begins to write (May 1634): Asmodaeus promises to "come out" of Jeanne's body. That will get him into the Bibliothèque Royale. Paris, Bibliothèque Nationale

20. Urbain Grandier, in the days of his success. Paris, Bibliothèque Nationale

21. The judges of Loudun. Paris, Bibliothèque Nationale

INTERROGATOIRE
DE
MAISTRE

VRBAIN GRANDIER
Preſtre, Curé de S. Pierre du marché de Loudun, & Chanoyne de
l'Egliſe ſainѣe Croix dudit lieu.

Auec les confrontations des Religieuſes
poſſedées contre ledit Grandier.

Enſemble la liſte & les noms des
Iuges deputez par ſa Majeſté.

❀

A PARIS,
Chez Eſtienne Hebert, & Iacques Povi-
lard, ruë des ſept Voyes.
M. DC. XXXIV.
Auec Permiſſion.

22. One of the pamphlets sold on the Pont-Neuf. Paris, Bibliothèque Nationale

23. Mgr de La Rocheposay, still the young bishop of Poitiers (1615). Time will make him grow stouter. Paris, Bibliothèque Nationale

24. Surin at the end of his adventures. Paris, Bibliothèque Nationale

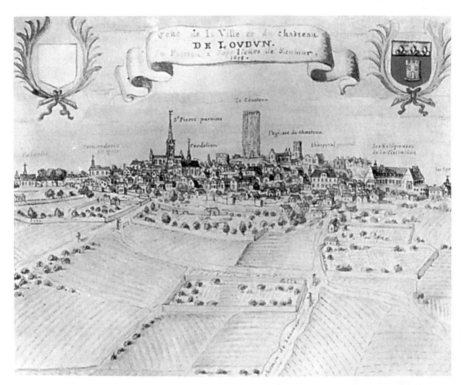

25. Loudun, a cluster of bell-towers surrounded by fields (1609). Paris, Bibliothèque Nationale

26. *Pourtraict représentant au vif l'execution faicte à Loudun en la personne de Urbain Grandier...* ["Portrait from life representing the execution in Loudun of the person of Urbain Grandier..."] (Poitiers: René Allain, 1634). Paris, Bibliothèque Nationale

27. *Effigie de la condemnation de mort et execution d'Urbain Grandier...* ["Effigy of the condemnation to death and execution of Urbain Grandier..."] (Paris: Jean de la Noüe, 1634). Paris, Bibliothèque Nationale

28. *Mère Jeanne des Anges*, a film by Jerzy Kawalerowicz, 1960. Source: Edimédia, Paris

~ 8 ~

The Medical Eye

Spring 1634

In mid-April a whole series of physicians is called on to auscultate, feel, observe, and medicate, while on another front the ranks of the exorcists are renewed and increased, with a view to organizing common sessions to be held in churches. Among the crowd of physicians are Charles Auger, François Carré, Alphonse Cosnier, Gabriel Coustier, François Duclos, Mathieu Fanton, Vincent de Fos, Jean-François Grolleau, Antoine Jacquet, Gaspard Joubert, and Daniel Rogier, along with the surgeons Allain, François Brion, and Maunoury, and the apothecary Pierre Adam. Others come from Poitiers, Tours, Saumur, Niort, La Flèche, Le Mans, Paris, Montpellier, and elsewhere. They will file report on report: the *Registres de la commission* (1634) list twenty-six of them, written and signed before Grandier's death, and they are not all mentioned there.[1] The list of medical publications is no less impressive.

Villages and Major Cities

The debates among physicians do more than reveal the new "curiosities" of a social category. The tragedy of Loudun is a scene in which the drama of a perturbation in knowledge is also represented. Something is breaking up, something being born in what is then called medicine. In this same year of 1632 Rembrandt paints *The Anatomy Lesson of Doctor Tulp,* the depiction of an epistemological moment. In Loudun, before the objects submitted to its diagnosis, a science betrays its ambitions, its divisions, its mutations in progress, the shifting or the stiffening of its concepts, and even its obsessions. But the doctrinal oppositions are connected, at least in public opinion, with a social cleavage between the city and the country. Witness the accusation made against the "possessionists" by the *Factum pour Maître Urbain Grandier* (August 1634), a lampoon published in many places:

> By what physicians are they served? One is from Fontevrault [Alphonse Cosnier], who has never had any letters and for that reason was forced to leave Saumur. The ones from Thouars are the same way, one [Jean-François Grolleau] having spent most of his youth measuring ribbon and hat cloth in a Loudun shop; the other [François Brion], equally ignorant and convicted of extreme incompetence by monseigneur the archbishop of Bordeaux and also a close relative of Trincant's wife. The one from Chinon, ignorant and kept out of work by those from town, even a bit out of his head. The one from Mirebeau [Antoine Jacquet], similarly, a relative of Mignon's sister. In short, all village physicians. . . .
>
> Instead of calling, in an affair of such great consequence, on some more learned, famous, and experienced physicians and apothecaries of the good neighboring cities, like Tours, Poitiers, Angers, or Saumur. But they didn't want such clear-sighted ones.[2]

Elsewhere the doctor from Châtellerault will be accused. Whatever the errors of fact or of judgment may be, the line of demarcation here is clear: to separate the bad from the good, the clever advocate uses a cliché, the depreciation of the "villages" in favor of the "towns," and bases his views on the hierarchy that ranks, by order of increasing importance, hamlets, villages, small towns (those that have markets), and cities. The physicians lose their proper names and find themselves assigned the common name of a category of place, which "classes" them and fixes their individual position in relation to a sociocultural center. That is almost enough to distinguish "the ignorant" from "the clear-sighted." Knowledge has its geography: around Loudun, a small circle of "villages"—Chinon, Fontevrault, Thouars, Mirebeau, Châtellerault—is contrasted with the larger circle of "major cities" and good-quality medicine: Angers, Saumur, Tours, Poitiers (see below, fig. 2).

Physicians, Surgeons, and Apothecaries

Another cleavage, more discreet but no less strict, is the socioprofessional distinction among doctors of medicine, surgeons, and apothecaries. At the bottom of the attestations, a punctilious etiquette dictates the order of signatures, as it does the order of entry at the top of official documents. First the doctors, with their titles. Then come the surgeons, the technicians of medicine, men of tools. Whereas doctors "possess," in the judicial sense of the term, sight and knowledge, surgeons receive the status of handworkers. The surgeon Dionis says it clearly: "The physicians took the whole theoretical science for their portion, leaving us the practice and the work of the operation of the hand." Many physicians even think that to do bloodletting lowers them to the level of craftsmen. Between saying or knowing, on the one hand, and doing or operating on the other, there is a distance that separates two professional categories in a finicky hierarchy.

As for the apothecaries, such as Pierre Adam, they do not contribute to the texts. They are excluded from the places in which "truth" is certified. Let us recall what the traditionalist Guy Patin (1600?–1672) says about them in his *Préceptes particuliers d'un médecin à son fils:*

> Pharmacy is a stumbling-block and a trap to a physician, who should wisely shield himself from it. Never do anything against your conscience and the honor of your profession in favor of an apothecary. . . . If you take away four boxes from their shop, all the rest is but charlatanism, painted and gilded boxes in which all you find is mouse droppings passed off as pepper and ginger. That invention of apothecary shops and specialties has only come into credit by the connivance of some physicians and the foolishness of the people, who want to be fooled. A physician cannot order much for a patient without wronging both him and his own conscience, and even most often he damns himself and kills his patient.[3]

Does the redistribution that changes the trades into "orders" correspond to a hierarchizing of science, technique, and commerce (or, as Patin puts it, the "shop")? Does it indicate, out of three ways of approaching the body—theoretical knowledge, intervention, drugs—a classification that favors for a time *representation?* At the highest level of science, as at the highest rank of the organization of the professions, there is the spectacle.

Seeing and Examining

The physicians' first task is "to see and examine," and hence to follow and note the spectacles of the body. They proceed in the manner of the authors who compose at that time a *Theatrum mundi* or a *Mirror of the World* (an earlier form of our present atlases) and place their work beneath the motto: *If thou wouldst see* (so Bouguereau, in his *Théâtre français*). They describe the patient as a ground, a terrain, with "emotions"

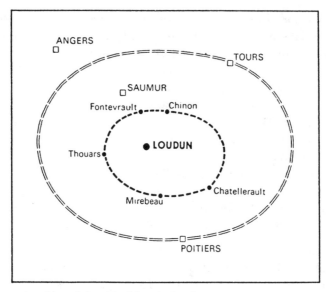

2. A geography of knowledge. Physicians in Loudun are classified as "the ignorant" or "the clear-sighted," according to whether they come from "villages" or from "major cities." But the distance also determines the authority.

or movements, irruptions, and so forth. But they do so in describing the terrain as it *appears* to them. Their testimonies are the image of an image: the textual images of visual ones. They relate the travels of the eye.

Thus, elementary though it be, this "certificate" and "testimony" given on January 30, 1634, by the first consultants:

> We, doctor of medicine and master surgeons undersigned, certify to all whom it may concern, that by virtue of the order of M. Laubardemont, councilor to the king in his State and Privy Councils, did go to the convent of the Ursuline ladies of that town of Loudun to see and examine the mother superior of said place, on whom we found several excoriations and scratches all over the face, particularly on both cheeks, on the chin and beneath the throat, which we saw more visibly after having made a lotion of water and wine, because of the blood that was dried there, and we remarked two on the right cheek that were somewhat deeper and wider than said others . . . etc. etc.
>
> To which above we hereby bear witness as containing truth. Witness our seals herein affixed. This thirtieth day of January of the year sixteen hundred thirty-four.
>
>   Dr. Rogier, Doctor of Medicine
>   Allain, Master Surgeon. Maunoury Master Surgeon.[4]

The meticulous "theater" of facts "considered" forms the first "truth" to which the physician "bears witness" and states that he "certifies to all." It will be all the more reliable, the more eyes there are—that is, the more physicians. How many things risk going unnoticed! They all must enter the "mirror" that gathers them together. The gazes are therefore multiplied and the body of consultants, reinforced. The written accounts, in turn, made up of the complementary journeys of so many eyes over the same surface, get longer. The narrative becomes cumulative. A lyricism of precision maintains the rhetoric that adds details endlessly, following the law of spatial dispersion.

Suspicion

Yet the relentless way in which a surer vision and a more ample observation are sought attests to worry as well. The need for certainty is also the admission of the fear of losing it. What is really seen? Illusion infiltrates perception. A suspicion undermines the eye's ambitions. There is a worm in the bright apple of vision.

Whatever may be the reflections this doubt will give rise to, and which we shall encounter, the spectacle takes on an ambiguous meaning as a result. Like so many figures of baroque art, "curiosity" is ambivalent: festive in one of its facets, it also has the face of anxiety.

From surprise to fright, that anxiety of the observer does not, for the most part, express itself directly. It is masked, and betrays itself in the object observed, to which the character of being frightful or surprising is attributed as to a cause. Thus in the report of Doctors Grolleau, Brion, and Duclos, dated April 17, 1634—a report too long to be reproduced in its entirety—"astonishment" (that is, in the seventeenth century, dread or stupefaction) and "horror" circulate, pass from the possessed to the examiner, from the latter to the public, so that it is impossible to assign them to any particular subject. In this story, there is fright, a fright that eludes localization and refers back globally to a certainty that should be there and is missing.

The physicians describe their observations during a celebration of the mass in the chapel of the Ursulines:

Astonishment and Fright

A little later, we equally admired the same movements in Elisabeth Blanchard, movements each one of which surprised her

with more horror and fright than the last. Which movements
and agitations continued in both said Françoise [Fillastreau]
and Elisabeth until after the communion of the mass, after having appeared in said Elisabeth so prodigiously and enormously
before the holy canon of the mass that said girl, by using her
feet and the top of her head, the only things holding her up,
with her belly high, arched herself backward, head first, squirm-
ing from her place to the height of the altar, having by an all
new and extraordinary manner of disproportion quickly as-
cended with the back of her head the two steps to reach the
feet of the priest, the end of whose alb she brusquely and
roughly pulled during the elevation, to interrupt him and keep
him from proceeding. And the Reverend Father Lactance, the
companion of the father and exorcist, desiring to pull her away
from there and keep her from committing further similar inso-
lences, said Blanchard brought him to the ground so roughly
that it was hard for him to get free from her hands.

Then, toward the end of the holy mass, Léonne Benjamine,
the sister of the preceding, began carrying on like the two others
with oaths, great blasphemies, and threats, which came out of
their mouths, to kill now one another, now the very girl out of
whose mouth these words were furiously proffered, saying: "By
God, I'll kill that girl."

All of which things we judge absolutely to surpass the forces
and means of nature, and to be of the same condition as the
ones we see daily with astonishment and fright in the persons
of said ladies, Ursuline nuns of this town.[5]

Judging

The "truth" announced and certified by these reports often carries, inscribed with all the rest on the table of exploratory successes, an apparently heterogeneous element: this surpasses nature. This big fish caught
in the net of the text has its place, like the others, beneath the sign
of what has been "remarked," as Doctor Cosnier says, or "judged and
remarked," as he also writes. This datum is dangerous. It is at once of
the order of what one sees and of the order of what one thinks. More
clearly, on April 14, 1634, the doctors of medicine D. Rogier, A. Cosnier,
F. Carré, F. Duclos, and F. Brion declare: "We have adjured that there
is something that goes beyond nature."[6]

But on November 30, 1632, Brion attested that he had gone

to see, in the convent of the Ursulines, madame the prioress, named Jeanne de Belciel, of the house of Cozes, and Sister Claire de Saint-Jean de Sazilly, the niece of M. de Villeneuve, the lieutenant of M. le maréchal de Brézé in Saumur, which two, having considered them both at rest and in the throes of their affliction, we judge (given the excesses that surpass the natural) that there is possession by evil spirits, which appeared to us by divers signs that we deduce as requested, as also other ladies, numbering four, that we have recognized as being obsessed. That which is above we say is true.[7]

Knowing in Order to See

In this medical deduction (in the seventeenth century, *to deduce* means "to describe"), the facts observed are as surely traced back to "that which surpasses the natural" as are the nuns to their family titles and names. That which is seen is "Jeanne of the house of Cozes," or Claire, "the niece of M. de Villeneuve, the lieutenant of M. le maréchal de Brézé." In social perception, the "girl" is the visibility of a family essence that is known. Similarly, it seems, the contortions and gesticulations give the immediate apprehension of a reality posited by a knowledge: that which surpasses the natural. Such is the case, at any rate, with the whole of medicine: it demands to recognize in the patient the nosological essences that it has defined and of which the patient presents an incarnation (more or less successful, depending on how complete the table of "signs" to be found there may be).

Observation is not thereby devalued. On the contrary, the physician seeks to fill what he knows with what he sees. He is in search of the manifestation of his nosological concepts. Mobilized by attention, he considers the deployment of a knowledge in the new and visible form of an appearing. In short, he discovers without learning. This enterprise is difficult, for one must distinguish how and at what points the indefinite series of spectacles scanned by the eye is articulated with the finite series of medical categories at the disposal of science. The medical "consideration" is thus the alloy of a seeing and a judging, or of a noticing and a thinking—but an alloy that will become more and more unstable before the "extraordinary" facts. For then one falls either into the simple re-cognition that accepts only the known portion of the visible, or else into the empirical recording of an unknown that throws knowledge off course, toward a different formalization, privileging experience. In the first case, the "judging" circumscribes and represses the "noticing"; in the second, observation compromises judgment.

"Beware of Becoming Empirical"

Everything turns on *experience,* a pivotal notion in the disputes that, faced with the extraordinary, call into question the status of perception and the definition of nature. Some will say, with Guy Patin (an extreme case, it is true):

> Beware of becoming empirical. Reason always and use experience only as the servant of the reason and science you have acquired. The sects of the methodists and the empiricist, if they be not subdued and do not obey dogmatics, are but vicious extremes that you must carefully avoid. Hippocrates spoke no truer words than: *Experimentum fallax.* A physician who does not reason is not a physician, he is but a charlatan. One must bleed, purge, apply cupping glasses, give wine or deny it to a patient by reason.[8]

That marvelous confidence in "acquired" science will not keep Patin from saying about Loudun: "I'll believe no man or woman to be demoniacal unless I see them, but I suspect there be no such thing."[9]

In order to believe, must one then see? Is what he knows not enough for him? But in reality his knowledge leads him to think he cannot see that. Would he trust in what he saw to the detriment of what he knows, or would he find in his "reason" and his "dogmatics" the means to reabsorb the threatening interrogation connected with the hypothesis of such a vision?

Accommodating the Uncanny: The Possible

The many physicians who gather together with an intent gaze around the gesticulations of Loudun—like Rembrandt's doctors around the cadaver—find themselves carried by their observations to the limits of their science. What criteria do they have to affirm that they have "never seen and observed anything above the common laws of nature" or the contrary? Fundamental problems are posed. On the one hand, they must decide on what is and is not possible in nature. How can they judge otherwise than on the basis of what they know? From this point of view, it is a question of knowing whether they can situate the extraordinary, which escapes them, within nosological categories, or whether they should locate it outside. Where is the most reasonable locus to make room for the uncanny—in what is theoretically assimilable, or in what is to be recognized as "different" or "supernatural"? Will the unknown be classified on the near side or the far side of what is posited as comprehensible in principle?

In itself, it is not obvious that the most totalizing option (everything is explainable in medical terms) is the most scientific: it refuses to set itself a limit, a zero degree, on which rigor would be founded; in saying that everything is "natural," it merely takes over in its own name the cosmological and all-encompassing model of a theology. This difficulty comes from the fact that two issues are lumped together: the establishment of a medical field and the determination of a natural order. There are sociocultural reasons for this. Every era imposes a particular kind of alternative.

The physician is led to take the place of the theologian, as the witness of a lay knowledge that takes up where clerical knowledge leaves off. Doctor Yvelin will soon say it clearly, with respect to the possession at Louviers:

> The physicians in this case have grave prerogatives above the ecclesiastics, for they know that if that melancholic humor stagnates within hypochondriacs, there arise from it vapors and winds of sufficiently malignant quality to produce all the effects that seem so uncanny and so extraordinary.[10]

Or else the physician, passing up that position to be taken—one that offers him, like the statesman, a very well-defined role—accepts the supernatural as a region of facts that adjoins his own domain; he recognizes in the theologian the proprietor of fiefdoms delimiting his own, and still requiring his allegiance in the name of God.

The Illusion of Seeing

On the other hand, suspicion is cast upon experience itself, which becomes questionable. What is the relationship between what *appears* and what *is?* An old question, one that is already present in the postnominalist philosophy of the period. The physicians express it in gliding from what they see to what they think they see. The treacherous mediation of this thinking introduces the permanent danger of illusion. When they inquire into the natural and the supernatural of observed facts, they must ask themselves what they really see. *Truthful, true, truth:* these words keep coming up, obsessively, at the end or in the heading of *Relations,* precisely admitting the fragile point and locus of lack—perception itself.

The abnormality of the facts and the contradictoriness of interpretations thus leave an opening in sight for doubt to slip through. Thus the

physicians, in their own way, share in the social anxiety of which possession is a symptom. In the ambient skepticism, they experience that un-
easiness as epistemological uncertainty: there is trickery. But where? The
question is not unlike the one that consisted in assigning a locus to the
unknown. For some, it is knowledge that is erroneous, and one should
return to a fideism, blindly trusting truths received from elsewhere. For
others, it is experience that puts us on the wrong track: *Experimentum
fallax,* as Patin said. Perception is misleading. Or, as Dr. Duncan will say
of Loudun, "the imagination errs, it is false, it is wounded and fools the
senses."[11] Unless perhaps illusion can be blamed on the actors, driven
back to the level of artifice and simulation, to which the observed facts
would then be attributed, thus eliminating the problem. This hypothesis
is by far the most tempting, but remains difficult to accept. It is no more
acceptable to the majority of physicians than is the "explanation" by the
miracle, though they do accept it as a nonnegligible element.

Feeling One's Way

Before being dealt with thematically, these problems arise through the
day-to-day examination of an exceptional case, tied to a professional
practice and also to questions of conscience. Such is the case in the
report, in which "Sieur Seguin, a physician in Tours," tries, by feeling
his way in the dark, to clarify and explain his personal position:

> Sir,
> It would be to deny the friendship I have sworn to you, were
> I to deny what you desire from me. It is true that, without your
> insistence, I would gladly have forborne interposing my puny
> judgment in a matter that involves devils, having seen nothing
> during my trip to Loudun that could instruct you further . . .
> other than what was published in various writings that circulate
> everywhere, and, I am sure, on the Pont-Neuf among other
> places. It is not as if you had not read the letter that M. Bardin
> wrote to his friends on this subject, of whom I believe you to
> be one. After which letter I do not claim to give you any other
> satisfaction than that of acquiescing to your wish.
> Now, in order not to repeat what he writes perfectly of the
> impossibility of trickery, I will add that I conversed with the ma-
> jority of those poor afflicted souls in their good intervals, during
> which they only answered me with such great naiveté that I do
> not think them capable of sustaining such a horrible wickedness
> for so long. Thus it is that on that score I am fully convinced,

though to tell the truth all the indiscreet zeal of one exorcist disturbed me a bit at the beginning.

A Sickness of the Soul?

For what touches the sickness of the soul, that is where I would be more hesitant, for I do not see it to be an absolute impossibility, as many do. For first, concerning the medical test, on which they based their report on the possession of the religious, I do not understand why they so necessarily ascribe a supernatural cause to the lack of effect of the purgative medicines prescribed by them in double doses. Theophrastes (*Lib. IX historiae plantarum,* cap. 18) relates several stories of persons who devoured maniples of hellebore, without being in any way affected by it, among others that of a certain Eudemus, who one day took, in the middle of the marketplace, twenty-two doses of hellebore, without departing thence all the morning, and upon coming back to his house, took a bath and supped as was his habit, without vomiting. Which he ascribes principally to custom, which is so powerful that it accustoms us to even the most present and strong poisons and renders them without effect.

So maybe these good religious, who are said to have been very sickly, were so accustomed to it that they no longer felt any change. Besides, perhaps the humors, not having been duly prepared, could not yield to the medicine, the action of which they thus entirely stop by their extreme resistance: and consequently I think that first test did not suffice to be sure that the Devil made that impeachment.

As for the onset of their great agitations, I find it nothing strange that they should be irregular and have no fixed period, but rather that they begin and end at a given moment, namely at the exorcist's command. Which I have often seen to happen, and sometimes not. Nevertheless it is certain that this would not usually happen by chance. Whence it is inferred that the cause of it must be other than sickness. Which I do not find that it be so indubitable as is supposed, and esteem that the imagination can be wounded and the reason troubled to the point of persuading themselves they are possessed by demons, so that the mind obsessed by that error betakes itself more willingly to occasions that stir up its illusion. The which is noted in almost all sicknesses of the spirit, which are brought on and redouble in intensity, according to the occurrence of divers objects for which it has a predilection. Thus so far, one could come to the conclusion that these poor girls fallen into such extravagancy of mind are driven to a fury when they are irritated by the exorcists.

In a similar way, it could be maintained that all the sudden changes that take place in them are the effects of that perverted imagination, at which one should not be astonished after what one sees every day of the force of the imagination of women, which, the more commonly it appears in that sex, the less reason there is now to say that it is the cause of that madness. That would be going too far in the direction of something I do not believe.

"There Must Be Some Deviltry Here"

For after all, considering that so extraordinary a folly could not be found in so great a number of different temperaments and conspire to one same thing without a wicked conspiracy, I resolved to believe there is in fact somewhat of the Devil in it, mistrusting rather him than the probity of several persons who have never given any cause to judge of them so badly.

It is true that there are things that shock that belief and have often puzzled me. But, when I go back over it and think whether these things come of the Devil's intrigue or of men worse than Beelzebub, they confirm what I thought and all the more so as they seem to destroy the truth, whose enemy is the demon.

So why then, somebody will say to me, does he so reproach those who do not believe the possession, going so far as to denounce them as magicians? I admit I am not clever enough to account for that arch-deception. It is a retaliation that carries beyond where it strikes, and that I find so dangerous that only God could remedy it. You may believe as you please about it. But again, there must be either devilish wickedness, or deviltry here. Otherwise, how could these girls understand a language we are assured they never learned, and answer on the spot all kinds of questions, even the loftiest questions of theology, as I have sometimes seen them do? How could they make movements so various and difficult, without having long studied them? I am not speaking of the supernatural ones, especially since I have not attended them, though they are attested to by

many people of merit, capable of judging in such matters. Nor
do I speak to you of divinations and other peculiar signs they
have given to most of the judges, among others M. le président
Cothereau, who remains convinced. They also responded in the
Topinambou language [the language of a Brazilian tribe],
which M. de Launay Razilly, whom I believe more than I do
myself, spoke to them, and whom I cite because you know him
for a man worthy of credence.

Of all that I have seen, the thing that seems to me the
strangest is the deep torpor into which they are sometimes sunk,
as in a lethargy, with at least no apparent sensation, though they
be pricked. At other times, they are in very violent, continual
agitations that last for two full hours, now throughout the body,
now in a part of it, and particularly the head, with no change of
pulse or breathing. Thus it must be concluded that the demon is
not only the moral cause, but truly the effective one, of all these
disstatic movements. There is what I know and think of this
whole affair, which I have represented to you with no other care
than for the truth.[12]

~ *9* ~

A Teratology of Truth

I. THE IMAGINATION

As for the truth, Dr. Seguin must discover it in "the great forest" of the Witches' Sabbath, which a possessed woman had one day given as a meeting-place to her interlocutors.[1] Physicians, exorcists, and theologians go around there with him. Three years later, Descartes also finds himself in a forest of impressions and knowledge, but, he says in the *Discourse on Method* (1637):

> Imitating . . . the travelers who, finding themselves lost in some forest, must not wander around in circles, now in this direction, now in that, nor even less remain in one place, but always walk the straightest way they can in one sole direction and not change for minor reasons, even though it may have been in the beginning nothing but chance that convinced them to choose it. For by this means, if they go not just where they desire, at least they arrive at last somewhere, where likely they will do better than in the middle of a forest.[2]

Quadrupedia

The erudite of Loudun adopt a different conduct. They reside in the world of the imagination and of lies. They linger there, eager to discover in the imaginary the reason that lies hidden there, "though the images be the most monstrous and strange in the world"[3]—or to recognize in the works of the Liar the truth they confess through the inversion or deformity of its signs. Their tactics is not to withdraw from such enchanted haunts. On the contrary, they come to them. They sojourn there, fascinated by the uncanny—something that is known to be a general phenomenon in this time of mannerism, baroque, and Gongorism. And being there, they practice a teratology of truth.

If medicine during this period is a philosophical locus, it is because sickness at this time has an essential relationship to truth. The learned who pass judgment on the possession seek not so much to extract the natural from evil and the authentic from deception as to recognize nature (or supernature) in its deformed state, and truth that has become monstrous or erroneous. A bold intent, to be sure; it risks turning into its opposite, for it leads them to ask whether nature is not fundamentally ailing, or whether truth is not an illusion that does not know it. Skepticism creeps in everywhere.

At the outset, then, there is an acceptance of a pathological language of truth, a demonic language of God, and also a bestial language of man. The physicians, convinced they are dealing with holy religious women, virgins and martyrs, speak of them as *quadrupedia*. The immense edifying discourse formed by the minutes is made up of the cries and gestures of beasts. It exhausts the animal repertory. It is the Noah's Ark of the imaginary of the period. As if admiration fixed upon monstrous life or monstrous truth lost sight of the human. Between the celestial beings and the beast, or between the combined elements of the cosmological and the "vital," there is an ellipsis of humankind.

But is it not precisely a question of defining what is human? In Loudun, we are far from the society that will allow Cyrano de Bergerac to affirm with assurance, in his letter *Contre les sorciers:* "One must only believe of a man that which is human, that is, possible."[4]

The necessity of finding one's way about in the immediate setting, in the forest of frenzied signs, directs all effort toward their interpretation. That pathological, demonic, or bestial language must be deciphered. All the tools of intellectual work are used to that end: the decoding of the foreign language of truth. Given the urgency of criteria and norms, every technique is made to serve in an enterprise of definition and identification. The physicians seem to forget that they are supposed to give care, it is so important to them to diagnose, and they are so much in demand to "render an opinion." The exorcists give priority to the demonstration the possessed allow them to carry out, rather than to their deliverance. The learned seek to designate what is true more than to eliminate evil. Identification wins out over therapy. The means of healing become the means of knowing.

Recovering the True

Perhaps the professional, medical, or liturgical practices are merely manifesting in this way—more blatantly than in other times and places—

their relationship with the social truth they presuppose and defend. Because the order to which they referred is weakening and crumbling, the therapeutic acts allow a hidden finality to appear. They substitute for an objective was not immediately theirs, but which their normal functioning implied—the establishing of a social certainty, the providing of a sure knowledge. The purge or the fumigation, the exorcism or the blessing becomes a "theoretical" operation and a procedure of investigation. They are used to reclaim possession of the true, even when it has changed into its opposite.

For the possession at Loudun strips the learned of their dignity: their knowledge has been possessed by the uncanny, just as the anthropology of the day sees in sickness the intruder installed within the patient, or in the devil the illegal colonizer of the Christian. The learned are at home in the monstrous, but on a property that has been taken from them by force, and their goal is to recover their possessions. They know those are theirs, but this is no longer visible. Hence they must reclaim their knowledge and see that their titles are recognized, precisely where their right is being hidden by an unjust occupant.

It is doubtless not insignificant that all these learned men in search of their adulterated truth—physicians, exorcists, theologians—speak Latin. Later, La Ménardière will publish translations of Trajan's *Panegyric* and of Pliny. Quillet will publish Latin poems, *Henriciados*, a translation of Juvenal's satires, and so forth. They are at home in that language of their learning and their leisure. In Loudun, the foreign language in which they must reclaim their property—a teratological, pathological, demonic, bestial language—tends to be French and the language of facts. They keep their distance from present experience by preserving the locus of their rights and their titles of ownership: Latin. Almost all the medical reports and all the theological consultations continue to be written in that language of their legitimacy. The exorcists usually address the possessed women in Latin only, a sign that they are there as representatives of the Church, the legal keeper of the revelations that have gone mad, and it is in Latin that they claim to force the Father of Lies to deliver up the truth. When both parties yield on this point, the assurance of a legitimacy will have disappeared.

The Remedy and Exorcism

This does not mean that, speaking the same language, the traditionalist doctors and theologians understand one another. They have common interests, but they are competitors. In the battle of each day, they confront each other's opposing show of rights. Thus, on May 20, 1634, after the "exit" of three demons from Jeanne des Anges through three wounds at her heart, one of the exorcised women warns the public about the physicians' knowledge:

> One of the exiting demons was constrained by the holy angel of the mother superior to declare that they planned to envenom the three wounds, and, by this means, cause the mother to die; that if some remedy were applied to heal them or lessen the pain the patient suffered, which was searing and continued for almost three weeks, that would allow them to accomplish their project; but that if nothing at all were done, at the end of three weeks, to the day, they would be entirely healed. The which turned out to be true to the letter. Not so much as a scar remained. The mother would very much have liked an attempt made for her suffering to be lessened by some human remedy, as her wounds were causing her burning pain, and lasting more than a fortnight. But they wanted to see if it were true that Satan had been coerced to declare his own malice.[5]

On another occasion, the exorcist demonstrates his celestial powers over the body, in opposition to the authority that orders potions or bleedings. Such is at least the understanding of the chronicler of this scene, in which the exorcist gives orders to the blood like Moses to the sea:

> She [Jeanne des Anges] was given a potion of antimony, prepared much stronger than is given to the most robust temperaments. She was observed and watched over for twentyfour hours, to see the working of the remedy. There was none. The next day the dosage was doubled, and on the third day, tripled. And with all that, it appeared that nothing came out of the patient. She did not feel the least movement from it, and appeared, during the three days, in her right mind and even-tempered. They had her bled from the arm, with all these messieurs present, and the exorcist father, who, when the blood was running its strongest, commanded the demon present in the body to stop it. At the instant of the command, the blood stopped and was held up above the arm for a rather long space of time. Then the exorcist, commanding to let the blood flow, the blood came as before. The divers commandments were repeated several times, as a result of which the prioress lost so great a quantity

of blood that the strongest body would have been noticeably
weakened by it, and the mother, though of a delicate complexion, was not at all weakened. The doctors, surprised and
astounded at seeing no effect from the antimony, nor from everything that happened during that bleeding, all admitted there
was nothing natural in it.[6]

A distinction must be made between two types of practices and theo-
ries—those of the physicians and those of the exorcist theologians—
even if they often belong to the same system of interpretation.

A Voyeur

Among the physicians, here is one who comes from Paris. Sieur Léon Le
Tourneur, a distinguished humanist, doctor of medicine of the faculty of
Paris, writes from Loudun on July 7, 1634, in sound and sonorous Latin:

> Whereas in Paris the mind is constantly occupied by the heaviest
> cares, as if crushed by the weight, and each one aspires to the
> leisure of some Ithaca, the only rest for weariness. . . . [M. Le
> Tourneur was leaving for a vacation on his island of Ulysses, his
> family Ithaca.]
>
> I was obliged, persuaded by the pressure of friends, and
> induced above all by the order received from superiors, to make
> a detour to Loudun for the purpose of examining the truth of
> that famous demonomany, most famous in all of France for two
> years already. In this memorable place [monumentum] I have
> spent a week, so great was the curiosity of so strange a spectacle.

He has come to "visit" this monumentum—in the medical sense of examining it. More than a tourist, he comes as a "voyeur." His vocabulary,
like that of his colleagues, is structured around the infinitely repeated
verbs: admirari, considerare, contemplari, examinare, explorare, inspectare, in-
vestigare, mirari, notare, observare, reperire, stupere (in or ad), videre, and so
on. But the operations of the gaze, accompanied by quasi-obsessive ad-
jectives (accurate, sagacissime) run up against the "trickery" of what appears. In particular, is not what the face shows a false appearance? A
medical science, metoposcopy, claims to found a diagnostic on the connections between the bodily organs and the parts of the face, but it is
strongly debated at the time. Sieur de la Forge, a physician who came
from La Flèche in June 1634, a great scrutinizer of faces, has confidence
in it. Le Tourneur seems to prefer a different way of reading (but is it

not even more uncertain?), the principle of which is that the parts of the face do not correspond to bodily "residences," but to vices and virtues:

> The forehead, the eyes, the facial expression, and lines of character often lie. In the virgins [of Loudun], however, the forehead speaks only of dignity; the eyes, of modesty; the cheeks, of decency; the mouth, of things grave and serious; the whole air of the face, of distance from imposture.[7]

For his part, Pilet de la Ménardière, doctor of the faculty of medicine of Nantes, either cannot or does not wish to believe "that my senses were charmed or that the books are deceitful."[8]

Making the Body Speak

But all this remains to be demonstrated. Mobilized in the defense of a certain theoretical knowledge on the terrain of sight, the physicians use their therapies as proofs. Therefore the practices are intended to make the body "speak," to make what is seen confess to what is known. Nothing is more harmful, in this respect, than lethargy, or, as noted by Doctor Pilet, Doctor Du Chesne, and still others, the "watchful sleep" into which the religious sink. Fumigations will awaken the sleeping, closed bodies. This olfactive technique (founded, once again, on the "virtue" of smells) passes from the physicians to the exorcists:

> Said Sister [Agnès] was surprised by lethargy and afterward by convulsions. And the lethargy having returned to her, said Father [Lactance] caused it to cease by fumigations that were followed by great convulsions.[9]

The procedure takes the form of torture when applied by Father Tranquille, an old hand at these battles with the devil, and who has a foot soldier's notion of them:

> His principle was that you had to force the possessing devils to speak frequently and to respond. . . . It happened from time to time that the prioress mother remained one or two days without the demons who were within her appearing to work her. If, during these times, some considerable visitors, whom the exorcist wanted to oblige, expressed their desire to see signs of the possession, he used all the invention he considered proper on the possessed woman to touch her humor and embitter her passions, giving as his reason that there was no other way to make these demons appear and speak.

For example, desiring to obtain that the mother should be put in external agitations surpassing the natural measure, he would provoke anger. To get Satan to talk, he would excite gaiety and joy. For anger, and to sour the humor of the possessed woman, he would use smoke produced by lighted candles of pitch resin, of dwarf elder sulfur, and similar things, having the possessed woman's face held over the smoke until, unable to withstand it longer and losing patience by the excess of pain, Satan appeared in her. For the other passions, he used means as little reasonable, which was learned when the poor girl, having no other defiance than her cries and lamentations, used them with all her strength. Those who heard her, running to her help, fell into astonishment to see such a thing, and that man dismissed them so brusquely and rudely that they were afraid to go back.[10]

Drugs

This aberrant case, armed with an apologetics, is the extreme consequence of a displacement in a therapeutic system: it attests a new usage of fumigation. The same is true of the drugs used by Drs. Rogier, Cosnier, Grolleau, Carré, Bion, Jacquet, and Duclos:

> To give medicaments, we proceeded by order, beginning with the lightest and taking into consideration the strength, age, temperament, and the peccant humor. Such medicaments were senna, rhubarb, agaric, starpethe, carthanus, and similar ones, as for splenetics, hepatics, cephalics, hyplerics, etc. Then stronger ones were used: scammony *(dacrydium)*, alkandal *(al-handual)*, and their composites, which are sold in the stores, without omitting hellebore and saffron from metals. All these medicaments were administered to no effect, as was noted above.[11]

These drugs are mainly purges: senna purges the black bile and the pituitary of the brain (madness is known to be "caused by the irregular conformation of the brain or by some cold or pituitary humor that overcomes it"); rhubarb, "heavy, hot and dry to the second degree," purges the bile (as does scammony); agaric purges phlegm, and so forth. Other physicians administer diaphoretic antimony, polychrest salt, and coloquint. Along with that, they make "a little insinuative, preparative, and softening clyster" or "a good detersive clyster."

In addition to the drugs, there are other techniques. Some physicians order a great many bleedings. The pulse and perspiration are the main objects of analysis, less frequently deglutition, excrement, urine: these are the basic examinations.

These various therapies intend to provide demonstrative tactics. They are to force the body to attest to the science that organizes them. Their objective is to have the body send back, as if by a mirror, the image of a theoretical knowledge. Should they be without effect, for example, that would confirm the supernatural character of the phenomenon, and it would equally confirm the theory that denies melancholy the capacity to produce them.

Defining What Proves

The definition of what can be demonstrative belongs to the learned man, since he himself defines what the causes are and what their effects. In his *Traité de la mélancholie,* Pilet de la Ménardière believes melancholy to be unable to produce the effects he witnesses in Loudun; therefore melancholy does not explain them, but something that transcends nature. In his *Discours de la possession des religieuses de Loudun,*[12] the Scotsman Marc Duncan, a philosopher and physician installed in Saumur, fashions for himself a theory of the imagination that allows him to bring into it all the facts from Loudun that are not the result of deception. The Latin *Satire* addressed in 1635 to the French clergy by Claude Quillet, then a physician in Chinon, and his *Relation de tout ce que j'ai veu à Loudun en neuf jours que j'ay visité les possédées* [Relation of All That I Saw in Loudun in the Nine Days during Which I Examined the Possessed Women] (1634) represent the same position for the same reasons.[13] Du Chesne is more uncertain, but since his general conceptions hesitate, he leans rather in the direction of the "possessionists."[14] François Pidoux, dean of the faculty of medicine of Poitiers, has no hesitation in firing off, against Duncan, his *In actiones Juliodunensium virginum . . . Exercitatio medica* (two editions the same year), and his *Deffensio* against Sieur Duval, who had called him an *ignorant* in a work that appeared under the pseudonym "Eulalius" ("he who speaks well").[15]

A Physics of Melancholy

The real debate is of a theoretical order. These physicians are philosophers, or they refer to a philosophy (to a cosmology) as to that which will decide the question posed by the observations made in Loudun. Thus writes Pilet de la Ménardière to his Parisian friend, Sieur Du Bois-

Daufin, in September 1634: "You who are well versed in natural philosophy, examine, I pray you, whether, according to [Aristotle's] physics, the
facts [of Loudun] can flow from a [natural] cause." And in his *Traité*,
he attacks the "ridiculous opinion [attributing the acts of the possessed
women to the black humor] that never had a foundation but in a popular error or in that of the philosophers of the sect of Pomponazzi."[16]

   Published in Basel in 1556, reissued in 1567, *De naturalium effectuum
(admirandorum) causis, sive de incantationibus* (The Causes of the Marvels
of Nature, or the Enchantments), by the Mantuan Pietro Pomponazzi,
is the target of La Ménardière's attack; the work is "indeed one of the
boldest among those which open the way of modern philosophy."[17] It
defines the causes among which the facts will be divided *qua* effects.
Pomponazzi's conception of the imagination, and even more of natural
determinism, leads him to classify under that cause perceived data, however strange they may appear. In 1516, in Paris, Vanini takes up his ideas,
and even copies his text, in his *De admirandis naturae reginae deaeque mor-
talium arcanis*. The quarrels precipitated by that thesis are situated on
the terrain of cosmological theory, not of observation. They define which
"truth" should be recognized in the most extraordinary symptoms. Thus
proceeds the Angevin Pierre Le Loyer, when he takes on Pomponazzi
(because he is in vogue among the learned) in his *IV Livres des spectres
ou apparitions et visions d'esprits, anges et démons* (Angers, 1586; Paris, 1605
and 1608)—a book from which Pilet de la Ménardière draws much of
his inspiration, though he says little of it.

   However it may be with this issue debated by all the contemporary
"philosophers," or with the systems that combine in a variety of ways the
temperaments (sanguine, melancholic, phlegmatic, and so forth), the
four elements (fire/hot, water/moist, air/cold, earth/dry), the humors
(bile, atrabile, pituit, blood), the "spirits" (natural, vital, or animal), and
so on, the essential is the epistemological decision that the observer of
the possessed has to face, and which forces the learned to take a position
on the possible, whether in the name of a challenged tradition or on
the strength of new theoretical options.

The Innocent Imagination

To restore the apparent facts to their "maternal cause"—such is the intent of Pilet de la Ménardière. As a convinced partisan of possession, he
challenges the view that the Loudun "prodigies" are "simply the effects
of a fickle humor, awakened solely by the power of imagination, upon
the view of the instruments and the speech of the persons serving in
exorcisms."

No, he answers, the "imagination" does not have this "power." He *knows* this:

> The imagination of which so much is noised and that is the ref-
> uge of those at the end of their finesses and not of their injus-
> tices in the affair before us [Loudun] has not so great a power
> as most men think. And it would require that in this case she
> be as mighty as the ideas of God himself for a melancholic to
> be possessed in fact because she thought she was. . . .
>
> The thoughts of men, though spiritual and in some way like
> the form that gives being, have not that virtue of making their
> beings of reason truly be. Otherwise, it would follow therefrom
> that if I imagined myself to be the castle of Sablé, I would be-
> come forthwith what I thought. And by the same consequence,
> one would not be sick so long as one thought oneself to be well,
> inasmuch as that thought, in tempering the humors or in expel-
> ling the other causes, would put us in the condition necessary
> for being in perfect health.

Imagination and Judgment

It is not an injustice to take away from the imagination an imaginary power that does not belong to her. . . .

Those who know her better know very well that her trade
is simply to conceive phantoms [what we would now call fanta-
sies] or the images that represent the things themselves. . . .
When the glass of a mirror represents the objects facing it as
they truly are, it cannot be accused of not being faithful, though
the images in its crystal be the most monstrous and strange in
the world. And if I had before my sight spectacles of painted
glass, I would be wrong to find it a bad thing that my eyes saw
all things to be the color of the glass, since their natural function
is to perceive their objects in the form of their appearance and
not enquire whether that form be false or true.

Thus, when in sleep that is engendered of the vapors rising
from the entrails, or in some incommodity that makes them rise
to the brain, as do melancholies, we imagine chimeras and other
things that are not at all, which the impurity of the fumes (which
are the material causes of the Ideas we have) cause to pass for
true in the court of judgment by depriving it of its freedom to
recognize its error, it is not the imagination, I mean the faculty

of the soul, that is blameworthy since she does not leave off properly carrying out her charge. . . .

But it is our judgment that makes the whole mistake (though it be innocent of it and only erred through the privation of its lights, which are put out or dimmed by darkness of the vapors) if, in examining the things of which he is the arbiter and controller general, he makes a false reasoning on the quality of the species and wrongly approves an erroneous vision that, properly speaking, should not be called fallacious but for the fact that reason did not rectify it, and it was unable to discern true being from apparent, and truth from falsehood.[18]

The Limits of Nature

The question arising from "experience" appealed to a theoretical decision that classed among the "possibles" all that was offered by sight. Here, in an analogous move, truth and falsehood are removed from the imagination as well as from sight, and attributed to judgment, the validity of which depends solely on its freedom and on reasoning. Closed up within the confines of the act of judgment and discursive thought, truth escapes the difficulties of observation. But it is tied to the solitary arbitration of the thinker, or to the correctness of reasoning whose premises can only be received (and from where?).

A Cartesian or pre-Cartesian situation! What is more, when La Ménardière attributes the facts of Loudun to a supernatural cause, the "truth" of which can be recognized in them, in so doing he sets limits to the (natural) region over which his knowledge extends. "I maintain [nature] in the things in which I know it to be well founded, and I am as scrupulous in avoiding taking anything away from it as I try to be equitable in not extending its domain to the detriment of supernatural causes."[19]

"To the Gentle Readers"

In his view, to be a "possessionist" is, in short, a decision that bases the possibility of reasoning on the reciprocal necessity of localizing the supernatural. He posits a reason in assigning it a locus in which judgment is "the controller general and arbiter." In his dedication, *Aux honnêtes gens* [To the gentle readers], he declares that his publication is a

separate piece taken from a work that has been ready for a long time and that you will see, if I feel compelled by reasons as cogent as those constraining me to give you this little word. . . . I am not at all unjust toward you in disposing of my work, and

> although everyone says children and books belong to the public,
> I am not of that opinion touching the latter. I think my books
> belong more to me than to others, since they issue from my
> mind which is naturally free, and exempt, by its condition, from
> the laws of human police.[20]

As the book was appearing anonymously, La Ménardière adds: "If this seem good to you, you will be curious enough to enquire who I am. And if it is not to your taste, it will be quite unnecessary for you to know the author. Adieu."[21]

He withdraws quietly from his writings as if to see them from the place of his retreat, the place whence "they issue," and with a different eye from that of the public. The cause of perceptible things has, in a sense, the same position in relation to its effects, which do not declare its proper name either, and only "speak" to the learned who knows the agent itself.

In 1638, having become councilor and physician to his royal highness Gaston d'Orléans, he published his *Raisonnements sur la nature des esprits*. Afterward, having been named the king's reader and elected a member of the Académie Française, he became more interested in poetry, to which he devoted his *Poétique* in 1640. In 1634, though a "possessionist," he is not necessarily retrograde. But he has to take a theoretical position before an extreme case.

Among the partisans of supernatural causality, there are options foreign, or even opposed, to his own. But like the options of the "antipossessionists," they are all conditioned by their relation to the split that has occurred between cause and effects. Hence, one must either see in experience the extravagant apparition of a "true being" determined by reason or, changing poles, make experience be the point of departure of a different reason. On the one hand, we see the adumbration of Cartesian rationalism, and on the other a positivism that, in Loudun, will take on an appearance now scientific, now "mystic." In reality, these options are mutually determining, because they cannot detach themselves from the problem, or, if you will, the system that governs them.

The Antipossessionists

The antipossessionists also rely on a theory of melancholy, of the imagination, of nature, ultimately, and therefore of the possible, when they utter their pronouncements on possession. But their option is the opposite of La Ménardière's. Far from setting a limit to reason in order to set up a domain in which natural knowledge would hold sway, they include the whole of the knowable in advance within a natural causality. This is a challenge, a daring choice of the mind, well before being the result of observation. This choice, made possible by the breakup of the religious homogeneity of society, is in most instances legible in a traditional, unchanged tabulation of facts.

In the "antipossessionist" perspective, the unknown or the uncanny is not attributed to a supernatural cause (but known from elsewhere), that is, to an outside nature; it is accommodated within natural knowledge, but as its future. In other words, the unknown does not belong to an other (revealed) knowledge. It belongs to the future of the same knowledge; it represents what the already defined power of reason has not yet reached. The fact is, the theory will make new technical procedures and "observations" possible, from the moment when the theory states that the facts cannot be supernatural.

The explanation of the Loudun prodigies, then, can in both camps account for the same facts, while attributing opposite meanings to them. For example, certain possessionists and certain antipossessionists will equally admit (will equally *see*) that such-and-such a religious is floating above the ground, but the former will declare it to be an effect of the Devil, while the latter will call it an effect of melancholy. La Ménardière notes that the girls give themselves over to extraordinary actions only if the exorcists address them as possessed women, and that the "means of calming" and pacifying these tempests that rage as high as heaven is to speak to these "spirits as if to the hosts of the earth" and to testify by one's gestures "that one gives absolutely no credence to there being any devils in those miserable bodies."[22]

And indeed La Ménardière concludes that the infernal powers manifest themselves exclusively when addressed by the Church, and that the regularity with which the convulsions occur when the exorcists call upon the devils excludes the explanation of the facts by the melancholic temperament of the possessed. Conversely, other deduce from the same fact that the exorcists, armed with Latin, with ornaments and sacred injunctions, impress the melancholic women, who are thereby induced to conform to the character expected of them.

Erotomania

To Claude Quillet, the diagnosis appears simple: hysteromania. This doctor from Chinon is only twenty-seven. A Rabelaisian character, a schemer, a poet, a man of tireless erudition, a lover of good food and good reasoning, he will set out on a brilliant career beginning in 1636, the date of his departure for Rome with the maréchal d'Estrées. His career will be favored by the indulgence of Richelieu, and his progress sustained by a network of connections won over by his free-ranging genius. He is "short, fat, red," but admired by Naudé for his frankness and his knowledge.

In his view, according to Naudé,

> it would be better to speak of hysteromania or erotomania. . . . Those poor she-devil religious, finding themselves shut up between four walls, go crazy, fall into a melancholic delirium, tortured by the urges of the flesh, and in reality what they need is a carnal remedy in order to be perfectly cured.[23]

That medic's quip will not prevent Quillet, in his *Callipaedia* (Paris, 1655–56), from attributing a determining influence on the conception of children to the signs of the zodiac. But he wants first to maintain that there is nothing that is not "natural" in Loudun, leaving open the question of which natural causes, to be specified subsequently, are manifested in the observed prodigies.

His neighbor and friend from Loudun, Ismaël Bouilliau, does likewise. Still filled with the fresh enthusiasm of a neophyte, this twenty-nine-year-old Catholic convert from Protestantism, ordained to the priesthood in 1630, an astronomer, fascinated by history and oriental languages, has been a faithful correspondent of Gassendi's since 1631. He is as keen on spreading his faith as on condemning the injustice of the case against his friend Grandier or the "superstition" of the pious, obsessed with miracles.

A Skeptic: Duncan

The best analysis of the events in Loudun comes from a senior member of the erudite group, who share common convictions and acquaintances: Marc Duncan. He has already published an abridged logic. He is interested in mathematics, philosophy, and theology as much as in medicine, which he practices in Saumur, where he lives with his wife. Soon he will be invited by King James I of Great Britain to serve as his regular physician. He will refuse, in order to remain in Saumur. His *Disours sur la possession des religieuses ursulines de Loudun* (1634) will cause him problems with his client the maréchale de Brézé; she is impressed by Laubardemont's criticisms. He writes on the subject:

> But let us assume there is no trickery or fabrication in this affair. Does it necessarily follow that these girls are possessed? Can it not be that, through folly and error of the imagination, the

women believe themselves to be possessed without being so? This happens frequently to spirits that are predisposed to folly, if they are closed up in a convent and become confused in meditation; and this in various ways.

First, it may occur after fasts, vigils, and deep meditations upon hell's punishments and devils, and their trickery, and God's judgments, and other, similar matters. It would be preferable that such spirits not give themselves over to solitary religious life, for ordinary contact with other people might serve to shield them from such ills.

Second, a word from their confessor, well said but ill interpreted, might give rise to it. For if he told them that certain evil desires, such as that of leaving the convent and getting married, desires they may have had and to which they may have confessed, come from the Devil's temptations and suggestions, then they, feeling these desires arise within them time after time, might come to believe themselves to be possessed, and their fear of hell might make them imagine they always have a devil by the tail.

Third, a confessor, seeing and hearing them say and do strange things, might, by ignorance and simplicity, believe them to be possessed or bewitched, and then persuade them of it, through the power he has over their spirits.

And it is in fact true that Sister Agnès has often said, when she was being exorcised, "that she was not possessed, but that they wanted to make her think she was, and that they forced her to let herself be exorcised." And on the twenty-sixth day of last June [1634], the exorcist having accidentally dropped some burning sulfur on Sister Claire's lip, she began to weep bitterly, saying "that since they said she was possessed, she was willing to believe there was some truth in it, but that she didn't deserve to be treated like that because of it."

Now, if such thoughts dominate the spirits of one or two of them, they rapidly spread to all the others. For the poor girls have a lot of faith in what their companions say, and daren't doubt the word of their mother superior. Whereupon they become frightened, and by dint of thinking of it day and night, they take their dreams for visions and their apprehensions for visits. And if they hear the sound of a mouse in the shadows, they think it is a demon, or if a cat gets up on their beds, they believe it is a magician who has come down the chimney to try their pudicity.[24]

Dreams and Books

The "force of the imagination," by which Pomponazzi had already explained miracles,[25] brings about, between people "very susceptible to impressions" due to confined quarters and contagion, two dangers, which in this case, as in the therapy of the day, call for aeration and separation. Specifically, spirits, like a kind of fluid, are transmitted by proximity. This "contagion" or "communication of spirits" forms, in Duncan's work, the basis of a mental and physical pathology. It will remain in this role for a long time. As late as 1677, Jean de Santeul submits the following "case" to Dr. Vallant, the Marquise de Sablé's physician:

> We beseech you, M. Vallant, to give your opinion on this circumstance. Two persons were very close to one another, so much so that they touched. One had the colic with rather violent contractions, and the other was in very good health. A half an hour or an hour thereafter, the person who was in good health complained of feeling as if her belly were pierced by darts and arrowheads. . . .
> Can we not rightfully attribute this sudden effect to the communication of spirits passing from one body to the other, and setting both in motion with the same movement? We take you, Monsieur, as judge, and gladly submit to your judgment, to which we defer completely.[26]

Beneath the symptoms, these "spirits" circulate. The physician possesses a knowledge of them, is qualified to judge them by reason of his information, and must reveal their presence in the distorted or strange surface of "appearances."

Thus it is not surprising that the imaginary, dreams or obsessions—those "books of the night," as Le Loyer calls them—should cause the learned to turn toward the printed book, the solidity of the written text made public, the established doctrine among men of science: whence the countless "authorities" whose works (especially ancient or specialized ones) adorn the libraries of physicians.[27] References to them fill the margins or the text of the physicians' "judgments" or "reasonings."

> If we are to give credence to the most learned physicians [according to *Factum pour Urbain Grandier*] a suffocation in the

womb, a Poitou colic, an ardent fever, an epileptic sickness can cause symptoms, convulsions, contortions, and grimaces far stranger than those that have appeared. . . . Witnesses to this are Simon Goulard, in part 2 of Book I of his *Histoires admirables;* Brasavole, in his *Commentaire* on Hipppocrates' sixty-fifth Aphorism, in his Fifth Book; Uvier, in Book III, chapter 15 of *L'imposture des diables,* and the learned surgeon Pigray, in chapter 6 of Book VII of his *Chirurgie.*[28]

From the books of day to those of night, from "authorities" to dreams, from the same to the other, the learned postulate the continuous text of a knowledge of which they are fearful of being dispossessed; they must constantly renew its reading (or its legend), by recognizing it in teratological forms.

II. THE LIAR

When the exorcist tries to get the truth out of the Liar, he, too, does battle book in hand—namely, the Gospels, the treatise of a theologian, Father Michaelis's *Histoire véritable,* or some other authority on demonology. According to the brochure titled *Lettre au Roy du sieur Grandier* (not by Grandier), "nothing was said that is not found word for word in the book by Father Michaelis, who wrote the *Histoire* of the possessed women of Provence, which is the original upon which the women from here are molded."[29]

The Certitudes of the Learned

To an even greater degree than the authors of the *Lettre* thought, the facts are molded on the book. The nature of the event—that is, the event itself—is dependent on a science that defines the nature of spirits. Whence the importance of the consultation requested from learned theologians from Paris, at the beginning of the affair. They are far from where the prodigies are taking place, but by that very fact situated in the locus from which a theoretical knowledge can give a name to what is manifested in Loudun. Such is the meaning of the response (in Latin, naturally) sent by the four physicians at the Sorbonne consulted in 1633 by the bishop of Poitiers:

> We, the undersigned doctors of theology of the venerable University of Paris, at the request of the most illustrious and most reverend father in Christ, D. D. Henri-Louis de Chasteignier-

Rocheposay, bishop of Poitiers by the grace of God and the Holy Apostolic See, after having seen and examined at great length the facts and accounts of the doctors of medicine and surgery of the house of the Ursulines of Loudun, have judged and do judge that two of these religious, to wit Mother Jeanne de Belciel, the superior of the Convent, and Sister Claire de Sazilly, are truly and really possessed of the Demon, and to be held and treated as energumens.

The Proofs of the Existence of the Devil

First, since according to the reports of the physicians, these two religious were seen by them and by many others suspended in the air for a quarter of an hour, so that their bodies must have been, despite their innate weight, raised up into the air and held suspended there. Since, obviously, that cannot occur naturally, some power superior to nature must have kept them in that state of suspension. That power can be none other than that of the Demon, as is clear from the other effects and adjurations or exorcisms. Though certain persons require that in addition to this remaining in the air, a sneeze should shake the energumen or energumens and bring the bodies down again, nevertheless the suspension and the remaining, without further support, amply suffice to prove possession by the Devil.

Second, because the above-mentioned religious, lying flat on their beds, raised up on their feet without any bending of the body or flexing of the limbs, a thing naturally impossible as is declared by both Aristotle in the *Mechanics* and elsewhere, and Galen in his book *On the Use of the Parts,* passim.

Let it not be said that dancers and tightrope walkers, to amaze a public of simple folk or get money from them, sometimes rise suddenly erect upon their feet, and that consequently that sudden rising of the religious cannot be taken as an infallible proof of diabolical possession. That objection is doubly refuted, as false and contrary to experience: on the one hand, when dancers rise to their feet, they are not lying down flat, but hold themselves in a curled position, as Trucardo de Naples has depicted it visually in a line drawing; on the other hand, in that rising up, a flexing in the middle of the trunk occurs that was not observed in the case of the above-mentioned religious, for they were lying completely flat, without any inward curving in any part of the body, at the moment when they went to an erect station in the presence of the observers and physicians, and, what is more important, they show no sign of flexing of the trunk or limbs. Therefore this rising is an infallible sign of the presence in the women of a stronger and loftier force in them than the force of nature, or (which amounts to the same thing) of their possession by the Devil.

Third, among the above-mentioned religious, during the time of the exorcisms, there occurred horrible convulsions, agitations, and contortions, which according to the doctors of medicine are never observed in the numerous cases of splenetic, uterine, epileptic, or other illnesses, without being accompanied by horrible movements of the face, the mouth, the eyes, and the cheeks. Furthermore, these agitations did not in the least alter the natural pulse of the arteries or make it any faster than normal; on the contrary, the pulse remained in the state proper to a body at rest and in perfect health, from the point of view of the movement of the systole and the diastole. Certainly this is proof that the agitation and torment of the above-mentioned religious does not come from nature (the impulsion of which would be reflected in some slight commotion) but by a superior agent, to wit the Devil. Especially since these violent and strange symptoms were induced by the force of exorcisms and adjurations and disappeared when they were broken off, at which time the religious returned to their state of inner calm. . . .

Salva Reverentia

Which is why, to each and every one it does or may concern, we attest that these two religious, Jeanne de Belciel and Claire de Sazilly, are truly and really seized and possessed by the Demon, and that this cannot be denied without malice or error by any person who examines these signs attentively and at length.

As for the four other religious of the same convent whom the doctors of medicine judge to be obsessed and not possessed, we do not wish to pass judgment, since the symptoms, in their case, are not as clear as for the two first ones. But if we are requested to render an opinion on the basis of the information received, we will say, with all the respect due to the doctors of medicine, that they seem to us to be possessed rather than obsessed. Obsession comes from the Devil *qua* external agent. Now, what the exorcisms or other actions cause to appear in these four nuns seems to come from an internal principle. But we suspend our judgment and prefer to let the above-mentioned doctors and other ocular witnesses pronounce.

Deliberated in Paris on this eleventh day of February of the year of our Lord sixteen hundred thirty-three.[30]

Adaptation

This strange diagnosis is signed by Antoine Martin and Jacques Charton, unremarkable professors, and by two famous Parisian theologians of the day: André Duval and Nicolas Isambert.

They too, and they particularly, have only the power to make a judgment. The facts come to them already tailored by an observation not their own. To what others—physicians—have already determined, they have only to add a meaning, of which they say, in the name of knowledge handed down to them, that it is the truth. But since in reality a truth is already posited by the very presentation of the facts, they must adjust their truth to the one imposed upon them.

As opposed to the doctors of medicine who adapt their optical "views" to their theoretical ones, and especially as opposed to the commissioner and the civil judges who mark out units by their very actions, the doctors of theology are restricted to aligning themselves, with their own argumentation, with judgments and facts established outside themselves— even though, in principle and *salva reverentia* [with all due respect], they note a divergence—totally hypothetical, moreover—in relation to the diagnosis pronounced by the physicians.

There is nothing surprising in the fact that the table of symptoms furnished by the medical eye seems to captivate and obsess theological reflection. That reflection is held by the glue of corporeal imagery, it sticks to those appearances, though it must hold them at a distance in order to confront them with doctrine taken from the books that say what is the nature of "true" beings.

From Exorcism to Magic

Two traits, among a score of others, reveal among the exorcists that ambiguous situation of theology before the facts and their medical observers: on the one hand, the distortion of exorcism, which, from being a liturgical act, a salvific or revelatory operation, becomes the arm of a theatrical combat, the admission of a loss through the operation of recovery; on the other hand, after the reversal of traditional positions, the conviction that the truth must be sought in the lie and it is the Liar who speaks it.

The exorcist, as we have seen, is moving in the direction of medical practices. He adopts the physician's fumigations and the apothecary's drugs as if, in placing himself on the Devil's terrain, he also accepted the physician's tactics. For example, when the religious falls into "lethargy," which makes it impossible for the action to proceed, the father "blesses sulfur, rue, and other drugs, to make fumigations and to burn, as on the previous day, the image of Béhéric [a demon] and of his companions painted on a leaf of paper with their names."[31]

This syncretism of magical and therapeutic procedures is to be found in all the minutes. In the past these techniques, foreign to the liturgy, were scarcely used. Could it be that at this time the exorcist is losing confidence in his own techniques, or that the latter cease being *practices*—that is, an act—to transform themselves into theater and into utterances without effect?

It is true that the exorcist has his own instruments and means. But while the physicians are put in the position of onlookers, and he in that of stage producer (as in the case of Father Gabriel Lactance: "said exorcist responded that several of the physicians [having] requested to be shown contortions, which they had heard others speak of with admiration, he desired to give them that satisfaction"),[32] he uses the sacred objects, the relics, the monstrance, the custodial, the host, as objects that act on the basis of a physical causality, just like fire, water, or smoke, more or less according to their proximity and the place on the body they approach. Only the Gospels seem to escape this reuse, but they are scarcely mentioned in the minutes, at the end of a sequence: in moments of calm, as a kind of respite, or intermission between the acts, the exorcist "says the Gospels contained in the ritual." The rest has the value of a tool to set in motion, stimulate, or dramatize the action:

> Said sister remained peaceful until said father having taken the holy sacrament and placed it on both the head and stomach of said sister, and commanding the demon to come out, she was thrown backward by a lethargy, which passed by fumigations. . . .
>
> And the exorcist, then having taken the holy sacrament constrained the Devil . . . to lift up the body of said sister.[33]

The Sacred Finger

Holy sacrament, fumigations, holy sacrament: the means alternate. Also included in the same series are the custodial, the host, relics, and an instrument of which much use is made—the *sacred finger* of the exorcist, priest, or bishop:

> Said bishop [Msgr. de La Rocheposay] took said sister, putting the sacred finger in her mouth, and [she] immediately falling into convulsions. . . .

> After several exorcisms during which said sister remained
> peaceable, said exorcist [one of the male religious] took her
> and, putting the sacred finger in her mouth, commanded Bé-
> hérit to manifest himself and rise to the upper parts. Said sister
> immediately fell into a very violent convulsion.[34]

The stereotypes of the phrase prolong the mechanism of the effects
that result from this finger. They form the setting, elsewhere, for other
objects, isolated like this finger, and that form the holy panoply of the
exorcist. These tools will be kept separate, themselves charged with a
power that seems to have been drawn out from the globality of the human or liturgical act and opposed to those other "objects"—the parts
of the body, the mouth, the head, or all the diabolical "residences."

They will follow their own itineraries. One of these can be found in
René d'Argenson, when that remarkable man mentions in his testament
(1652), among all his possessions, the reliquary whose "virtue" he saw,
probably when he was the *intendant* of Saintonge and Poitou (1633–34),
doubtless in Loudun, where at least La Trémoille relatives came:

> My reliquary of the true cross that I normally carry with me and
> that was given to me by the late Madame de La Tremoille, the
> abbess of Sainte-Croix de Poitiers, of the virtue of which reli-
> quary I saw a miraculous proof on a person possessed by the
> Devil.[35]

To Heal Language

But what does the virtue of all these relics obtain? They infiltrate the
interval between a question and an answer; their function is to "produce"
or constrain confession. According to the minutes—the reports that best
express the practice of the exorcists and their views—the instrument
intervenes when the Latin of the churchmen does not obtain the state-
ment that would meet their expectations. It allows the disconnected
parts of the religious discourse to "agree"; it forces the differences of
language to be no more than a negation (an inverted and diabolical
image) of the articles of faith—which is blasphemy—and, in a second
phase of the operation, to negate themselves and return precisely to the
point of departure—which is the devil's "confession."

Therefore there must first be a demoniacal utterance, and that implies
a struggle against silence, the "lethargy" or the refusals of the religious.
Next it is necessary that that utterance turn against itself and announce
the sufferings of hell, the glory of the Redeemer and Mary's virginal

power. The sacred objects or the drugs inaugurate, maintain, and rectify the course whenever there are accidents or halts. Like blows, they "correct" from without, physically, all error or suspension, in that daily promenade. Technical artifice assures the artificial construction of a language.

It is in this that the exorcism of Loudun departs from the tradition and even inverts it. In the past, with the sobriety of the liturgical acts, God's word had the efficacy to heal the soul and sometimes the body of the possessed woman presented to the benediction and the reading from the Gospel. In Loudun, the first objective is no longer the healing of the possessed, but the healing of language. Whence the reversal or reorientation of meaning: the goal of action becomes the firming up of the word, shaken by doubt, whereas in the past the sacerdotal word was, by a common faith, oriented toward a sanctifying and pacifying action. In exorcism, the *deed* and the *word* switch places.

The Vanishing of Practice

If we leave aside the steps that prepared this inversion, we observe that in Loudun exorcism no longer *does* anything. The agents fade into the background, are no more than roles in a system whose elements are organized in such a way as to say the same thing. Both the exorcists and the possessed women are the characters and vehicles of truths that must reemerge from out of their negation, reappear beyond silence and blasphemy, return just as they were, where they seemed to have been lost. The religious language must speak and be repeated. It is the subject-object that every action, every actor in particular, serves.

The priority of action in the older practice of exorcism is followed by that of verbal manifestation. In place of the private, even secret nature of the liturgical gesture, driving the devil out in the name of Jesus Christ and giving the Christian the salutary "benediction," there now appears the tragedy of language, the fragmentation of which must be compensated for by the reiteration of the same truths in each one of the parties that make up the spectacle—the exorcists, the possessed women, the public, and so on. Each partner in the *mise-en-scène* must reflect back the same image, the same Yes/Amen, the same affirmation, in order to guarantee the truth of speech as it is used in the peculiar locus the Church has become.

The decisive point in this operation is clearly the relation to the lie. Exorcism consists in struggling against the lie. But the former is dangerously compromised along with the latter. Between truth and lying, between the witnesses of the True and the Liar, the hand-to-hand combat is so intimate, so indecisive ultimately, that the exorcist, faced with those possessed by the demon, no longer knows whether he is confronted with the Other or the Same. Perhaps by dint of trying to confirm himself by assimilating the adversary, he is caught up in his own artifices, thus depriving himself of the means of being assured. He employs so much clever trickery with the Liar in order to force him to be nothing but a witness to the truth, he is so bent on resetting his reality in trickery itself, that he can no longer discern whether he is being fooled by his own artifices, whether he is a victim of the Enemy's ruse, whether his truth is falsified by illusion—or whether, on the contrary, he is deceiving the deceiver and constraining the liar. Is this not an admission that, in defending the truth, he does not know where it is?

Constraining the Liar

The battle for truth is expressed, among the exorcists, in a military vocabulary that corresponds, for them, to what the lexical repertory of seeing represents for the physicians. But everything hinges on a central problem: Can the Liar be made to tell the truth? This problem has registers that are less explicit, but just as fundamental. Does the bestial language of the possessed women (who claw, bite, crawl, hiss, and bark) express a divine truth about human beings? Are the foreign languages spoken by the demons the translation, and in some sense the negative, of the revelations conveyed in the Latin of the Church? But these questions, which challenge the functioning of exorcism, are treated and discussed in the context of the power of the Church, "our Holy Mother the Church," to constrain the "Father of Lies" to speak the truth.

At an initial stage, the truth revealed by the demon is that of hidden events and secret thoughts. That is what the *Lettre d'un magistrat à Mademoiselle de la Motte Le Voyer, à Paris* attempts (after many others) to demonstrate: "in which it is spoken of various revelations of secret things, done by the possessed women to Grandier's judges (August 2, 1634)."[36] The *Lettre* relates that Mlle de Rasilly "has in her possession a thing that astonishes the most learned theologians of God, to wit that the Devil divines the thoughts of the exorcist without the latter's manifesting them by signs and words. Nevertheless Saint Thomas and the greatest theologians hold that the Devil cannot know what we think within ourselves."[37]

"Very Secret Particulars"

This disturbing proximity between the thought of the exorcist and the speech of the possessed will be the first experience of Surin in Loudun,

at the end of 1634. He has just arrived from Marennes, where he was
the spiritual director of Madeleine Boinet, one of those unlettered mystics who fascinate him,[38] and he is quite "astonished" by what he hears
in Loudun:

> The first [demon] who presented himself said to him: why had
> he left in Marennes good souls whom he cultivated, to come
> here and amuse himself with mad girls. And on the subject of
> those good, pious souls who were in Marennes, he was not long
> in discovering very secret particulars about the people who were
> there, of whom the possessed girl [Jeanne des Anges] had no
> knowledge nor had ever heard of. [Really? In fact, the prioress
> was clever and had gathered information.]
>
> Particularly, he drew out a letter from that girl that had told
> him he would suffer much in that employment [of exorcist]
> and, holding it in his hand, he showed it to this demon, who
> said to him:
>
> "There is a letter from your pious girl."
> He followed up with: "*Quaenam illa est?*" ["Who is she?"]
> He answered: "Your Madeleine."
> He added: "*Dic proprium nomen.*" ["Say her proper name."]
> He then said in a furor: "Your Boinette."
>
> That pious girl's name was Madeleine Boinet, who had
> since been sent to Bordeaux. . . . After that discussion with the
> mother, the father was not long in affirming earnestly, particu-
> larly to the unbelievers who were countless, that he could not
> be in any doubt as to the possession. Those same demons that
> were in the mother spoke to him of several things that had hap-
> pened during the time he was in Marennes and that he only
> knew very secretly. The demons said them to him, so that [he,
> too, being seduced by that truth coming out of its nocturnal
> secrecy, rendered up and, as the texts tell us, "vomited" by his
> adversary] he had the torch in his eyes to see the truth of the
> demons residing in those bodies.[39]

Controversy with the Atheist

But from the (surprising) fact that secrets emerge in this way from residences occupied by the demons, can one move to a *right*? Do the exorcists have the right to require the truth, which might be unduly falsified
and hidden in these lost bodies? Or—another form of the same question—can they legitimately rely, as if they were "truths," on utterances

brought to light by constraint? What is symbolically at stake through the right to require and extract the truth from the Liar is the relationship of the "Christian truth" to the other, the "atheist" or the unbeliever. This right to make the blasphemer say the Christian profession of faith and to force him to give his consent is inscribed here, though in a theatrical and demonological mode, in the same line as the great contemporary apologetic undertaking. For example, in that same year of 1634, Jean de Silhon declares in his treatise *De l'immortalité de l'âme:*

> Never has the faith been in greater need of being vivified. Never has religion been more dangerously sinned against. It is no longer the roof or the fortifications that are being battered; they are attacking the foot of the wall, undermining the foundations; they're trying to blow up the entire edifice.[40]

And he fully intends to oppose the attacker, to force out of him "the consent of all ages and all nations," and to reveal in his adversaries the "belief" they refuse, and to say the truth that, present within them despite themselves, must be confessed by them in spite of their denials. In Loudun, the Devil holds the same place as does the atheist in Silhon's apologetics. Hence it is not a secondary question, this issue of the right of the Church (of the exorcist, of the theologian) to constrain the Liar or the lie to speak the truth.

A Diabolical Dogma

Ismaël Bouilliau envisages the problem from a legal point of view when he judges it to be intolerable that Grandier's trial should be based on "the deposition of the devils alone, to which the judges have given credence, against the express doctrine of Saint Thomas and of the faculty of Paris."[41]

A just protest, but in reality the "depositions of the devils" enter neither into the reasons adduced nor into the legal proofs for the condemnation pronounced by the judges. The question arises rather from a theological point of view. Bouilliau adds, in this regard, that the exorcists' confidence in the "truths" extracted from the demon rests on a "dangerous, impious, erroneous, execrable, and abominable doctrine, which makes Christians idolatrous, ruins the Christian religion in its foundations, opens the door to calumny, and will, unless God in his providence remedies this ill, cause the Devil to immolate human victims, no longer under the name of Moloch, but with the help of a diabolical and infernal dogma."[42]

The *Remarques et considérations servant à la justification du curé de Loudun* (1634) say as much:

> I am astonished at how readily people believe in the Devil, particularly when he accuses the curé or slanders honest folk, making the condition of the Christians worse than that of the pagans who believed in the Devil, but thought him to be God. And we are told that the Devil is a liar and a maligner, and nevertheless we are supposed to believe what he says, particularly when it is something to harm the curé or when he slanders the most virtuous, but if he speaks in defense of Grandier, he is a liar. . . .
>
> Thus they would dethrone God, who can say nothing but truth, to put in his place the Devil, who says nothing but deceit and vanity, and that vanity must be believed to be truth.[43]

Truth and vanity crisscross, as do paganism and Christianity. On this subject, a recent authority is cited by Grandier himself: the *Refutation de l'erreur du Vulgaire touchant les responses des diables exorcisez*, published in Rouen in 1618 by "Frère Sanson Birette, un Religieux du Couvent des Augustins de Barfleur." On the basis of an ample dossier that includes the names St. John Chrysostom, St. Thomas Aquinas, and consultations with the Sorbonne, Friar Sanson concluded: "It is therefore as true that an exorcised Devil can lie, as it is false that exorcism always constrains to him tell the truth."[44]

The Mélange

This *always* translates rather precisely the Thomist principle according to which "one must not believe the demon even if he says true things."[45] There is some truth there, but where? And how can it be discerned? The demon is the sphinx of a truth mixed with lies, as is the imagination, according to Pascal: "mistress of error and falsehood, and all the more deceitful in that it is not always so, for it would be an infallible rule of truth if it were an infallible one of lies."[46]

Jean-Joseph Surin also considers the mélange of truth and falsehood to be the essential datum of experience, upon which he means to establish a science. He concedes, as to devils, that they do not always lie:

> Now, for determining when they are telling the truth and when they are not, it is difficult to give a certain and indubitable rule.
>
> But by the experience that God has given me in this matter, I can say that when the exorcist does his duty well and conducts

himself with a disinterested and prudent spirit, our Lord obliges them to do what the Church desires, and that often, for the good of souls, God constrains them to say, when they least want to, very great truths. And when the things they say are found to be in agreement with what the faith teaches us, we can have great assurance.[47]

Of the three criteria combined here, is the first ("when the exorcist does his duty") ever assured? The second (the Church desires or orders it) is relativized by an *often* that indicates a global perspective and thus leaves each particular case undecided. As for the "great assurance" obtained by the third (agreement with the teachings of the Church), it is identified with the great assurance that has as its basis and measure "what faith teaches us." Personal disinterestedness and prudence, ecclesiastical mission and ordination, faithfulness to the doctrine: nothing, in these three points, goes beyond the rules of preaching as they are understood in the treatises of the seventeenth century. That is doubtless Surin's intent: he preaches a truth henceforth hidden ("mystic") to a society in which the public is becoming "unbelieving," and a truth to be uttered in the language of communication between dispersed experiences, since the discourses swirl in the definition of essences without any relationship with what is happening.

But what service do the devils render a truth defined, believed, or recognized without them?

The manuals that the exorcists have in hand—from the *Manuale exorcistarum ac parochorum* by the Franciscan Candido Brognoli de Bergame (Bergamo, 1551) to the *Manuale exorcismorum* by Maximilien de Eynatten (Antwerp, 1635)—do not shed much light on this point. Like all manuals, they attest, by their severity with respect to the truths one would ask of the possessed women, a practice long left behind.

In reality, the request of the exorcists in Loudun is connected with the social situation of these years. During a period that ends around 1650, but whose trends will reappear toward the end of the century, the Christian truth becomes embroiled in the confused mass of ideas, daring, and divisions of all sorts. In the experience of the believers, that truth seems to lose its way in lies. Further, an atheist seems to inhabit the most spiritual. To have to find the truth in lies is a religious situation that is symbolized by the labor of discerning truths mixed in with the statements of the possessed. But the practice of exorcism betrays two very different reactions.

The Locus of Knowledge

For some, the important thing is the "new locus of truth constituted by the mixture with the lie." Hence they will move from public displays to a search for the truth in embryonic form in the duplicities of the heart, given in the radicality of a choice and formulable thanks to recognitions made possible by spiritual communications. Surin is the first to take this step, condemning the public spectacles, and preferring in their place the retreat of private conversations and the preparation for decisive choices. He thus elaborates an "experimental science."

The Defense of a Power

For others, it is first of all a question of a threatened power, that of the Church. For them, the truths are not affected by the situation that changes, unknown to them, the internal conditions of the quest in spirit and in truth. Defined, circumscribed, and owned by the ecclesiastical institutions and discourses, those truths are not the object of new inquiry. The whole problem seems to come from without, and from unexpected forces that are arising. It is a question not of truth, but of power.

Two words recur continually in the discussions: *power* and *constraint.* One repeats: "The Church has the power to constrain the demon." Making abstraction of personal motivations, the phrase has its logic. To repress the adversary who is threatening a "legitimacy," that is what the exorcism mimes. It uses the holy sacrament as one would wield a scepter or a weapon. Father Tranquille writes in his *Véritable relation des justes procédures observées au fait de la possession des Ursulines de Loudun* (1634):

> To know whether one can use the deposition of devils who have been legitimately adjured by the Church and whether they tell the truth, I do not touch upon this matter. I refer the reader to a little work printed in Poiters, done recently, the title of which is: *Briefve Intelligence de l'opinion de trois docteurs de Sorbonne, et du livre du Père Birette touchant les diables exorcisez.*
>
> Only I will say in passing that never have the devils wished to swear a lie, having been adjured on the holy sacrament. . . . One of these devils, accusing the exorcist of being a magician, the exorcist having said to him that he would pass for one if he said so, having been adjured on the holy sacrament to tell the truth, he never wanted to go beyond that, and was constrained to take back what he had said.[48]

More broadly, André Duval contrasted jurisdiction with the danger to which temporal jurisdictions exposed the Church. On February 16, 1620, he declared:

> To prevent the exorcism of demoniacs is to deprive the infidels and heretics of a miracle that exorcisms perform ordinarily and that becomes a manifest proof for them of the divinity of the Church; it is, furthermore, to recognize that the demoniacs are under temporal jurisdiction, which is false.[49]

Tranquille sees the Loudun affair more accurately when he says that the victory over the demons "is a work of God since it is the work of the king"; that "M. de Laubardemont conducted the trial by the royal roads of justice and piety"; that thus justice "has come to Loudun . . . with its usual weapon, the sword and the scales, to pronounce an edict against hell."[50] The effectiveness of power is clearly on that side, political.

The action that would defend the old ecclesiastical power over truth is therefore forced to change into a spectacle. It is progressively displaced in the direction of what is said, and distanced from what is done. The only thing left for it to do is to benefit from an external reinforcement, that of the king, which it decorates with providence and with which, in reality, it aligns itself. The theatralization of exorcism is reinforced by the refusal to admit a problem of truth that is posed in new terms. It is the product of a halt, the symptom of a dispossession denied. The representation of power is all the more spectacular in that it betrays the anguish of losing it—or of having lost it.

~ 10 ~

The Judgment of the Sorcerer

July 8–August 18, 1634

The trial begins on July 8 with the commission that designates Grandier's judges:

> Another and new commission of the eighth of July, one thousand six hundred thirty-four, signed Louis, and, lower: by the king, Phélypeaux, and sealed with the Great Seal,
>
> by which his majesty delegates and deputes:
>
> said Sieur de Laubardemont,
>
> Sieurs Roatin, Richard, and Chevalier, councilors at the Presidial Court of Poitiers.
>
> Houmain, *lieutenant criminel* at the Presidial Court of Orléans,
>
> Cothereau, president at the Presidial Court of Tours,
>
> Pequineau, *lieutenant particulier,*
>
> de Burges, councilor at said Court [of Tours],
>
> Texier, *lieutenant général* at the Court of Saint-Maixent,
>
> Dreux, *lieutenant général* at the Court of Chinon,
>
> de La Barre, *lieutenant particulier* at said Court,
>
> de La Picherie, *lieutenant particulier* and criminal assessor at the Court of Châtellerault,
>
> Rivarin, *lieutenant général* at the Court of Beaufort,
>
> to all together . . . conduct and complete the trial of said Grandier and his accomplices until definitive sentence and execution thereof exclusively, any and all oppositions and appeals notwithstanding, for which there shall be no deferment.[1]

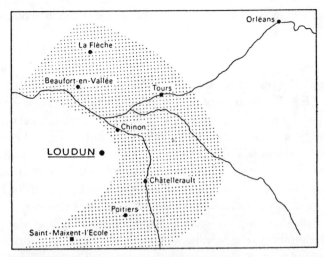

3. Presidial courts of members of the Extraordinary Commission, the Catholic resistance against Loudun—the spearhead of the Protestant advance.

The Priesthood of Judges

These commissioners, all foreign to the place of the trial, come from towns forming a semicircle west of Loudun, and thus represent approximately the frontier of the regions with a Catholic majority before the Protestant advance of Loudun: Beaufort-en-Vallée, Chinon, Tours, Orléans, Châtellerault, Poitiers and Saint-Maixent-l'Ecole (see fig. 3).

According to certain pamphlets, several residents of Loudun, proposed to serve on the commission, withdrew: Auguste du Moustier de Bourgneuf (president of the Élus) and Charles Chauvet (assessor). Sieur Constant, a magistrate in Poitiers, was alleged to have done the same, along with Pierre Fournier, originally named(?) prosecutor of the commission. In fact, Jacques de Nyau, councilor at the Presidial Court of La Flèche, was assigned to this last post.

Those appointed to the commission are all, as president, lieutenants or councilors, serving on presidial courts, local tribunals limited to small matters and each made up, in theory, of nine magistrates. The office that belongs to them, and that they had to purchase, requires of them a task that is neither very remunerative nor very demanding. In Marennes, they boast at the time of "the sweetness of an idle life that is found in that employment."[2]

Do these judges inscribed in the hierarchy of the royal justice belong to the petite bourgeoisie then imbued with a "spirit of repudiation" that prompts so many of them to dissociate themselves from the commoners? In any case, they have their "lands": Chevalier is Sieur de Tessec; de La Barre, Sieur de Brisé; Roatin, Sieur de Jorigny; and so forth. It has been claimed that Dreux, La Barre, and Houmain were men of ambition and libertines.[3] The proofs are lacking. De Nyau, the treasurer of the fabric of a church in La Flèche, accused of having misappropriated the sacred vessels, was aquitted by the parliament of Paris. More than evidence of his morality, we have in this circumstance an indication of his support and socio-religious position in La Flèche. Similarly, there are indications that Texier was a member of the Compagnie du Saint-Sacrement in Saint-Maixent; Roatin was closely associated with the Jesuits of Poitiers and engaged in the campaigns of the Counter-Reformation.

Above all, their appointment to the commission grants the judges, facing the suspect priest, a veritable priesthood. Before the sorcerer and the possessed women, they exercise the public ministry of divine justice, spiritual guidance, and pastoral "remonstrance." They are convinced that they are safeguarding an imperiled religion, a compromised order, and souls seized by the Devil. These laymen are ordained to a priesthood that takes over where that of the clerics left off; they combat the blasphemous curé and thus conform to the mission of which Laubardemont avails himself as the minister of a new sacred power.[4]

Repressing Criticism

The creation of this "foreign" tribunal, of which Laubardemont appears to make his crown and his cover, stirs up opposition: placards and libels sprout up in the little streets, posted anonymously, printed without the author's name, distributed on the sly. Reacting to one of these papers found on the doors of the church of Sainte-Croix, the commissioner has the following order posted everywhere, read during the sermon, and shouted out on the street corners. Still today the manuscript bears the trace of having been glued up by the sergeants and lacerated by readers:

> By the King and M. de Laubardemont, councilor to his majesty in his State and Privy Councils, and commissioner deputed by his majesty for the exorcisms being performed in the town of Loudun under his authority, it is expressly forbidden to all manner of persons, of whatever quality and condition they may be, to oppose by word or deed or otherwise act against the Ursuline religious and other persons of said Loudun who are afflicted by evil spirits, their exorcists or those assisting them, whether it be in the place in which they are exorcised or elsewhere, in what-

ever way and manner it may be, under penalty of ten thousand pounds and more, and corporal punishment if it be the case.

And in order that no one claim ignorance of the present edict, it shall be read and published this day in the sermons of the parochial churches of said town, and posted on their doors as well as elsewhere where needed.

Loudun, the second Sunday of July, XVI hundred thirty-four.[5]

After that edict, which runs through all the possible outlets for criticism in order to close them off, the work of the tribunal begins on July 26, with a liturgical gathering in the church of the Carmelites, including a mass, sermon, communion, and solemn procession. Until the judgment is pronounced, the magistrates will go every Sunday and feastday to one of the churches of the town to adore the holy sacrament, attend a mass to the holy spirit, and hear the preaching of one or another of the exorcists.

Fifty Quires of Large Paper

Immediately after the religious ceremony, the judges proceed to the reading of the royal edict constituting their commission, designate Houmain and Texier as reporters of the trial, begin hearing witnesses, and above all begin examining the voluminous file prepared for them by Laubardemont (who will take the precaution of not involving himself in their deliberations). A vast undertaking:

> The acts of the proceedings carried out until the death of Grandier, though very succinct, contain fifty quires of large paper [each "quire" is the equivalent of ninety-six pages], and it took the judges eighteen full days to report the trial, though they devoted six hours a day to it.[6]

These "fifty quires of large paper" are about what a historian can still study.

> "I know from a good source," writes Father Du Pont on July 15, "that there were three different inquests for the crime of magic alone, in one of which seventy-five witnesses were heard, and in the other twenty-two or twenty-three, and in the third, ten or eleven."[7]

"It Is God's Will"

In the first days of July, La Rocheposay left Loudun, where he was directing the exorcisms.

A fortnight ago monseigneur our bishop has withdrawn from
Loudun in order to leave all freedom and authority to the commissioner judges who went there to try Grandier. The exorcists
have the order from said prelate to give entire satisfaction to
whatever the judges want and desire for their enlightenment.
Hence at present said commissioners write the minutes [of the
exorcisms] and M. de Laubardemont does not involve himself,
in order to close the mouths of the slanderers.

The judges, then, have the devils questioned on whatever
they please and in the manner they wish, and sometimes they
interrogate them themselves. . . . Since the judges have been
there, the marvels have increased to such a degree that it appears that God wishes to work some great thing. As for the possession, they have all the proofs of it they wanted, and have been
promptly obeyed by the devils, who since their arrival have become much more supple.[8]

Laubardemont steps out of the way, La Rocheposay bows out, the
devils become more "supple": what authority, all of a sudden, for these
good gentlemen of neighboring presidial courts! But the commissioner
closes the mouths of criticism and has the doors guarded behind them;
the bishop leaves after having left the imposing testament of his absolute conviction; the devils, who are subtle, flatter these lawyers, harbin-
gers of victory and deliverance. From July 26 to August 18, the date of
the sentence, the judges are shut in by the minutes written by possessionists, the fantastic confrontation with the demons, and the opinion
of those who have "experience." Half foreigners to the town, "protected"
and insulated from its rumors (and even if they wanted to hear them,
would they have the time?), they are honored in advance as the sacrificers of a salutary victim not their own. In a holy struggle, these fictive
dispensers of justice receive a role that was already set for them long
before they were designated. Prisoners of this fearsome and providential
personage, are they flattered by it? Conscious of it, terrorized by it? All
we will know of is their sense of "relief" after the rendering of the sentence.

Speechlessness

More than they, Grandier, the accused, is also shut in, uninformed of
what is going on, turned over to his mother's action and information, as

the judges are to Laubardemont's. On July 28 or 29, he writes to Jeanne Estièvre:

Mother,

Monsieur the king's deputed prosecutor gave me your letter in which you tell me my papers were found in my bedroom, and those that could serve to justify me kept so that they could be handed over to me. But they have not been given me.

Also, when I get them, I am not at all in a state to write.

As for statements of the case, I cannot say anything other than what I said during the trial, which consists in two matters.

First, they interrogated me on the facts of my first accusation, to which I answered, and said I was found to be fully justified, which must be shown by producing my four sentences of absolution. To wit, two from the Presidial Court of Poitiers, and two others from monsieur the archbishop of Bordeaux. If the gentlemen commissioners are doubtful of their fairness, they can by their authority bring the trial that is in the Registry of the Court of Parliament [of Paris], with my civil production, which serves to show the wrongful procedure that was then made against me.

The second matter is touching magic and the illness of the religious. Of which I have nothing to say but a very constant truth, which is that I am completely innocent of it, and falsely accused, of which I have made my complaint to the judiciary, which must be brought to light by using the minutes of the bailiff in which are included all the requests I presented both to the royal judges and to monseigneur the archbishop, of which I once gave an official copy to Msgr. de Laubardemont, which the king's prosecutor told me he also produced.

Please make a request that these be used by our prosecutor who will do what he deems best. My responses contain my defenses and reasons. I did not advance anything that I do not justify by writings and witnesses if my aforesaid monseigneurs give me a way of doing so.

Beyond that, I rest for all things upon God's providence, the testimony of my conscience, and the fairness of my judges, for whose enlightenment I pray to God continually and for the safeguarding of my good mother to whom may it be God's will

to restore me soon, so that I may fulfill toward her better than
I have done the duties of her son and servant,

Grandier.

[He adds in a postscript:] Inasmuch as I know nothing, here,
of what is going on in the world, if something has happened in
public forum that might be useful, we should avail ourselves of
it as the counsel thinks best.[9]

The adversaries are equally blind, though for different reasons. How
could they come together, even though a confrontation is organized
later on, in August? Moreover, in this text, one of the last we have from
him, Grandier repeats: "I know nothing. . . . I have nothing to say." These
are the penultimate words of the "fine talker." Things present themselves
to him differently from the discourses in which he circulated with such
ease. These things remained hidden, lying in wait in the little society
which he fled in defying it. Now that the reality is revealed in the form
of a violence that, from his point of view, is blind, his ability to speak
deserts him. He "surrenders himself" to that force that is other. In the
same gesture, he yields the floor to his mother, who doubtless was always
the one who truly had it.

The Triumph of Truth

Around the prison in which Grandier is confined and the churches that
circumscribe the exorcisms, life in the town ebbs and flows, swept by
opposing currents, swollen by waves of curious visitors, filled with contradictory tales and rumors. Assemblies meet. The libels become increasingly violent. During the first days of August, Father Tranquille publishes
(anonymously, of course) his *Véritable relation des justes procédures observées
au fait de la possession des Ursulines de Loudun,* which appears in Poitiers,
before being reprinted in La Flèche and then in Paris, and completed
by the *Thèses générales touchant les diables exorcisés,* first printed separately.
A military vocabulary shines forth with a dangerous brilliance through
the thickness of his argumentation. The prologue sounds already like a
song of war and victory:

The history of the possessed girls of Loudun is the most memo-
rable and famous in this genre that has taken place in several
centuries. Hell having perceived itself to be reduced to despair
in that place by the fall of heresy, and unable to prevent the
Catholic truth from triumphing over error, desired to make a

second attempt to bring magic to credibility, in order to vomit its rage more freely against heaven and the innocents.

It appears that that city is fatal and deadly, in that it was the place in which the Evil Spirit conceived its pernicious plans for the heresy, and is it not again in the same town that the Devils gathered to wage war on God by the use of magic. . . ?[10]

The struggle against the devils aims, according to the author, at fostering "public tranquility," but it has been known for a long time that, in the lexicon of occupying forces, *repress* and *pacify* are two synonyms, and with what meaning they are charged.

In Grandier's Corner

The opposing party also distributes libels, justificatory pamphlets, and denunciations in this early August:

> *Factum pour Maître Urbain Grandier, prêtre, curé de l'église de Saint-Pierre-du-Marché de Loudun et l'un des chanoines de l'église Sainte-Croix dudit lieu.* Printed in-quarto, 12 pp.[11]
> *Remarques et considérations servant à la justification du curé de Loudun, autres que celles contenues en son Factum.* Printed in-quarto, 8 pp.[12]
> *Conclusions à fins absolutoires, mises par-devant les commissaires du procès par Urbain Grandier.* Document, 8 pp.[13]

These brief works, distributed everywhere, even recopied because the printed copies were insufficient, had Grandier as their object and not their author. Others speak of him. He himself no longer speaks. These violent texts—solidly argued, moreover—aggravate his case before the judiciary; they hurry him to his death almost as much as the mobilizations for the extermination of the Devil. They are presented to him anyway. He writes of them to his lawyer, the prosecutor Jean Moreau:

> Monsieur Moreau,
>
> I signed the *Conclusions* with the precautionary remarks that you will see written in my hand. I do not know whether that will be well, as I do not understand the forms. I did not want to sign the *Factum,* in order not to offend anyone. See what I say about that in the margin to the *Conclusions,* and communicate the whole thing to the counsel to see if there be anything in it that would be unfavorable to me. Make my presentation, please, and forget nothing appertaining to it.
>
> Your servant,
>
> Grandier.

> This Wednesday of eleven o'clock in the morning, August
> 9, from my prison.[14]

Hounded, isolated, he can no longer recognize his defenders. The preceding evening, they had organized a meeting at the *hôtel de ville* of Loudun, called by the bailiff Cerisay, announced in the town by the trumpeter Briault, and immediately declared illegal by the *lieutenant criminel* Hervé and by the lawyer Menuau, who nevertheless attended.

A considerable crowd gathers there. It is inaugurated by the bailiff as a protest against procedures that threaten the entire town, against Tranquille's booklet and his insulting preaching, and against a situation that calls for a recourse to the king, but turns into a polemic between Huguenots and Catholics. Rather skillfully, Hervé accuses the "so-called reformed" religion of fomenting a gathering hostile to the authority of the king and calumnious of Catholic priests. Finally Hervé and Menuau are forced to leave, faced with a hostile crowd made up in large part, as it will be said in a possessionist account, of children and workers or *manacles* incapable of judging.[15] A long address to the king is then presented and approved, along with a *Censure* of Father Tranquille's booklet; the bailiff and Chauvet, his assessor, take the responsibility for conveying it to Paris immediately, which they do by August 9:

"Our Interests"

> Sir,
>   The officers and inhabitants of your town find themselves at last obliged to have recourse to Your Majesty, in pointing out to him most humbly that, in the exorcisms that are being performed in said town to the religious of Sainte-Ursule and a few other lay girls . . ., a thing most harmful to the public and to the peace of your faithful subjects is being done, to wit that certain of the exorcists, abusing their ministry and the authority of the Church, are asking during the exorcisms questions that tend to defame the best families of said town, and M. de Laubardemont, councilor deputed by Your Majesty, has had such faith in the statements and responses that, on false information given by them, he is reported to have entered the house of a gentlewoman [Madeleine de Brou] with great uproar and a large following to perquisition imaginary books of magic. As yet more gentlewomen are said to have been arrested, in the church and the doors closed, to perquisition certain supposed magical pacts similarly imaginary.

Since then, this ill has progressed so much that such consideration is today given to denunciations, testimonies, and indications about said demons, that a booklet has been printed (Father Tranquille's *Relation*) and distributed in said town by which they are trying to implant this belief in the minds of the judges: that the demons, duly exorcised, tell the truth. . . .

Therefore the supplicants, impelled by their own interest, given that if these demons are authorized in their responses and oracles, the good people and the most virtuous of innocents, and to which consequently said demons have a more deadly hatred, will remain prey to their wickedness, request and most humbly beseech Your Majesty to interpose his royal authority to put a stop to these abuses and profanations of the exorcisms that are performed daily in Loudun in the presence of the holy sacrament, in which His Majesty will imitate the zeal of the emperor Charlemagne, one of his very august forebears, who stopped and forbade the abuse that was committed in his day in the application of certain sacraments, the use and purpose of which were being perverted from the design and end to which they were instituted.

For these reasons, Sir, may it please Your Majesty to order said faculty of Paris to see said book, and *Censure* thereto attached, to interpose abundantly his decree and judgment upon the above propositions, doctrines, and resolutions.[16]

A Dead Man on Reprieve

Grandier is never named in that supplication of citizens "impelled by their own interests," but they know how to appeal to Louis XIII as a reformer and restorer of religion. If the bailiff also took (this is uncertain) a *Lettre au Roi du sieur Grandier accusé de magie*,[17] that letter, which also circulates in Loudun, is not from the curé; it constitutes a systematic attack on notables or families of the town, particularly Hervé, Menuau, and Mesmin de Silly. The accused address themselves immediately to Laubardemont, to bring his attention to

three defamatory libels, directed both against the suppliants and other qualified persons, a *Factum* and a printed work entitled *Estonnements* [that is, the *Remarques et considérations*], with a hand-written *Requête* [the *Lettre*], all three composed by unknown authors and who would deserve corporal punishment as

being full of falsehoods and suppositions, tending toward sedi-
tion and popular emotion.

They request that these libels be suppressed, torn up and
cast into the fire, with open declaration that they hereby make
to be a party against the authors of said libels, if they can be
discovered.[18]

Grandier is already the absent figure from these wars in which the
adversaries find in the darkness of anonymous pamphlets, as the religious found behind the mask of possessed women, a means of spewing
forth their demons. A dead man on reprieve, eliminated from the discourse of which he is the cause and the occasion, he seems, by this veil
already thrown over the victim, to make possible the plague, the smell
of which "occupies" the houses of Loudun with its pestilential stench.

The Possession at Loudun

In order for the dossier to upon which the commission is to pronounce
itself to be complete, one document is missing: the official judgment of
the bishop of Poitiers. He sends it from Dissey, his country estate.

We, Henry Louis, by divine mercy bishop of Poitiers, certify to
whom it may concern

that although previously, after having seen, carefully considered, and diligently examined with capable persons the minutes taken by the venerable deans of Champigny and Thouars
of our diocese sent by us and deputed to attend the exorcisms
of some Ursuline religious of the town of Loudun that M. Barré,
a doctor of theology, had by our order exorcised in their presence in said town, we, in agreement with the determination of
messieurs from the Sorbonne of Paris who on the basis of the
present minutes had judged and declared those religious to be
truly possessed, swore the same.

Nevertheless, given that since then, during the two and a
half months that we have sojourned in said town of Loudun,
where we went in order to again, in our presence, have said
Ursuline religious and some laywomen also tormented in the
same way be exorcised, and continually, in the morning and in
the evening, we attended and in some cases ourself exorcised,
and we recognized clearly the truth of said possession by a great
number of extraordinary actions, circumstances, and other supernatural things that occurred in our presence.

> For these abundant reasons, we declare said religious to be
> truly tormented and possessed by the demons and evil spirits
> and desire to procure their deliverance. . . .
>> Executed in Dissey, this tenth day of August, 1634.[19]

Here, too, from his hierarchical superior, there is no mention of the
curé. But if there is possession, the sorcerer must be punished. It is left
to the civil justice to find the courage to give him his name.

An Excepted Crime

The criminal commission that will judge Grandier has superseded the
ordinary jurisdictions (in particular the parliament of Paris) and brings
into play the personal justice of the king, on whom it is entirely dependent. Though it is "extraordinary," depriving the accused of the usual
guarantees, the procedure is nonetheless regular. It has its precedents,
particularly in affairs of sorcery or possession.[20] It will bring to its legal
conclusion an affair that had two phases: the first, from October 1632
to March 1633, characterized by the search for a competent authority,
was marked by the order of the archbishop de Sourdis of December 27,
1632; the second, opened by the commission of November 30, 1633,
included the time of the judicial inquiry and hearing of the case, confided to Laubardemont, and distinct from that, the time of the judgment, which is the charge of the tribunal designated on July 8, 1634.

The case involves what is, in the juridic sense of these terms, an *excepted*
and *supernatural crime,* requiring therefore an extraordinary treatment
and implying the search for accomplices, always presumed. The suspect
is in this case a cleric. But that does not place him beyond civil jurisdictions. Since the sixteenth century, the latter are not only recognized as
being competent for lay suspects by all of French jurisprudence (which
denies the pontifical protests favoring ecclesiastical tribunals, the Inqui-
sition, and so forth); as councilor Pierre de Lancre says clearly, their
competency extends "even to the priest" *(etiam in presbytero)* in cases of
"privileged offense, enormous crime," murder, and therefore sorcery as
well:

> When the crime is notably atrocious and grave and, as we say,
> privileged (as we have earlier shown magic spells to be), the
> canonists [the jurists] themselves maintain that the secular
> judge must hear it. . . .
>> I am well aware that the presbyterial dignity, the sacrosanct
> character of the sacerdotal and priestly order which the Savior

in his Church gave us for a sacrament, hold in horror and exe-
cration the profane and bloody hands of the secular judges. . . .

But when it is a question of a qualified homicide, of an
assassination and ambush, of an adultery, sodomy, forgery of
titles and magic spells . . . where there is impiety, imposture,
scandal, sodomy, adultery, heresy, apostasy, corruption of the
youth, and a hundred and one other crimes of which the ecclesiastical judge has no knowledge and is not accustomed to treating, it is reasonable to keep it and treat it before the royal judges.

Indeed, we are now at the point where the prelates, in
France, are subject to the laws and customs of the country in
which they reside and to the king's orders. . . .

Even the priests and other ecclesiastics, in order to save and
protect themselves from the ecclesiastical jurisdiction, consider
it a great privilege to be able to have recourse to and place themselves under the protection of the temporal jurisdiction.[21]

Jean Bodin said as much in 1580, in his *Démonomanie des sorciers* (IV,
5); Jean Desloix also, in his *Speculum inquisitionum,* which had just been
published in translation (Lyons, 1634). Martin del Rio, a Jesuit, advised
recourse to a double jurisdiction *(mixti fori)* in his *Disquisitionum magicarum libri sex* (Lyons, 1608), but in fact the ecclesiastical judges "often
show small ardor to repress sorcery."[22]

The Argumentation

On what "proofs" can the judgment that the commissioners are to pronounce be based? They were presented by one of them, Dreux, as it
seems,[23] the *lieutenant général* of Chinon, in the *Extrait* of proofs that are
in Grandier's trial:

As the foundation of the entire proceedings of Sieur de Laubardemont is the possession of the Ursuline religious, and that it
is the subject of the trial whose inquiry he has extraordinarily
conducted against the curé of Loudun, it was necessary to establish the truth in that matter by witnesses such as are desirable
in that matter.[24]

Thus begins the report that, while requiring verification from other
sources, furnishes a rather clear picture of the questions to be dealt with,
and the criteria by which they resolved them. Two problems are clearly
distinguished: the authenticity of the possession and Grandier's guilt.

The first question is not directly within their province. They therefore turn to the competent authority. They cite the following: the *sentence en décret* of the bishop of Poitiers (August 10, 1634); the opinion of the doctors at the Sorbonne (February 11, 1633); the attestations of approved exorcists (Lactance, Elisée, Tranquille, and "a Carmelite"); the declarations of a few theologians (Father Gilbert Rousseau, rector of the college of Poitiers, the prior of the Jacobins of Tours, and Revol, a doctor at the Sorbonne); certificates of the many physicians who esteem that the facts transcend nature.

The second point, the true object of judgment, can be illuminated by the depositions of witnesses *(ordinary proofs)*, or by marks or scars found on the suspect *(extraordinary proofs)*, or by his confession.

The Ordinary Proofs

The harvest of *preuves ordinaires* results first from successive inquiries and the hearing of witnesses. Essentially, they bring out the seduction carried out by Grandier, to the point where out of his church "he made a place of pleasure and a bordel open to all his concubines"; this power of a "fascinating sorcerer" holds the attention more than does misconduct.

> Thus a woman says that one day, after having received communion from the accused who fixed his gaze upon her during that action, she was immediately surprised by a violent love for him, which began by a little shiver through all her limbs.
> The other said that having been stopped by him on the street, he shook her hand and immediately she was also seized by a great passion for him.[25]

Another testimony: a lawyer "testifies to having seen the accused read books by Agrippa." That is, Cornelius Agrippa, the great theoretician of *Philosophie occulte* (1531). The lawyer, in clarifying his deposition, nearly annuls it, but the retraction will not be retained:

> It is true that [the lawyer] somewhat explained himself upon confrontation and said that he believes the books by Agrippa of which he had heard, according to his deposition, are *De Vanitate scientiarum*. But that explanation is very suspect, because the lawyer had left Loudun and would not submit to the confrontation till after having been forced to do so.

The Truth of the Possessed Women

Another source of ordinary proofs is constituted by the depositions of the nuns and laywomen possessed outside of the exorcisms, texts in which "there is not a word but merits consideration": their obsessive love for Grandier, their nocturnal visions, the blows they mysteriously received, and so forth. The reporter underscores an episode from these depositions before Laubardemont (December 1633–January 1634).

> Now, outside all the accidents by which the good religious were tormented, I find none more strange than what happened to the prioress mother and Sister de Sazilly. The former, the day after having submitted her deposition, when Sieur de Laubardemont was receiving that of another religious, put on a shirt, bareheaded, with a rope around her neck and a candle in her hand, and remained in that state the space of two hours, in the middle of the courtyard where it was raining abundantly. And when the door of the parlor was opened, she dashed to it and fell to her knees before Sieur Laubardemont, telling him she had come to atone for the offense she had committed in accusing the innocent Grandier. Then, withdrawing, she tied the rope to a tree in the garden, where she would have strangled herself, had the other sisters not come running.

The oddity of this accident is considered an indication of the power exercised by the sorcerer! This is followed by some attestations of Barré tending to suggest the identity of the suspect. But the "declarations made by the demons at the exorcisms" are not retained, "leaving the most refined to examine whether one can believe what comes from the Father of Lies, whether the demons duly exorcised are obliged to tell the truth, and whether the conditions required to make an exorcism perfect are as possible as they are necessary."

The Extraordinary Proofs

Despite everything, the ordinary proofs appear more indicative than probing. It is necessary to move on to the *extraordinary proofs*. One of them is the scar that the sorcerer allegedly bears on his body for having signed a pact with the Devil in blood. On April 25, in giving the pact, the "demon Asmodaeus" had declared that the blood visible on the pact came from a cut that Grandier had made on the thumb of his right hand to sign it. Laubardemont, some physicians and exorcists, a whole little troupe, then proceeded to the prison, and the curé, on whom they observed the scar in the place indicated, gave embarrassed explanations: a wound from a pin, he thought. No, the physicians declared the cut was made by a knife. Doubtless, Grandier resumed, he had cut himself cutting the bread with a knife one of his wardens had given him. In any case, as Jacques d'Autun repeats in *L'incrédulité savante et la crédulité ignorante au sujet des magiciens et sorciers* [Learned Incredulity and Ignorant Credulity on the Subject of Magicians and Sorcerers],[26] it is very difficult to distinguish between this type of mark and simple scars.

More reliable are "indolent marks," spots that do not bleed. Pierre de Lancre said that in practice "there are no proofs that I find more certain that those."[27]

These indolent marks, the object of an entire literature, of Jacques Fontaine's *Discours des marques des sorciers* (which appears to have been used in Loudun)[28] in particular, obey precise rules.

The Indolent Marks

> The depth of these marks is approximately three or four fingers in the part that seems dead or insensitive, since all the iron of an awl that is plunged into it causes neither water nor blood to come out, nor causes any pain to the sorcerer.[29]

The search for these regions snatched away by the Devil from the laws of nature had been made on the curé following the information furnished by the "demon Asmodaeus," possessing Jeanne des Anges, in the course of the exorcism of the preceding April 26. The surgeon Maunoury, charged with that "visit," accompanied by physicians, "had Grandier stripped naked, blindfolded, and shaved everywhere and stuck down to the bones in several places on his body."[30]

Maunoury was accused of having simulated a prick at certain points of the body, so that they would appear insensitive because the victim ceased to cry out. Despite Grandier's request of August 11, they refused to repeat the experiment. The April examination was deemed in order and its result constitutes the argument that the *Extrait* seals:

> Eight physicians were sent to visit the accused, who gave their report, by which they declare that among all the marks found on his person, those of the shoulder and the secret members [genitals] are suspect to them, because a needle having been introduced into the former to the depth of a thumb-width, the feeling was dull, and not at the level of the one the accused had testified to having felt when he was sounded in the other parts, and from neither did any blood issue when the needle was withdrawn.

The insensibility of the body thus corresponds, in the sorcerer, to the unconsciousness or "lethargy" of spirit among the possessed women. Of speech, nothing human remains. It is the needle that will found the judgment by transpiercing the surface. In the end, it alone will draw the least indecisive proofs from the body, when neither reasoning nor testimonies will demonstrate. The surgeon's instrument, producing alternating cries and silence, "makes [the body] speak" and "constrains the devil": it thus attains the two objectives by which the exorcists are obsessed. But it is blind, the weapon that imposes its law and "subdues" the devil.

"There," concludes the *Extrait*, "is the major portion of the proofs upon which the sentence of August 7 is based."

It is necessary to stretch to the maximum the relative indices, since the complete proofs are lacking. The objects seized at the curé's residence appear to be indices too distant and not very reliable. The pacts are only mentioned indirectly, although they usually constitute one of the essential pieces of evidence in a sorcery case. Finally and above all, the confession is missing.

The Judgment

On August 15, 16, and 17, confronted with his judges, Grandier admits, once again, his misconduct and "weaknesses of nature," but once again denies having committed the crime of which he is accused. On the fifteenth, he confesses and takes communion. On the following day, Father Archange comes to tell him of the imminence of the condemnation; he will leave with the curé's response:

> If I must die, I pray to God that it is for the expiation of my sins and my crimes.[31]

The judges meet at the convent of the Carmelites on Friday, August 18, 1634, at five o'clock in the morning, to render their verdict. The day before, in Poitiers, M. de Cursay, accused of magic, was aquitted after the speech for the defense by Maître Lemaistre: "Powerful proofs," he said, "are necessary to make anyone believe that a Christian could have committed this sort of idolatry." But on August 8, in Paris, the Chambre de l'Arsenal sentenced two men, one of whom was a priest, accused of having acted against Cardinal de Richelieu in their house by invocations, spells, and magic, to be hanged, their bodies burned, and their ashes cast to the winds.[32]

The commissioners, stuffed with demonological literature, learned that "the crime of evil spells is all the more enormous in that in it alone are combined all the circumstances and crimes of apostasy, heresy, sacrilege, blasphemy, homicide, even often parricide, carnal fornication against nature, and hatred against God."[33]

By everything their dossier repeats, the provincial lawyers, gathered around the commissioner, are faced with the antisociety, confronted with the very crime that is a plurality, the gathering into one of all crimes.

The Sentence

At dawn, they make their pronouncement. After their judgment, it is Laubardemont's responsibility to execute it. He goes to the prison, preceded by the surgeon Fourneau, who was sent for by two guards for the complete shaving of the condemned man. At about seven o'clock, the carriage of the commissioner, escorted by royal police agents, crosses the already busy streets, conveying Laubardemont to the Palais de Justice. La Grange, the provost of Chinon, Grisard, a police officer of the guards, and the curé. The last is brought into the courtroom. The judges are there. The exorcists also, in vestments, and a large public. Grandier kneels and, with head uncovered, hears the reading of the judgment by the clerk of court Nozay.

> Seen by us, commissioners deputed by the king, sovereign judges in this case, in accordance with the letters patent of the king of the eighth of July one thousand six hundred thirty-four, the criminal trial brought at the request of his majesty's prosecutor, plaintiff and accuser for the crime of magic, enchantments, irreligion, impiety, sacrilege, and other offense and abominable crimes, on one side, and Maître Urbain Grandier, a priest, curé of at the church of Saint-Pierre in Loudun and one of the canons of the church of Sainte-Croix of said place, prisoner, defendant, and accused, on the other,
>
> We, without regard to said request of the eleventh of the instant month of August [the request to repeat the testing of the marks], have declared and do declare said Urbain Grandier duly attaint and convicted of the crime of magic, evil spells, and possession befallen by his doing upon the persons of some Ursuline religious women of this town of Loudun and other seculars mentioned at the trial. Together with other offenses and crimes resulting from the same crime.
>
> For reparation of which, we have condemned and do condemn him to make honorable amend, bareheaded and in a

shirt, the rope about his neck, holding in his hands a burning pitch firebrand weighing two pounds, before the principal doors of the churches Saint-Pierre-du-Marché and Sainte-Ursule of this town of Loudun, and there, on his knees, ask forgiveness of God, the king, and justice. Which being done, to be led to the public courtyard of Sainte-Croix of that town, to be tied to a stake on a pile of wood, which to that end will be erected at said place, and there his body be burned alive with the pacts and magic figures remaining with the clerk of court, together with the book written by his hand, composed against the celibacy of priests, and his ashes cast to the winds.

We have declared and do declare each and every one of his belongings be acquired and confiscated by the king, upon which previously is to be taken the sum of 150 pounds *tournois* to be used for the purchase of a plate of copper in which shall be engraved the present judgment in excerpt, and posted in an eminent place in said church of the Ursulines, there to remain in perpetuity.

And before the execution of said judgment, we order that said Grandier be applied to the question ordinary and extraordinary on the truth of his accomplices.

Pronounced in said Loudun this eighteenth day of August one thousand six hundred thirty-four.[34]

~ 11 ~

The Execution: Legend and History

August 18, 1634

This death escapes history. Of the execution nothing but later accounts are extant. They leave the event itself blank. The ambiguity of Grandier's words and gestures during those hours is all the more serious for being that of a vanished subject, broken up in the testimonies of others.

His *ultima verba* [last words] come to us through hagiographic discourse or apologies for the condemnation, prominently exhibiting the "truth" in their titles—a memoir *in truth* "of what took place," a *truthful* relation—but vying for his remains and inventing utterances for the image to be circulated.

Death and Legend

Is it true that, in the morning, before the sentence, he waved aside first Texier, the *lieutenant général* at Saint-Maixent, and then the Capuchin Archange, both of whom had come to urge him to prepare himself for the end, and, according to Father Du Pont,

> The Capuchin father having made response to him that the question was to die well, he said to him, pulling him up by the nose: "You are bothering me. Leave me alone."

But the same Archange—who was, moreover, persuaded that the curé "died impenitent and satanically"—will make the deposition that at that early-morning hour of August 18, "upon the exhortations made to him by Father Archange, he [Grandier] said to him: 'May it be God's will that he be glorified today by my constancy.' "[1]

Is the response he supposedly addressed to the judges after the reading of the sentence authentic? Can we rely on the transcription of it given in the *Mesmoire de ce qui s'est passé à l'exécution de l'arrest contre M. Urbain Grandier?*

> Messieurs,
>
> I call God the Father, the Son, and the Holy Ghost and the Virgin, my only advocate, to witness that I have never been a magician or cast spells or known other magic than that of the Holy Scripture, which I have always preached. I acknowledge my Savior and beseech him that I may be worthy of the blood of his passion.[2]

The Voice of Laubardemont

The account closest in date to the execution is from Saturday, August 19. Angevin, the royal notary, wrote it, but it conveys the thought and words of Laubardemont:

> Minutes of the question and death of Grandier, the curé of Saint-Pierre du Marché of Loudun, executed yesterday, for the crime of magic and others, of which we have, by order of Maître Laubardemont, councilor to the king in his State and Privy Councils, commissioner in that case, and other commissioners appointed by his majesty for the judgment of the trial, taken minutes of what took place the day of yesterday and today touching said execution of the person of said Grandier, the circumstance and related facts thereof, having called with us F. Gayet our clerk of court, in the following manner:
>
> To wit, that we, councilor and commissioner aforementioned, declare we were present yesterday from seven to eight o'clock in the morning, in the hall of audience of the bailiwick of Loudun, when the reading was done to said Grandier of the judgment of death rendered against him, and that, said reading done, [Grandier] begged said Sieur de Laubardemont not to have him burned alive, for fear lest he fall into despair.[3]

That demand had legal precedents. In Lorraine, before sorcerers or witches, the judges in many cases took care to mitigate the death of the condemned, and even more to preserve in them the virtue of hope. In that spirit and "to avoid a despair" that would have brought about the eternal damnation of the sorcerer, they would often abridge the sufferings of his last moments, and decided that after "having but felt the heat of the fire" he would be strangled before his body was caught up in the flames.[4] The motivation was religious.

Grandier, according to the minutes,

> did not say he was unjustly condemned. To whom said Sieur [de Laubardemont] pointed out that it only depended upon him [Grandier] to obtain that favor by confessing that he was guilty of the crime of magic for which he had been condemned to death.
>
> [Grandier] responded that he had never committed said crime.
>
> We pointed out to him that there had been thirteen of us judges at the judgment of his trial, and that of one accord we had all declared him to be duly attaint and convicted of the crimes of magic, evil spells, of being the author of the possession of some Ursuline religious and other seculars mentioned during the trial, and we told him often that we were very assured that he was a magician.
>
> The which he once responded to us that he could not remove from us that belief.[5]

The Question

The judgment included "the preliminary question ordinary and extraordinary." According to current legal practices, that was not abnormal. Torture is ordered when there is a death sentence, but also when there is suspicion of accomplices not yet disclosed. Only infants, deaf-mutes, children under the age of puberty, and pregnant women were excepted. Grandier does not belong to the excepted categories, and his crime is of the kind that implies accomplices. Of these, a trace was sought in vain in his papers and among his circle. Father Du Pont, curious about all the rumors, claims that one of the judges, "of whom I am a friend, gave me to understand, though darkly [the good father can catch the least implications and interpret the silences of his friend, without any doubt Sieur Roatin] that the main proofs and depositions of the witnesses touch not only said Grandier, but several other persons of whom some are of very great quality, whom one cannot place under arrest without an express order from his majesty, to whom the trial has been sent."[6]

Thus the "ordinary" question, to which the sentence adds the "extraordinary," is not only a corporal punishment; it is intended to facilitate the discovery of still further "truths," in particular the "school of magic" that is the object of the Loudun "rumor." The torture consists in driving a series of increasingly large wedges between the boards within which the legs are enclosed and the legs, until the bones break.

Outside the Laws

Degradation, traditional when a priest was turned over to the ordeal, was omitted by Laubardemont, either because it appeared odious and was less practiced, or because it could allow the person charged to have recourse to the ecclesiastical jursidiction.[7] No religious authority intervened on behalf of the curé. The archbishop of Bordeaux was silent, for political reasons, it appears. He was in violent conflict (1633–34) with the governer of Guyenne, Jean-Louis de Nogaret, duc d'Épernon, and too much in need of the support of Richelieu to take on Laubardemont, who was, additionally, the governer's political adversary.

Grandier, alone, is turned over to the judiciary. D'Angevin continues his minutes, dictated by the commissioner:

> And we noticed that he did not look at the picture of the crucifix, which was a painting that was attached to the wall; and that before he was put to the question, Father Lactance, a religious, exhorted him to say the prayer of the guardian angel [the Hail Mary] which he did not know, so said father had him say it word for word after him.
>
> We saw that he was put to the question of the boot ordinary and extraordinary, for the space of three-quarters of an hour, without confessing said crime. He said several times that he had committed greater and more shameful ones, and it being inquired of him what they were, he said these words: "It is from fragility," and confessed to other crimes mentioned in his interrogation.
>
> That he never pronounced the names Jesus, Mary, though he often said these words: "My God of heaven and earth, give me strength." His eyes, during the question, were flashing, horrible and terrifying; he moaned and cried aloud greatly, and yet produced no tears, though he was urged to weep when often he sighed and sobbed, so Father Lactance, a Recollect religious, who exorcised the instruments used in the question, performed a particular exorcism, to express tears from his eyes, which contained nothing but these words: "*Si es innoxius, infunde lacrymas*" ["if you are innocent, shed tears"].
>
> That, during said question, he begged said Father Lactance to kiss him, and that said father approached him and kissed him thrice. We saw no sign of penitence, and he neither by utter-

ances nor gestures asked for a priest, either before or after said question.

That being out of said question, looking at his legs, he said: "My Lords, *attendite et videte si est dolor sicut dolor meus.*"

The Passion

"Behold, and see if there be any sorrow like unto my sorrow": this biblical verse is repeated in the liturgy of Holy Week, in which it forms part of the first Nocturn of the Office of Tenebrae, celebrated during the night that follows Good Friday. The crowd of the faithful sang the canticle of lamentations ascribed to "the Man of Sorrows": "O ye that pass by the way, stop. . . . Peoples of the universe, behold, and see if there be any sorrow like unto my sorrow." Grandier takes up this call of the Suffering Servant as his own and addresses it to the witnesses of the "question."

> Said Grandier was immediately led to the high room of said hall of audience to warm him, in which room we went to visit him at two o'clock in the afternoon, and, seeing that often he spoke favorably of God, we rebuked him, since on that same morning we were very certain that he was a magician, and on that basis, we knew very well that when he spoke of God favorably he meant to speak of the Devil, and when he detested the Devil he meant to detest God; and that what we were telling him was true.
>
> To which he made no response, other than to pray to the God of Heaven and Earth to help him.[8]

Language has lost meaning. In any case, Laubardemont's logic has, in the Devil, the means for determining what the condemned man "means" by words that affirm the opposite.

The Execution

The crowd is waiting: six thousand people, according to some; twelve thousand, according to others. At four or five o'clock in the afternoon, Grandier is dressed in a shirt infused with sulfur, and, with a rope around his neck, taken down to the palace courtyard, where a tipcart drawn by six mules will take him, following the prescriptions of the sentence, to the church of Saint-Pierre-du-Marché, then to the Ursuline chapel, and finally to the public square, the Marché Sainte-Croix.

In the eyes of the thousands of spectators who are present, what is happening? What do they see? The curé is lost in that crowd, though all eyes are focused on him.

Here is Royal Notary Angevin's version:

> Said Grandier, being led to the ordeal, before the door of Saint-Pierre-du-Marché, of which he was the curé, to make the *amende honorable* in keeping with said sentence, said Father [Lactance] entreated said Grandier to say: "*cor mundum crea in me, Deus*" ["God, make my heart pure"]. Because of which said Grandier turned his back to him and said with a sort of disdain: "Well then, Father, *cor mundum crea in me Deus.*"

At the Place du Marché, About Five in the Afternoon,

> We declare that Grandier being tied to a stake to be burned, said Father Lactance exorcised the wood to be used to burn him; that Father Tranquille, a Capuchin religious and warden of the Capuchin fathers of La Rochelle, a preacher on mission in Poitou who, with his companion Father Patience, attended said Grandier from the time of his being submitted to the question till the moment of his execution, a period of about six hours, did not see him perform any act of contrition for his sins.
>
> He therefore began to urge him to recommend his soul to God. He held a wooden crucifix up to him, from which [the curé] turned his head; said Grandier, having perceived that said father was displeased with his disdain of the crucifix, turned toward it, and said father urged him to kiss it, which he did, as if with regret.

Last Moments

Said Father Lactance, a Recollect, told us that yesterday, at the moment of Urbain Grandier's death, said Grandier being bound to the stake where he was to be burned, he, exorcising the wood that was to serve to burn the body of said Grandier, for fear lest the heat and activity of the fire be suspended by the Devil, saw a black fly as big as a nut that fell brusquely upon the book of exorcisms:

> that, during said time, he had admonished said Grandier that paradise was still open to him if he turned back to God. Who responded with these words:

"I am going this hour to paradise."[9]

Amid the malignancy of the priests, what meaning does Grandier give to this new reemployment of Jesus' phrase: "Verily I say unto thee. To day shalt thou be with me in paradise"?[10]

Eyes on God

The *Relation véritable de ce qui s'est passé en la mort du curé de Loudun, bruslé le vendredy 18 aoust 1634* accentuates this parallel:

At about three or four o'clock in the afternoon, he was taken down and put in a tipcart, and brought before the door of the church of Saint-Pierre, where a good Cordelier [Grillau] awaited him. And when he was put on the ground in fulfillment of the order, this good father asked him whether he did not wish to die happy, and whether he was asking God's forgiveness for all his sins; that he should now confess them; that he was at death's door; that he should not depart with anything on his conscience; that he assured him on God's behalf of his salvation if he departed in repentance.

So he said: "My sweet Savior Jesus Christ, Holy Virgin, you see my heart. I ask pardon."

Then he said: "Good-bye, Father. Pray to God for me and console my poor mother."

Then he was put back into the cart and driven before the church of the Ursulines, where he was again implored to recognize his infamy and not die impenitent. "I hope," said he, "that my God, my Creator, Savior and Redeemer will pardon me. He alone knows that I am innocent. I will not say anything but what I have said. Do not disturb me further. I see my God reaching his arms out to me."

The father [in other accounts, it is the clerk of court] who was with him to take his confession told him: "How now, Sir, do you not wish to ask these girls' pardon?" "Ah, Father," answered he, "I never offended them."

He was put back in the tipcart where he was on his back, his eyes looking heavenward, having always God upon his lips. Passing before the house of his lawyer who was at his window, he said to him: "Monsieur Curé, keep your eyes on God. Do not make murmur against him. This is how he tests his children." The sufferer gave him response: "Monsieur, my hope is in God. He will not forsake me." He prayed to God continually, and even

when he was put in the cart he kept saying litanies to the Blessed
Virgin.

Having reached the public courtyard, he is put on the pyre
where he had the greatest assurance of all, and kept on saying:
"My sweet Jesus, do not abandon me, have pity on me." And he
was for a long time exorcised by the Recollect [Lactance], to
whom he said: "Father, you labor in vain. There is no devil in
me. I have renounced him. My God knows this. I will say nothing
but what I have already told you." He had a *Salve Regina* sung,
and the hymn *Ave maris stella,* praying continually. Finally, after
several interrogations, he beseeched the Recollect father to
give him the kiss of peace, which the father refused three or
four times. At last he condescended and said to him: "Monsieur,
here is the fire. There is no longer any salvation for you. Convert."

And indeed the Recollect and the two Capuchins each took
a wisp of straw and lit the woodpile themselves. Seeing which,
said curé said: "The promise made to me is not being kept,"
which was to strangle him first. And being in the flames, he said
these words more: "Lord Jesus Christ, I commend my soul to
thy hands. Send your angels, my God, that they may carry it
before thy face, and pardon my enemies." These are his last
words.[11]

According to Father Du Pont,

He attested in all things that he did not fear death, nor what
follows it, but feared greatly to be burned alive and did nothing
but beg to be strangled, as M. de Laubardemont had promised
him, if he converted. The opposite took place. For the fire or
the Devil cut the rope in an instant, and so quickly that the fire
was scarcely lit before he fell into it and was burned alive without
crying out. Only a few heard that he said: "Ah, my God."[12]

The Cost of the Dead Man

The ashes were thrown to the winds, the traces of the sorcerer wiped
clean, because contagious. The public square was swept clean of them.
But not the memory: the polemic will multiply, a literature will proliferate, born precisely out of that dangerous absence. There also remain
the marks of the work of Loudun that was connected with the "affair"
and continued after it. Such as these receipts, dated August 24, 1634:

I, the undersigned, acknowledge having had and received the sum of 19 livres 16 sols for the wood that was used in the burning of Master Urbain Grandier, the stake to which he was tied and other wood. . . .

Deliard[13]

I, the undersigned, Jan Verdier, prosecutor at the Court of Loudun, having charge of Pierre Morin, my sister, acknowledge having received . . . the sum of 108 sous, 6 deniers, for the day's expenses of five horses for the archers of monsieur the provost of Chinon, the day of the execution of M. Urbain Grandier, curé of Saint-Pierre-du-Marché of Loudun, and for the day of his mules, carts, and servants who led said Grandier to the ordeal. . . .

Verdier[14]

The event remains minutely recorded in the accounting. The "objective" history of the dead man is that of his cost.

The Meaning of the Dead Man

At the same time, letters, pamphlets, *Récits,* and *Relations* of all kinds spread throughout France. A letter from Ismaël Bouilliau, dated September 7, circulates immediately. During the same month, according to a private journal of daily events, "news of the ordeal of Urbain Grandier reaches Lyons. Here are the terms in which Ismaël Bouilliau, of Loudun . . ., etc."[15] In his letter, the erudite youth mentioned the information received from Loudun by his Huguenot brother. He writes to Gassendi: "Since I am on that virtue of patience, I will give you here an excerpt of a letter that a brother of mine wrote me on the subject of the death of M. Urbain Grandier."

The information is amplified and disseminated through letters that are excerpts of letters and chronicles that are copies of copies. But it begins to circulate under the sign of exemplarity. Bouilliau includes it in the subject-matter of patience, a stoic virtue:

I cannot refrain from speaking to you about the late M. Urbain Grandier, who died either as an angel, if angels could die, or like a devil, if they were mortal, for if that man was innocent, he most certainly used the greatest virtue there is among all the virtues. His constancy, when I think of it, overwhelms me.

That he should be condemned to the most cruel ordeal imaginable, and, beforehand, put to the question in order to find out his accomplices, that he should have endured the extraordinary torture without being spared, and that such agony should be unable to draw an untoward word from him, on the contrary an uninterrupted perseverance without the least vacillation, accompanied by prayers and meditations worthy of his spirit—that makes me say that there are few similar examples, for he knew he was to die, and was not in the least enticed by the world to endure such hardships, so that there was but that sole constant virtue that was able to bind him to such a resolution, together with a desire to leave behind a belief in his innocence.

I saw him at the stake speak boldly, I even saw the fire lit without his showing any apprehension of it, but he rather said aloud: "Lord Jesus, I commend my soul to thy hands." A witness asked for his pardon, as well as that of the others. He answered in these terms: "My friend, I pardon you as willingly as I believe firmly my God will pardon me and receive me today in paradise."

This makes me say, if he died innocent, that he died as a good man, and that he attested to an incredible virtue. If he died guilty, he died bedeviled, having used his so excellent gifts to maintain his wickedness. The devils say he is in hell where he suffers greatly, but many doubt it, having heard him speak as a Christian, added to the fact that it would be a sin against charity. Some say that when he called upon God he meant a diabolical deity and a trinity of the same sort; but others of his hearers say that he was once told by a man of wit and learning who heard him speak of God that the Jews reproached our Lord for having called upon Elijah. Grandier answered: "I call upon God who created me through his son Jesus Christ, my Savior, son of the Blessed Virgin, and know no other." He confessed that he had been a man, that he had loved women, but that since his Poitiers sentence [January 3, 1630], he had withdrawn from that and caused no offense, and denied, as they say, being a sorcerer or magician or committing sacrilege.[16]

~ 12 ~

After Death, Literature

Death seems to free speech. Once the execution has run its course, a literature proliferates. It relates what was, pleads in favor of what should have been done, profits from this dead man. It describes the events, justifying or condemning them. But everything it *says* is expressed in the past tense and is made possible only by an *action* that has been posited, irreversible and definitive: Urbain Grandier was burned.

The Press Set Free

The circulation of that little press is bound up with the fact that the event took place. Because Laubardemont won, he can be accused in the epigrams that the day of August 18 not only occasions, but also condones:

> Vous tous qui voyez la misère
> De ce corps qu'on brûle aujourd'hui
> Apprenez que son Commissaire
> Mérite mieux la mort qui lui.[1]
>
> [All you who see the misery
> of this body one burns today
> learn that its commissioner
> deserves death more than he.]

Because Grandier was in fact killed, he can become a literary object, in the hagiographic poem that seems to hesitate still between two interpretations, and that reuses the episodes of his "passion" (for example, the rumor, spread in the town, according to which someone held a crucifix reddened in the fire up to the curé at the stake, and that he rejected it, spitting on it):

L'enfer a révélé que, par d'horribles trames
Je fis pacte avec Lui pour débaucher les femmes.
De ce dernier délit, personne ne se plaint;
Et dans l'injuste arrêt qui me livre au supplice,
Le démon qui m'accuse est auteur et complice,
Et reçu pour témoin du crime qu'il a feint.

L'Anglais, pour se venger, fit brûler la Pucelle.
De pareilles fureurs m'ont fait flamber comme elle.
Même crime nous fut imputé faussement.
Paris la canonise et Londres la déteste.
Dans Loudun, l'un me croit enchanteur manifeste,
L'autre m'absout. Un tiers suspend son jugement.

Comme Hercule, je fus insensé pour les femmes.
Je suis mort, comme lui, consumé par les flammes.
Mais son trépas le fit placer au rang des dieux.
Du mien l'on a voilé si bien les injustices
Qu'on ne sait si les feux, funestes ou propices,
M'ont noirci pour les enfers ou purgé pour les cieux.

En vain, dans les tourments, a relui ma constance.
C'est un magique effet, je meurs sans repentance.
Mes discours ne sont point du style des sermons.
Baisant le crucifix, je lui crache à la joue.
Levant les yeux au ciel, je fais aux saints la moue.
Quand j'invoque mon Dieu, j'invoque les démons.

D'autres, moins prévenus, disent, malgré l'envie,
qu'on peut louer ma mort sans approuver ma vie,
Qu'être bien résigné marque Espérance et Foi,
Que pardonner, souffrir sans crainte, sans murmure,
Est Charité parfaite, et que l'âme s'épure
Quoique ayant mal vécu, en mourant comme moi.[2]

[Hell has revealed that by horrible schemes I made a pact with it to debauch women. Of this last offense, no one complains; and in the unjust ruling that delivers me to the ordeal, the demon who accuses me is the author and accomplice, and accepted as a witness for the crime he has feigned.

The English, to avenge themselves, had Joan of Arc burned. Similar furors have made me burn like her. The same crime was falsely ascribed to us. Paris canonizes her and London detests her. In Loudun, one believes me a patent bewitcher, the other absolves me. A third suspends judgment.

Like Hercules, I was mad about women. I am dead, like him, consumed by flames. But his death placed him in the rank of the gods. Of my death they have so well veiled the injustices, that one doesn't know if the fire, deadly or propitious, has blackened me for hell or purged me for heaven.

In vain in the torments my constancy shone: it's a magic effect, I die unrepentant. The style of my speech is not that of sermons. Kissing the crucifix, I spit at it. Raising my eyes to heaven, I make faces at the saints. When I invoke God, I am invoking the demons.

Others, less biased, say, despite envy, that one can praise my death without approving my life, that to be fully resigned indicates hope and faith, that to pardon, suffer without fear, without complaint, is perfect charity, and that the soul is purified, though having lived badly, in dying as I did.]

The Time of the Gazettes

In the town of Théophraste Renaudot, in that city in which the industry of parchment is so prosperous, on "rue de la Parcheminerie, the street that stinks," as they say, all types of press, of libels and disputes, come out of the silence and stupor, and flow out over the facts. They develop a local style. It is the same throughout the region of Poitou. According to a contemporary,

> [t]hese Poitevins are generally rather strong and robust, haughty, capable of vengeance, fond of lawsuits and novelty. They are subtle and keen of spirit, which is why they often have witty sayings and a strong inclination for letters and the sciences. . . . The peasant is rude and malicious, and more experienced in wrangling than all the clerks in a Clerk's Office.[3]

The literature that Naudé will call *la gazette des sots* [the gazette of fools] has, then, a vast and capable readership. Its domain grows wider. On all sides, publishers print the papers that come in from Loudun, Poitiers, Chinon, or Saumur. Dr. Seguin, on October 14, 1634, speaks to his Parisian friend of "divers writings that are circulating everywhere, and, I am sure, on the Pont-Neuf, as well as elsewhere."[4]

The Pont-Neuf is the Parisian rallying-place for the traffic of libels, of "popular pieces," of secondhand books spread out on trestle tables or lined up on the parapet.[5]

Seguin adds, after having aroused the curiosity of his correspondent, Sieur Quentin: "I beseech you not to share this with any but our friends."[6] This is a manner of speaking, for he knows very well what the fate of his letter will to be published in the *Mercure françois* of 1634. Father Du Pont does likewise when, on August 29, he writes from Poitiers to his Parisian friend M. Hubert. He announces sensational news to him and, in a second, purely rhetorical moment, claims to withdraw from circulation so many "marvels" and "peculiarities":

> If, in the three trips I have taken to Loudun, I had not myself seen what went on, I would not have wanted to believe it. If you share my letters with some of your friends, I beg you not to let

them make copies, as my intention is that they should never be printed.[7]

The unknown author, "N.," when he sends his *lettre à ses amis* on August 25, no longer even dissimulates the public for which his chronicle is intended: "It does indeed appear that this will be an article for the next *Gazette*"[8]—Renaudot's *Gazette*, naturally, founded in 1631 and which, since 1634, includes a monthly supplement of *Extraordinaires*. N. is thinking, then, of a newspaper that is less official and less serious than the *Mercure françois*.

It will become the custom to supply the public with "papers" coming from Loudun. They make their way into the correspondence and archives of the erudite: the Du Puy brothers, Mersenne, and in particular Peiresc, who collects and preserves them. Public attention exerts its power even over those who suffer from it and intend to avoid it. In 1635 Surin, who has been ill since the beginning of his stay in Loudun, will speak of the "blow my spirit suffered, having learned that a letter I had written to a man as if to a confessor has been brought to the knowledge of everyone."[9]

A Library

It is impossible to analyze in detail the indefinite diffraction of the event through the diversity of so many accounts and apologies, or its distortions in the course of their itineraries through the networks that convey them. Moreover, through their resurgence in new editions, their traces or copies, and textual modifications due to changes of milieu, interests, or periods, these pieces bring to light, like the voyages of a visible element through the opacity of the body, the socio-religious circuits and, at certain dates, the splits in mentality that diversify the public to which these "revised and corrected" texts are addressed.

The whole of this press dossier, taken together, is already the characteristic document of a moment in history. From the disappearance of the sorcerer till the end of 1634, the following pieces were redacted, collated, or printed. The portion presented here, in the approximate order of being placed into circulation, obviously constitutes only the remainder of a literature that is the most fleeting and ephemeral of all:

Interrogatoire de Maistre Urbain Grandier, prestre curé de S. Pierre du Marché de Loudun . . . avec les confrontations des religieuses possédées contre ledit Grandier . . . (Paris: E. Hevert and J. Poullard, 1634).
Factum pour Maistre Urbain Grandier (no place or date, but in fact published in Paris).
Requeste de Grandier, curé de Loudun . . . au Roy (a text that also circulated

under the title *Lettre de U. Grandier*, very probably printed in Paris, 1634).

Remarques et considerations servans à la justification du Curé de Loudun, autres que celles contenues en son Factum . . . (no place or date, but very probably printed in Paris, 1634).

Extrait des Registres de la Commission ordonnée par le Roy, pour le Jugement du procez criminel fait à l'encontre de Maistre Urbain Grandier et ses complices (published at least in Poitiers, by J. Thoreau and the widow of Antoine Mesnier, and in Paris).[10]

Extrait des preuves qui sont au procès de Grandier (apparently, Poitiers).[11]

Arrest de condamnation de mort contre Maistre Urbain Grandier, prestre, curé de l'église Sainct-Pierre-du Marché de Loudun et l'un des chanoines . . ., atteint et convaincu du crime de magie et autres mentionnés au procès (Paris: Etienne Habert and Jacques Poullard) (also several other towns).[12]

Procès verbal de la question et mort de Grandier, written by Angevin, royal notary (August 18, 1634).[13]

Effigie de la condamnation de mort et exécution d'Urbain Grandier, curé de l'Eglise de Saint-Pierre-du-Marché de Loudun, atteint et convaincu de Magie, sortilèges et maléfices, lequel a été bruslé vif en ladite ville, le 18 Aoust 1634, folio engraving with caption and lament (sold in Paris, chez Jean de la Noüe, engraver, Place Maubert aux Trois Faucelles, 1634).[14]

Pourtraict représentant au vif l'exécution faicte à Loudun en la personne de Urbain Grandier . . . (printed and engraved in Poitiers: René Allain, 1634).[15]

Exorcisme des possédées pendant le supplice d'Urbain Grandier, showing how the possessed women, exorcised "while Grandier was on the iron chair," tied to the stake, made the devils joyous, worried, happy at the end ("clapping their hands") at Grandier's damnation: "Il est à nous, il est à nous" ["He's ours, he's ours"].[16]

Procès-verbal de l'exorcisme de Jeanne des Anges et de la sœur Agnès, redacted by Houmain, *lieutenant général* of Orléans. According to this text, one sole demon remains in the possessed women, the others having left to conduct Grandier to hell.[17]

L'Ombre d'Urbain Grandier. Sa rencontre et conférence avec Gaufridi en l'autre monde (no indication of place, 1634).[18]

Le Grand miracle arrivé en la ville de Loudun, en la personne d'Isabelle Blanchard, fille séculière recevant le Saint Sacrement de l'autel, et le procès-verbal fait sur ce sujet par M. de Laubardemont. Avec l'exorcisme fait à ladite possédée [August 22, 1634] (Poitiers: R. Allain, 1634, very probably two successive editions).[19] *La Coppie du procez-verbal* . . . [by Laubardemont] *22 aoust 1634* (Poitiers, printed separately).

Letter of a resident of Poitiers on Grandier's execution.[20]

Three letters addressed from Tours by Father Louis de Saint-Bernard, a Feuillant religious, to the reverend father de Saint-Bernard, a religious of the same order, in Paris.[21]

Lettre de N. à ses amis sur ce qui s'est passé à Loudun, printed item (no place or date [1634]).[22]

Coppie d'une lettre escrite à une religieuse urseline du monastère de Dijon, sur le sujet des possédées de Loudun, printed item (no place, 1634).[23]

Discours faict par le Père Archange, Capucin, à Monseignr. l'Evesque de Chartres, à Chinon, le quatriesme jour de 7bre 1634, sur la mort de Grandier.[24]

Relation de ce qui s'est passé au voyage de Messieurs de Chartres, de Nimes et des Roches, à Chinon et à Loudun (September 7, 1634).[25]

Letter from M. Pilet de la Mesnardière to M. du Bois-Daufin on the possessed women (September 17, 1634).[26]

Letter from Sieur Seguin, a physician in Tours, to Sieur Quentin in Paris (October 14, 1634), published in the *Mercure françois* of 1634.[27]

Discours de la possession des religieuses Ursulines de Lodun [by Marc Duncan, a physician], (Saumur: probably published by Lesnier, 1634).[28]

Récit véritable de ce qui s'est passé à Loudun contre Maistre Urbain Grandier, prestre, curé de l'Eglise de S. Pierre de Loudun . . . (Paris: Pierre Targa, official printer of the diocese of Paris, 1634).[29]

Véritable relation des justes procédures observées au fait de la possession des ursulines de Loudun et au procès de Grandier (2nd ed., or complete ed., after a first, Poitou ed. prior to the death of Grandier and titled *Résumé des doctrines exposées depuis le début des Possessions des Ursulines*), by the R. P. Tr. R.C. [Reverent Father Tranquille, Capuchin religious] (Paris: J. Martin; Poitiers: J. Thoreau and the widow Mesnier; and La Flèche: G. Griveau, 1634).[30]

La Démonomanie de Loudun, qui montre la véritable possession des religieuses Ursulines et autres séculières . . ., 2nd ed., expanded by several proofs. *La mort de Grandier Autheur de leur possession* (La Flèche: chez Georges Griveau, 1634). The first publication seems to have been prior to Grandier's death. The author, anonymous, must be one of the usual Loudun exorcists.[31]

Relation véritable de ce qui s'est passé en la mort du curé de Loudun, bruslé tout vif le vendredy 18 aoust 1634. . . .[32]

Relation du procès et de la mort de Grandier.[33]

Extrait des choses remarquables qui se sont passées après la mort de Grandier.[34]

Mémoire au vray de ce qui s'est passé en la mort de Mre. Urbain Grandier, curé de Saint-Pierre-du-Marché de Loudun. . . .[35]

Mesmoire de ce qui s'est passé à l'exécution de l'arrest contre Me Urbain Grandier, prestre. . . .[36]

Discours sur l'histoire de la diablerie de Loudun et sur la mort de Me. Urbain, curé de ladite ville, fait par Pierre Champion, procureur audit Loudun, pour sa satisfaction.[37]

This literary production is still limited to an area defined by the printing centers: Poitiers, Saumur, La Flèche, and chiefly Paris, with expansions toward Bordeaux, Dijon, Lyons, Aix-en-Provence. From 1635 to 1637 the publication sites alone describe a larger circle, with Bordeaux, Tours, Orléans, Rouen, Lyons, and so on, in addition to the preceding. But the important thing is, beginning in 1634, that first proliferation around the locus of the dead man (see fig. 4 on pp. 187–89).

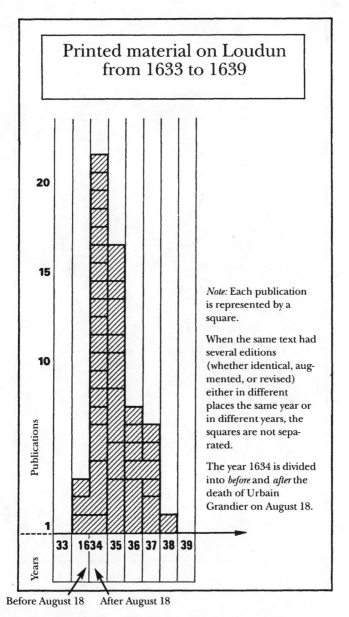

Before August 18   After August 18

4. Printed material on Loudun (1633–39) *(figure continues)*.

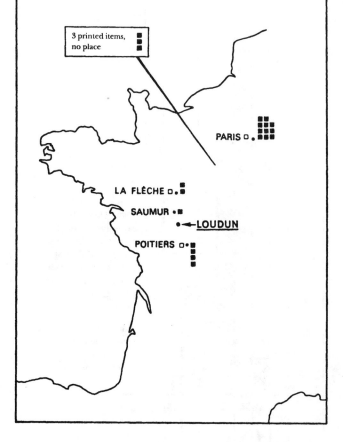

Printed material on Loudun (1634)

□ Appeared before August 18, 1634 = 3
■ Appeared after August 18, 1634 = 21

3 printed items, no place ■■

PARIS □

LA FLÈCHE □ ■

SAUMUR ■

←LOUDUN

POITIERS □ ■

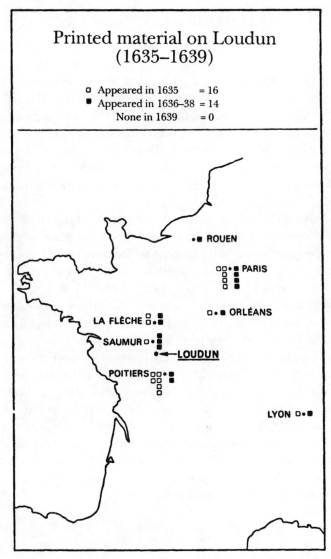

Printed material on Loudun
(1635–1639)

□ Appeared in 1635   = 16
■ Appeared in 1636–38 = 14
None in 1639   = 0

ROUEN

PARIS

ORLÉANS

LA FLÈCHE

SAUMUR

LOUDUN

POITIERS

LYON

Note: These maps obviously include only publications that have survived or for which there is positive evidence—the quantifiable remains of a "press" that was much more extensive.

Urbain Grandier's "Tomb"

The void left by Grandier's disappearance was filled by that multiplication of writings. A function of language, to say the absent? But the literary
event that follows the historical act has a more precise meaning, which
sketches out the future of the affair. Perhaps the authors themselves do
not fully realize it: Laubardemont will go after the Grandier family for
a few weeks; the exorcists will continue their exorcisms, which, unknown
to them, are undergoing a metamorphosis; d'Armagnac will try another
hand, but the game is lost. In reality, the time of action, in Loudun, is
already posited as over by all these writings that speak of it in the past
tense.

The real conflicts will move on to other terrains. *L'affaire Grandier* has
become the object of papers that have precisely the effect of removing
it from operative history and placing it in "dossiers," or the discourse of
history. Henceforth, metamorphosed into a story, it will serve to designate other wars: to feed the opposition to Richelieu on other fronts; to
struggle against Laubardemont's subsequent activities; to mobilize opinion against the libertine spirit or against the politico-religious associations in the process of formation.

To the rapid rise of verbal polemic, to its growth in surface extension,
there corresponds a fragmentation of opposing parties and convictions.
The camps lose, with Grandier, what constituted them as adversaries.
They break up because of his absence. The public forum of a bipolar
confrontation breaks down into individual opinions or groups that become isolated and pursue a marginal existence. The discourse of the pro
and con is fragmented along the lines of private curiosities or edifying
objectives. The drama disintegrates into individual tourism, popular mis-
sions, mystic communications, and so forth.

The Feast of Fire

The dead man prompts speech, but in discordant voices. After having
united such divergent interests against him during his life, he is, by his
disappearance, the revealer of these divergences. His presence gave
them a single objective, founded in ambiguity, and his absence causes
their dispersion. Why? That fact is the problem of Loudun. But light is
shed on it by the relationship between its two moments.

Evoking the "covenant" that the ecclesiastical authority seals with the
royal authority at the altar on which the victim is burned, on August 18,
Father Tranquille dares to write: "These two powers, joining hands,

make a St. Elmo's fire that lulls the storms and restores to us the fair weather of public tranquility."[38]

Like those St. Elmo's fires sailors saw surging from the mast tops after tempests and to which they attributed the power to "restore the fair weather,"[39] the burning of the sorcerer at the stake has here the sense of a cosmic feast at the very moment when the Synodal Constitutions and the Diocesan Catechisms are beginning to condemn the great "joy-fires" *(ignes jucunditatis)* and "odoriferous fumigations" intended to ward off storms as well as demons.[40]

In order to regain the cohesion of a cosmos, a divided and troubled society created a "deviant" and sacrificed him to itself. It recovers by excluding him. It targeted the "fine talker" precisely because he manifested in his statements the instability of the traditional beliefs and rules. In order that there might be a recognized law (but not necessarily the one he violated), he had to die. An old social reflex, which functions all the more surely, the greater the uncertainty. The death of the "sorcerer" (there are all kinds of them) "satisfies" the group—an anonymous god that has taken the place of the ancient gods and received from them its needs and its pleasures.

The liturgy Tranquille speaks of requires that a victim be burned for the relief of the collectivity. For the latter, it is a festival. The death of a man allows the group to survive. There are times when the burning of a dummy suffices. At other times, the uncertainty of the representations is such that the destruction of an effigy is no longer satisfactory. The act of a real crime is necessary, the return to those "primitive" beginnings that, in the mythologies, associate the birth of a history or a people with a criminal transgression, an excommunication by murder.

The Proof That There Is Order

The execution was not a moment of fictive cohesion. Quite to the contrary, it was a *test*, frightening but decisive, demonstrating a reason that has the force of law. It is not the law that one expected. But the essential is attained; *there is order*, that of the royal power. Then discussions are allowed; speech acquires the freedom to disperse words and convictions to the four winds; alliances can be broken. All this is allowed by the reconstitution of a ground and a frame of reference, by the unveiling of a force that will henceforth carry, in place of the religious authority, the organization of the city and the weight of language. The discourses resume their rumors and disputes as soon as a terrain is given them: that reason of State which founds the very critique of which it is the

object. Conversely, the "spiritual power," the fragility of which was a
source of concern, moves patently onto the side of these discourses. It
is one more voice in an order it ceases to sustain, which permits many
other voices, and assumes the power to authorize them or exert its con-
trol over them.

Thus, the obscure complicities secured in anonymity on August 18
fell apart. From the act that united them for a moment, heterogeneous
groups profited, each one for itself. They obtained for their own individual languages their condition of possibility. Henceforth, in dispersing,
a literature can, without danger, convey the dead man that is its guarantee at the same time as an object and an argument.

The Law of Unanimity

Laubardemont himself is the first witness of that exploitation. On August
20 he announces the unanimous condemnation to Richelieu, dis-
patching to him in Paris M. Richard, one of the judges, a councilor at
the Presidial Court of Poitiers:

Monseigneur,

Your Eminence has shown such pious and charitable feelings toward the evil befallen the Ursuline religious of this town
and other laypersons afflicted by the evil spirits that I thought
he would take pleasure in being personally informed on what
took place at the judgment of the trial I brought and instructed
against the author of this evil spell, having begged Sieur Richard, councilor at Poitiers and among those present at the judgment, to go and give an account of it to Your Eminence, and,
by his Eminence's favor, should it please him, to the king.

And as it is the virtue proper to Your Eminence to ever
derive good from evil, I am sure, Monseigneur, that beyond the
relief of these poor creatures, in the service of whom you have
enjoined us to employ our efforts with the ministers of the
Church who toil ceaselessly toward that end, you will work, with
the industry and wise providence that God has given you, the
miracles that we have received and yet expect from his hand
for the universal good of the Catholic Religion. That occasion,
Monseigneur, has already produced the conversion of ten persons of different qualities and sex.

We will not stop at that, if it please God. Since, through the
force of your courage and very generous conduct, He has entirely extinguished the faction of the Huguenots, He will give

you the resolution to convert them to Him by the authority of his miracles and the power He has given his Church.

I shall dare tell you that, knowing you to the degree that in my lowliness I can know the greatness of Your Eminence, I promised myself as the end of that work the conversation [the conversion] of all the heretics of the kingdom, which, after such evident miracles, will need no more than the order of the sovereign to return to the bosom of their mother who ever has her arms open to welcome them.

But what? Monseigneur, I go perhaps too far, and beyond the terms of my commission. Please pardon my zeal and the ardent desire I have for your glory. You give us every day new reasons to admire your virtue. I cannot do otherwise than pray daily for the prosperity of your administration.

If it please you, Monseigneur, that I should speak to you of our affair, I will say to Your Eminence that we have lived here in great order and police, and with such union that it has seemed we were all moved by a self-same spirit. We had but one opinion on all things and especially in the judgment of the trial. The ruling passed with a common voice though each of these messieurs, numbering fourteen, gave his reasons with such sufficiency that I dare assert nothing was said by anyone on this occasion that was not worthy of your hearing.[41]

The Field of Honor

An edifying literature. Moreover, Laubardemont exploits the victory by pushing for the purchase of a new house for the Ursulines. On September 20 he writes of it to Michel Le Masle, "councilor to the king in his councils, superintendent general of the house of monseigneur the very eminent cardinal," and who has been made prior of Les Roches [he is henceforth referred to as "des Roches"], near Fontevrault:

Monsieur,
This porter will present you with the plan that, following your order, I had drawn up of the grounds you were pleased to visit, being in this town. It is sufficient to build a very fine convent.[42]

He also gives thought to replacing members of the team of exorcists. Father Lactance died on September 18, seized by a strange "delirium." Father Tranquille, too, already exhausted, will die insane on May 31,

1638, after what Laubardemont himself will call a long "obsession,"[43] and will then be celebrated by Father Eléazar of Loudun (*Relation de la mort du père Tranquille* [Poitiers, 1638]) as a hero fallen in the field of honor. Also, "frenzy" affects Maunoury, the surgeon; Louis Chauvet, the civil lieutenant; and others. Deprived of its anchor in a real action, the discourse of possession drifts aimlessly, swirls dizzily, and pulls down into its vertigo those who had been supported by it. In the political realm, fresh troops are needed, as Laubardemont says to des Roches:

> Shortly after the death of Father Lactance, a Recollect, one of their exorcists, I dispatched M. de Morans to M. de Poitiers in order to ask him to do all he could to engage the Jesuit fathers to take part in this work. I even wrote Father Rousseau, the rector of the college of Poitiers, a very specific letter, and made him the most honorable offers I could imagine for their satisfaction. I await the answer today, and hope indeed that it will be favorable, so that by the offices of these good fathers, who have the well-earned reputation of being masters of the sciences, the public will receive the testimonies of the truth of that possession with less contradiction.
>
> As for myself . . . as I have expected no temporal reward in my work, unless it be that which I receive within myself, in faithfully satisfying the commands of the king and of monseigneur the cardinal, who have done me the honor of putting me into that employment, I receive every day from God such good feelings of piety and charity that I cannot be in the least shaken by the discourses of the world in the resolution I have to seek his glory in the end of this work.[44]

Good Feelings

Piety, in Laubardemont, is married to power; hence it is *solid*. He nonetheless brings proceedings against René, Grandier's brother, and Madeleine de Brou, his mistress. When the royal judges of the Grands Jours in Poitiers, toward the end of 1634, presume to add the affair of Mlle de Brou to those they rule on without appeal ("there being," the cardinal will say, "a [great] number of villains hanged and 233 gentlemen and powerful personages seized of body and goods"), the commissioner protests:

> We hope now, Monseigneur [he writes to Richelieu] that, considering the enterprise that messieurs of the Grands Jours have,

of late, undertaken to take over that affair to the detriment of the power I have in hand, you will judge that it could have no other than very bad results if the course were not ruled by the sovereign power of which you are the very worthy and very faithful dispenser.

Which is what I very humbly beseech of you, Monseigneur, and to be pleased to allow me to point out, with all respect, that several of these messieurs having come here, have done, even in public, indecent and reprehensible things that I nevertheless tried to cover up with silence and other licit means.[45]

Admirable delicacy! He finds, at will, the "good feelings of piety and charity" he needs. Floating, the language of devotion is fixed by service to the king, and this service requires the success of his good servants. Hypocrite or sincere (the documents taken as a whole make sincerity more probable), Laubardemont uses devotion as the need arises. Judging by his correspondence with the prioress of Loudun up until 1653,[46] he does not appear to encounter any inner resistance on the part of his religion. All opposition—even, later, that of Saint-Cyran or of Saint Vincent de Paul—seems to him to come from without, as does the Devil.

The Grace of Success

On the other hand, Laubardemont receives from religion all the justifications or "sensible consolations" desirable. In 1644 he will even write the spiritual history of the possession, a *Journal* that intertwines the "lights" received from heaven and the political struggles, and of which he will converse at length with his protégée Jeanne des Anges.[47] There he holds, in an equilibrium that no "discourse of the world" can "shake," but that rests in the last analysis on the "happiness of success," the rendezvous and criterion of all other forms of happiness.

Installed in this system, he is "faithful," as Richelieu says. He does not abandon those whom he defends. For twenty years he will be the defender of the Ursulines. Nor does he release his jaws from those he bites. After the execution of Urbain Grandier, he arrests his mistress on August 19; he prosecutes his mother, who is obliged to go into exile; he would like to condemn his brother René, who escapes from prison on February 20, 1635. The cardinal has to order him to desist.

One may wonder how the baron will withstand, in his Parisian hotel on the rue des Filles-Saint-Thomas, the years of disfavor and semi-retreat that follow Richelieu's death (1642–53).

He is stunned to see that good persons should be the victims of fate. He writes to the cardinal on Father Tranquille:

> Father Tranquille is now suffering the same vexations as the poor girls. His body is agitated, without pain, in a most prodigious fashion. I have seen nothing, Monseigneur, in all this affair that has given me more astonishment than the accident that has befallen this good religious.[48]

From the Supernatural to the Bizarre

As the political trial comes to a close, the discourse of the possession loses its seriousness. Once the juridical and royal apparatus that drew a public to the theater of Loudun for a question of life or death has disappeared, aren't the exorcists and the possessed still present and masked in the town whose "feast" is now over? The same facts, which yesterday "surpassed nature," do they not become "bizarre," according to the expression of Peiresc in 1635? A new curiosity motivates the visitors, more and more numerous, attracted by the literature on Loudun.

The situation insidiously takes on the form of the insane for the actors who have identified a question of truth with a problem of power. When the civil authorities begin to drop out and lose interest in the demonological shows; when yesterday's sorcerer is transformed into today's martyr by the crowd, always touched with tenderness for those whose death it has brought about; when in Chinon, in December, in order to cut short what might otherwise have become another Loudun affair, it is deemed sufficient to have the religious women "tormented by demons" whipped: what then is left of the discourse credited with a power of its own?

Because the sorcerer was not the cause but the product of the possession, his death cannot bring it to an end. It continues, then, without him. But, however it may be with individual cases, it changes in nature. From the exorcism of August 20 on, the evolution clearly moves in two directions.

Miracles

There is no longer any room for denunciations, even if they concern accomplices of the sorcerer. Yet a series of miracles is inaugurated by the host spotted with blood that the demon possessing the laywoman Elisabeth Blanchard brings back. This series will be spread out over a period of three years. Thus, some religious women will be miraculously healed. Or again, the devils, as they come out, will increase the number of stigmata on the bodies of the possessed women, who are progressively covered with these decorations commemorating the victories over hell. Jeanne des Anges will be the most famous beneficiary of miracles, and until the end of her life will be visited as the memorial of these divine struggles.

The miracle represents not only the celestial supplement that usually accompanies the doubts or anxieties of all groups of this sort. It restores a justification, but an internal one, since people can no longer count on the one that, thanks to the ambiguity of a moment, came from outside. Possession survives, then, by becoming marginalized. It accepts the isolation. It loses its confidence in the civil power or rational demonstrations. The accent is placed on the danger of incredulity, on opposition to the "discourses of the world," on the simple faith without which the eyes cannot see.

Edification

The other direction completes and prolongs the first. Less polemical, possession turns toward "edification." In giving back the host, spotted with the sacred blood, Elisabeth's devil becomes a preacher:

> Must devils give Christians lessons? In Heaven, the angels rejoice
> at this great miracle. The Divine Almighty forces me to say it,
> to my confusion.

He "sheds abundant tears," according to the account, and "addressing those present":

> You have not the least devotion to the Holy Sacrament!
> — "Volo," said Father Thomas, "ut adores Jesum Christum et sanguinem ejus." ["I want you to adore Jesus Christ and his blood."]
> — "I adore the blood of Jesus Christ which He shed to make the infidels believe, and whosoever does not believe it, it shall be his condemnation."[49]

The minutes are immediately published in Poitiers: Le grand miracle arrivé en la ville de Loudun en la personne d'Elizabeth Blanchard. This sixteen-page booklet will be followed by many others—a whole pious literature thanks to the good offices of the devils. Gradually their "avowals" will become more catechistic. The "confessions" of the devil Lorou will constitute a boring collection of sermons, but they will go through all the articles of faith.[50]

This mutation is just beginning. It will take place amid confusion. Its end is still distant. The coming of the Jesuits will mark its first decisive stage. Not because they are "masters of the sciences," as Laubardemont thought. For if henceforth it is a question of knowledge rather than power, this knowledge will come from preachers and missionaries.

Among them, Father Surin adds his own personal note. This d'Artagnan of *mystics*[51] is also a wounded genius. He discovers in Loudun, in the face-to-face encounter with the possessed women, the name of the anguish in which he is then living. With a gesture typical of him, he throws himself forward: "To bear the words of love on your part, I will go, gold trumpet in hand, to the middle of the public fora."

He finds a forum. The fact of its being already encircled by criticism or irony does not trouble him, but rather reassures him. He dreams of a spiritual adventure into which he can throw himself, taking all risks, "finding no thing more beautiful than the blow of a sword transfixing my body, killing me."

At first, his drastic choices will not be accepted. However, he creates a new mobilization. He invests this language cast adrift with a transitory meaning. That will not suffice to stabilize it. Between the struggle against the sorcerer and the popular mission, he introduces into the history of Loudun a time of spirituality, in many respects equivocal also, because fragmentary and hence ephemeral. In its own way, this mystical episode prepares nonetheless for the normalization of Loudun, the slippage from action to the normal function of speech, the passage from possession to the mission, and in the same movement, the agile metamorphosis of the possessed Jeanne des Anges to a witness to the miracles of God, to an inspired oracle, a director of conscience.

～ 13 ～

The Time of Spirituality: Father Surin

"A theater to which all sorts of people came running":[1] That is Loudun, according to Surin, at the time when he too arrives, in December 1634, in the town that emerges like an island huddled about its donjon in the middle of the icy plain.

He himself describes the circumstances of his nomination to Loudun, at a time when—sick, worn out by excessive tension, yet recognized as an exceptional, though somewhat unsettling, religious—he had been removed from Bordeaux since 1632 for health reasons:

The Appeal

Upon which [Surin relates] the king, having knowledge of what was going on, and M. le cardinal de Richelieu thought of using the Jesuit fathers for the exorcism of these girls and his majesty wrote to that end to the provincial of Guyenne, telling him of his will that he depute someone for the help and relief of these poor possessed girls. Monsieur the cardinal wrote of it also, and upon this the father provincial, who was Father Arnault Bohyre, took council with himself and fixed his thought on Father Surin, who at the time was in the Marennes residence, preaching to the people. He assented, following the custom in matters of consequence, to take the counsel of his advisers. But none of them was of the opinion that this father should be sent, both because he was young, being only thirty-three years old, and because they did not judge him to have the necessary qualities for that function. Nevertheless, the father provincial held to his judgment and asked the superior of Marennes, upon reading his letter, to send Father Surin to Poitiers to exorcise the possessed religious in Loudun.

At the moment when the father superior came to Father Surin to announce that employment to him, that father was before the holy sacrament, praying to our Lord to put him someplace where he could do service; for he was extremely travailed and indisposed. When the father superior told him that, he had nothing to reply; though the thing seemed to him far beyond his strength, nonetheless he told him he was prepared to leave. But as it was nearly night and the season of Advent, it was agreed that he would depart the following day, which was done, for the father slept that night in La Rochelle. He went on foot, hoping to make the entire trip in this manner, but he found he had misjudged, for he was so exhausted from that day's journey to La Rochelle that he had to take a horse to get to Poitiers, where he was given for a companion Father Bachelerie, older than he; and both of them went as soon as possible to Loudun. In the meanwhile, the father provincial, having thought the matter over, wrote on the day after the father left to the superior of Marennes that, if Father Surin had not yet left, he should keep him there, and that he had changed his wishes. However, the father had left, and the first wish had its effect, for he also sent the order that, if he had already left, he should leave it that way.

As soon as he had accepted that order, seeing that it was a thing beyond his strength in every way, the father proposed to put his main effort in being at the feet of our Lord to request his help and, on his behalf, to speak to the soul that was to be entrusted to him and persuade her to devote herself to prayer and penitence, and by these arms combat the Devil rather than by the apparatus of exorcism, for which he felt no capacity; for his head was so bad he could not read for a quarter of an hour at a time. . . .

During this time the mother [Jeanne des Anges], who was wily and naturally adroit, resolved at first to treat that father with all civility, but not to open her heart to him. And thus she continued in that practice, till our Lord gave the father a key to enter into that heart, and do his work there. He began his exorcism on the day of St. Thomas [December 21, 1634], shortly before Christmas.[2]

"Marvelous Terrible and Marvelous Sweet"

Surin is a radical; he will have none of a "half-service." For him, "the time is short and the work is great." In a few weeks, he will say this clearly to one of his correspondents, Françoise Milon:

> I pray that Love, victorious in Heaven and on Earth, will take upon your soul an absolute empire. Submit to Him, and give Him all the power you can give over you. Yield all your rights to Him. Let yourself be vanquished by his charms. Suffer Him to strip you of everything, to separate you from everything, to ravish you from yourself. . . .
>
> His work is to destroy, to ravage, to abolish, and then to remake, reestablish, resuscitate. He is marvelous terrible and marvelous sweet; and the more He is terrible, the more He is desirable and attractive. In his executions, He is like a king who, marching at the head of his armies, makes all give way before him. His sweet affections are so charming they make hearts swoon. If He will have subjects, it is to make them know of his Kingdom. If He takes away everything, it is to communicate Himself without limits. If He separates, it is to join to Himself what He separates from all the rest. He is avaricious and liberal, generous and jealous of his interests. He demands all and gives all. Nothing can fill Him, and yet He is content with little, for he needs nothing. . . .
>
> Nothing is more agreeable to me than to speak to you of Him, and I will do so with all my heart, if you send me news of you. Let us but take care that our letters fall only into the hands of the trustworthy, for in mine there are sometimes certain expressions by which some minds might be scandalized.[3]

He therefore "got under way with that idea of working more by an inner path than by the tumult of words, and of winning the hearts and affections of those souls vexed by the demon, and of persuading them to devote themselves to prayer and God's presence, and thus resist the power of hell."[4]

Winning Hearts

The idea, or the "intuition," as he calls it, is new with respect to the technique of public exorcisms. Upon his arrival, shortly before Christmas of 1634, the first contacts confirm it:

The first time he attended an exorcism, . . . God gave him so great a tenderness toward them [the possessed women], because of the great misery of their state, that he could not refrain from shedding many tears upon seeing them, and felt moved by an extreme affection to relieve them.

He was led by M. de Laubardemont, who was a commissioner of the king charged with bringing the authors of this evil spell to justice, to visit the mother prioress, whom he found in a very calm disposition, and having the free use of her mind. At the first sight of her, he found himself marvelously touched by the desire to help that soul, and to make efforts to convey her to the experiences of the good things hidden in God's inner Kingdom.[5]

He is exalted by that encounter with the possessed woman who has been turned over to his care, "looking at that soul with an eye (as it seemed to him) of charity," and also persuaded, "by the experience he had had of himself for the past twenty-five years," that he "could not continue more than a day in that exercise" in the way the exorcists already at work understood it. Surin takes absolute positions; he goes to the extreme:

In the first place, he resolved to be continually in prayer, demanding our Lord that it please Him to give him that soul [Jeanne des Anges] and, in her, to accomplish the work for which He had wanted to die on the cross. That prayer never stopped, except for the time of the exorcism, which was very short. He felt himself impelled to be ever on his knees before God and felt so attached to that enterprise that he hardly ever departed from it. He implored God with tears to give him that girl so that he might make her into a perfect religious, and was moved to pray for that with such ardor that one day he could not keep from offering himself to the Divine Majesty to be burdened with the evil of that poor girl and to participate in all her temptations and suffering, to the point of asking to be possessed by the devil, provided He agreed to give him the freedom to enter into her and devote himself to her soul. From that moment on, there was born in the heart of that father a paternal love for that afflicted soul, which made him desire to suffer a strange thing for her, and he considered that his greatest happiness would be to imitate Jesus Christ, who, to withdraw souls

from Satan's captivity, had suffered death, having taken their
infirmities upon himself.[6]

He is first and foremost a spiritual director, determined to "conduct
himself like a minister of the Church directing souls." Though he maintains the exorcisms that constrain the "possessed" to bow down before
the holy sacrament, he prefers a different "battery" and a different "manner of combat": "he would put himself at the ear of the possessed, in
the presence of the holy sacrament, and there he would discourse in
Latin of the inner life, of the good things that are found in the divine
union, and similar subjects, in a soft voice."[7]

"Give No Orders"

[Above all, he] constructed his plan and proposed to follow a
form of conduct, in the cultivation of that soul, in complete
conformity with that of God, employing the greatest gentleness
he could, attracting that soul by sweet words to the things per-
taining to her salvation and perfection, and leaving her freedom
in all things. He applied himself to discovering the movements
of grace that would grow from the seeds planted by his discourse, and then to following them. His first project was to establish in that soul a solid will to attain inner perfection, without
proposing anything particular to her, treating in general how
good it was to belong to God; to which the mother gave audi-
ence as much as the demons allowed her to, and little by little
this desire to be entirely God's took form within her. The father,
not only at these beginning stages, but also in all of his conduct,
maintained that practice of not giving her any orders.

He never told her directly: "Do this." But he disposed her to "make
proposals herself." He believed that "love was the great artisan in in that
task."[8]

In the Camp of the Possession

Parachuted into the camp of the possession, Father Surin can change
the methods, but not the terrain. He can give it a spiritual sense, but
he remains no less subject to the law of that "place," which a history has
progressively circumscribed. He is *inside*. He thinks in consequence. Not
for a second does he doubt the reality of the possession. How could
he, without betraying the cause he received the mission of defending?
Encountering the tourists of Loudun, "he could not understand how

several wise persons, even fathers of the Company [of Jesus], several of whom had been there a full fortnight for these spectacles, had recommended to him so strongly not to let himself be taken by surprise, but to examine carefully to see if there was not some fiction in all that."[9]

Besides, for him, is it not a revelation? From out of the dark struggle he has carried on for years with himself, seeking God in the depths of anguish, beating at the doors of his own limits, he *perceives* at last the true adversary. One morning day breaks in Loudun, and makes him visible, as it did to Jacob, the enemy of the night.

A Colony

But Surin's interpretation primarily reveals the economic and social condition of the exorcists in Loudun. Their isolation in the town increases at the same time that curious folk come from more distant places. The possession, a spectacle for out-of-towners, is no longer the affair of the residents of Loudun (except for the local merchants), but rather a dependence nourished and sought after by outsiders: conducted henceforth by these austere and learned religious who replace the colorful local figures; financed by Paris, or by unknown funds, or by sums levied on the town; offered to a public of city-dwellers, gentlemen, men of erudition, adventurers or tourists who stop for one, five, eight, or fifteen days (these are the usual lengths of stay).

It even becomes obnoxious. To the first group of exorcists, Fathers Surin and Bachelerie, five other Jesuits are to be added, in response to reports (December 26, January 5 and 18) from the bishop of Nîmes to Richelieu. Plus two Carmelite fathers. Plus aides. Now, by decree, Laubardemont presumes to requisition from the local people lodgings for all this fine gentry. He enjoins the municipality to ready "twelve or fifteen houses and rooms and quarters" and, in the meantime, "declares to be at the costs and expense of said township" the ecclesiastics, "their retainers and train, inasmuch as several of said exorcists have already arrived and were obliged, for lack of other lodgings, to stay in the inns."[10]

After a cool welcome, they are put up in the castle, a place of honor and solitude at the height of the town.

Laubardemont, having failed to receive the funds intended for the purchase of a new convent from M. des Roches, also decides to seize "the college building," the Protestant school, to house his Ursulines. He calls out the archers of Poitiers against the mob of Huguenot women.

Finally, appeal is made to the Royal Treasury. Msgr. Anthyme Cohon, the bishop of Nîmes, having been well informed by Jeanne des Anges in the course of a trip through Loudun in late December, sets forth the situation for the cardinal:

> The pensions of all the religious women, both professed and novice, amount to 900 *livres*. On which they owe each year, for the residence of their house, the sum of 250 *livres* in interest. The mother superior told me that with 2,000 *livres* per year, she can maintain her community respectably. Thus, she needs about 500 *écus* from charity, during the course of the evil, to keep out of extreme misery.

Jeanne has a cool head when she is not on stage. As for the exorcists, the bishop continues,

> His Excellency will, if he pleases, order through M. de Bullion [Claude de Bullion, superintendent of finances] a certain and insured fund for their food, which M. de Laubardemont will procure from the lowest bidder and at a discount for the six Jesuit fathers and Sieurs Du Pin [of the Oratory of Tours] and Morans [of the diocese of Poitiers]. Because for the Capuchins and for the Carmelite fathers, Monseigneur will pay for their upkeep as he wishes, assigning for that purpose some part of funds to their convents, which make withdrawals and pay for their food.[11]

The result: From his privy purse, "the king gave appointment for the upkeep of the Jesuit fathers, who created a community in Loudun, and monseigneur the cardinal gave 2,000 francs per year to the religious women."[12]

A financial and psychological enclave organizes itself, more and more cut off from the local life, except for purposes of profit, of piety (as when one makes a pilgrimage), or leisure (as when one goes to the circus). It is in this closed field that Surin plants his *mystics*.

A Strange Dialogue

"Father Surin spends his life in continual fasting and prayers for the relief of the mother superior," writes Msgr. Cohon to Richelieu.[13] Wounded, uncertain of his strength, the Jesuit throws himself into a "battle" of souls. He also knows the importance of the stakes. The bishop expresses this in speaking of Jeanne des Anges: "All the pacts are addressed to her alone, and hence we conjecture that after her deliverance, that of the others will follow unhindered."[14]

She knows it as well as, or even better than, the Jesuit. She resists him. As is her custom, she "applies herself to knowing his mood" and, by "a thousand and one little dodges," she eludes him. She "does not take pleasure in his wanting to penetrate [her] interior." She "avoids as far as possible speaking to him" while he "seeks her at all times." Patient, he keeps on. She resists stubbornly, but finally "there is formed in [her] so great a despair . . . that [she] resolves to bring about her own death."[15] Which is a way of saying that she gives in.

Jeanne's resistance was less dangerous for him than her assent becomes. A strange dialogue begins, and goes on for hours, days, weeks. He begins praying before her. In the presence of a witness who is not an interlocutor, he gives voice to spiritual flights he never allowed himself, or was never able, to express. Little by little, she lets herself be won over by a passion of which, shrewd little girl that she was, she had never suspected the existence. But also, in this face-to-face encounter that is not one, he immerses himself; he is elated; he wears himself out; in one movement, he pursues the logic of redemption to its conclusion, which entails that the doctor must take the illness upon himself to cure it; he sympathizes with the affliction of the hysteric and denies himself the means of resisting it. On her part, anticipating the experience she senses, once again "taking her cue from his mood," she already play-acts what she is beginning to desire, and these first fruits, interspersed with posturing, prematurely excite the confessor, awaiting them with wide-eyed attention. Is he not finding his own words in her? Thus, the more he draws her to his own heights, the more he is deluding her; but since she sees the gestures in which she puts an uncertain sincerity authenticated by him, why would she hesitate, despite her doubts, to think she has arrived? Does she know what it is?

The Exorcist Obsessed

By January 1635 he begins to be "obsessed by the devil, suffering strange effects": cephalalgies, dyspnoeas, fits of trembling, sudden walking problems, coenaesthesic hallucinations. He is giving in. In March it gets worse:

> It happened, then [he relates, casting a quasi-medical eye himself as if upon an object that is breaking], around the time of Lent, that one evening, having lain down in his bed to sleep as usual, he began to feel the presence of the demon, who first began to walk on him as would an animal, and, from on top of the covers, to press down on him at different points on his head

and body, as would a cat with his paws. This did not surprise
him much. But after that, he felt on his skin as if a snake had
crawled in and wrapped himself around, and by its bites, more
poisonous than painful, gave him much suffering.[16]

Then the affliction moves from night to day, from the private to the
public:

> Besides that, when I would leave the house and walk to see the
> mother, he [the devil] would go into my feet and make them
> heavy, as if my shoes were leaden.
>
>   When I was at the exorcism [there are still a few more] and
> was performing it, reciting what is in the ritual, he would leave
> the possessed mother in a moment and slip into me, and would
> always begin his operation with the bottom of the stomach, and
> there he would always inflict such pain that I could have no
> peace unless I lay on the ground. And, lying down, the agitations
> would seize me in all my limbs.[17]

Surin's state deteriorates, the prioress's improves. To Laubardemont,
who sends her a "beautiful chasuble" for the convent, she writes on May
8 of her fear that the Jesuit's misfortunes "may scare off others from
devoting themselves to this toilsome labor."[18] On May 3 Surin writes to
Father Doni d'Attichy, an old friend who is living in Amiens at the time:

"Two Souls within Me"

> For three and a half months, I have never been without a devil
> at my side as I am performing my duties. Things have gotten to
> the point where God has allowed, I believe because of my sins,
> something that has perhaps never been seen in the Church: that
> in the exercise of my ministry the devil passes from the body of
> the possessed person and, coming into mine, assaults me,
> knocks me over backward, and agitates and tortures me visibly,
> possessing me for several hours like an energumen.
>
>   I cannot explain to you what happens in me during this
> time and how that spirit unites itself with mine without depriving
> me either of my senses or of my freedom of soul, and becoming
> nevertheless as another myself, and as if I had two souls, one of
> which is dispossessed of its body and the use of its organs, and
> stands aside, watching the doings of the one that has entered
> it. These two spirits do battle with each other in the same field
> that is the body; and the soul itself is as if divided and, by a part

of itself, is the subject of diabolical impressions and, by the
other, the subject of movements that are its own or that God
gives it. At the same time, I feel a great peace beneath the good
pleasure of God, and, without knowing how, an extreme rage
and aversion for Him, and that shows itself as impetuous out-
bursts to separate myself from Him that astonish those who see
them; at the same time a great joy and sweetness and, on the
other hand, a sadness that shows itself by lamentations and cries
like those of the damned. I feel the state of damnation and know
it, and feel as if pierced by arrows of despair in this foreign soul
that seems to be mine, and the other soul, which finds itself in
full confidence, scoffs at such feelings, and curses in all freedom
Him who causes them. I even feel that the same cries that leave
my mouth come equally from these two souls, and am unable
to tell if it be happiness that draws them forth or the extreme
furor that fills me. . . .

When the other possessed see me in that state, it is a pleasure to see how they triumph and how the devils make sport of
me: "Physician, heal thyself! Get up in the pulpit straightaway.
How lovely 'twill be to hear *that* preach, after having rolled about
in public!" . . .

That is where I am at this time, almost every day. Great
disputes are arising about it. *"Et factus sum magna quaestio"* ["And
I became a great question"]: whether there is possession;
whether such mishaps can befall the ministers of the Church.
Some say it is a chastisement of God on me and punishment for
some illusion; others say other things; and I remain where I am
and would not change my fortune with another, being firmly
persuaded that there is nothing better than being reduced to
great extremity. The one I am in is such that I have very few
free operations; when I want to speak, I am cut short; at table,
I cannot carry a morsel to my mouth; at confession, all at once
I forget my sins, and I can feel the devil coming and going in
me as in his house. No sooner do I gather my thoughts for meditation, than he is there; in prayer he takes a thought away from
me when he pleases; when my heart begins to swell in God, he
fills it with rage; he makes me sleep when he will; he wakes me
when he will; and publicly, by the mouth of his possessed, he
brags he is my master, to which I have nothing to gainsay, having
the reproach of my conscience and on my head the sentence

pronounced against sinners. I must suffer it, and revere the order of divine providence to which all creatures must submit.[19]

The New Enigma

Factus sum magna quaestio: it is the new interrogation of Loudun. Father
d'Attichy, who has many literary connections, passes the letter on. This
text circulates, as many others of Surin already have. Numerous contemporary copies still exist. It is immediately published in Poitiers, in Paris.
The letter traverses the pious milieux, moves on to the curious and the
learned. On July 1, 1635, Father Mersenne writes to Peiresc, who, from
Aix-en-Provence, had already obtained information about Loudun in
1634 from Father Gilles de Loches: "I do not know . . . whether you
know that a Jesuit father, having gone to Loudun to exorcise, was himself
possessed or obsessed, as is shown by his own letters."[20]

Peiresc answers Mersenne on July 17: "If the possession or obsession
of this good exorcising father has progress, it will be more notable than
all other things of that nature, which commonly befall the very weak
spirits of little womenfolk."[21]

On July 24 he again writes one of his Parisian correspondents, M. de
Saint-Sauveur Du Puy, an erudite and bibliophile like himself:

> This little printed work by Father Surin is indeed bizarre. An-
> other written account was being circulated here that seems to
> be from him, and that is not badly composed. You have it here,
> though I have no doubt that it is already known to you; but just
> in case you may not have seen it, perhaps you would not be
> displeased to see it, in connection with the other one.[22]

Another publication of 1635, published in Poitiers, Paris, and Lyons,
the *Relation véritable de ce qui s'est passé aux exorcismes des religieuses possédées
de Loudun en la présence de Monsieur, frère unique du roi*, devotes much
space to the "case" of the Jesuit, given that on that day, May 10, the
wounded exorcist is again "thrown to the ground on his back" and "again
thrown onto the pavement, in the presence of his highness [Monsieur,
the king's only brother] and his court."[23] While the shows go on for the
public's satisfaction, Surin is going under. He is a humiliated child who
continues his correspondence with Father d'Attichy, asking for advice,
as do many others, to whom the sick man still has time to respond:

> I pray our Lord that it please Him to bind your soul to his with
> so many chains of gold of his love that it never escapes him. If

I could serve in that respect in anything, I refuse nothing. May
Your Reverence conduct himself as if I were his slave. . . . That
is my condition toward Your Reverence, added to that of being
his very humble brother.[24]

He can write to Laubardemont, in September: "We who treat what is
most important, we know something entirely different about it than the
spectators of the exorcisms."[25]

The Literature of "Triumph"

Meanwhile, on the terrain to which piety has withdrawn, the victories
multiply, interspersed with exits of the devils, miracles, and conversions
celebrated in the publications of a press that is henceforth specialized:

> *Relation de la sortie du démon Balaam du corps de la mère prieure des ursulines
> de Loudun* . . . (Paris and Poitier, 1635).
>
> *Copie d'une lettre escrite à Mgr. l'évesque de Poitiers par un des Pères Jésuites
> qui exorcisent à Loudun, contenant un bref récit de l'éjection de Léviatan,
> chef de cinquante démons* . . . (Paris: J. Martin, 1635; Poitiers: the widow
> Mesnier; and Orléans).
>
> *Traitté de la Melancholie, sçavoir si elle est la cause des Effets que l'on remarque
> dans les Possédées de Loudun. Tiré des Reflexions de M.* [Pilet de la Ménar-
> dière] *sur le Discours de M. D.* [Duncan] (La Flèche: M. Guyot and
> G. Laboë, 1635).
>
> *Les miraculeux Effects de l'Eglise Romaine sur les Estranges, horribles et effroy-
> ables actions des Demons et Princes des diables en la possession des Religieuses
> Ursulines et Filles séculières de la ville de Loudum, recueillis par M. de la
> Foucardière, prieur de Croysay, docteur en théologie* (Paris: Claude Morlot,
> 1635).
>
> *Lettre du R. P. Seurin, Jésuite, exorciste des religieuses ursulines à Loudun,
> écrite à un sien ami, où se voient les choses étranges arivées en sa personne,
> lesquelles excitent puissamment à la foi et à la crainte des jugements de Dieu*
> (Poitiers and Paris, 1635).
>
> *Relation véritable de ce qui s'est passé aux exorcismes des religieuses ursulines
> possédées de Loudun en la présence de Monsieur, frère unique du Roi, avec
> l'attestation des Exorcistes,* (Paris: J. Martin ["close to the copy printed
> in Poitiers"]; Lyons: J. Jacquemeton; and Poitiers, 1635).
>
> *In Actiones Juliodunensium Virginum, Francisci Pidoux, Doctoris Medici Picta-
> viensis, Exercitatio Medica* (Poitiers: J. Thoreau; 2nd ed. [apparently],
> 1635).
>
> *Relation de la sortie du Demon Balam du corps de la Mère Prieure des Ursulines
> de Loudun et ses épouvantables mouvemens et contorsions en l'Exorcisme.
> Avec l'Extrait du procès verbal* . . . (Paris: J. Martin; and Poitiers, 1635).
>
> Guillaume Rivet (pastor of the Reformed Church of Taillebourg) com-
> poses *La Defence des Droits de Dieu contre les inventions et artifices du Sieur*

Tranquille, supérieur des Capucins de La Rochelle (Saumur: Lesnier and Desbordes, 1635).

Admirable changement d'un jeune avocat en la cour [of Poitiers], *nouvellement opéré par le moyen d'un démon nommé Cédon dans les exorcismes des religieuses possédées de Loudun. Avec deux discours du même démon* . . . (La Flèche: G. Griveau, 1636; and Paris: J. Brunet, 1637).

La gloire de saint Joseph. Sur la relation authentique et véritable de ce qui s'est passé en la sortie d'Isacaron qui possédait le corps de la Mère Prieure des Religieuses Ursulines de Loudun . . . (dedicated to Msgr. the duc d'Orléans, the king's only brother) (Saumur: Louis Macé, 1636; Paris: J. Martin; Lyons: Claude Cayne; and so on).

Récit véritable de ce qui s'est passé à Loudun aux exorcismes des filles possédées, ensemble le miracle qui s'y est fait en présence de tous les assistants, by J. D. P. C. (letter from a Carmelite of Poitiers to a religious of his order) (Orléans: René Fremont, 1636).

Germana Deffensio Exercitationum Francisci Pidoux in Actiones Juliodunensium Virginum adversus Ulalium [Duval, a lawyer of Poitiers], preceded by a *Speculum mentis Eulalii Pictaviensis* (nonpaginated) (Poitiers: J. Thoreau, 1636).

Apologie pour M. Duncan, docteur en médecine, contre le Traité de la Melancholie du Sieur de la Mesnardière (no place, no date, but probably Saumur, 1636).

La guérison miraculeuse de soeur Jeanne des Anges . . . *par l'onction de Saint Joseph* (Saumur: Macé, 1637).

Les interrogatoires et exorcismes nouvellement faits à un démon . . . *avec les réponses du démon au R. P. Matthieu de Luché, capucin exorciste,* . . . *au grand estonnement du peuple* (Paris: J. Brunet; and La Flèche, 1637).

Les Miraculeux effets de la Vierge, de saint Joseph et de saint François dans le soulagement et délivrance des Filles Ursulines . . . (Paris, 1637).

Représentation et sommaire des signes miraculeux qui ont esté faits à la gloire de Dieu et de son Eglise en la sortie des sept démons qui possédaient le corps de la mère prieure des religieuses ursulines de Loudun (Rouen: D. Ferrand [1637]).[26]

Relation de la mort du P. Tranquille, l'un des exorcistes de Loudun . . . (Poitiers, 1638). Account sent by Father Benoît of Loudun to Father Eléazar of Loudun.

As much the word *miracle,* the name of the prioress shines forth on all the posters of these booklets. Her portrait is contained in the next to last. In the course of a succession of suspenses, illnesses and cures, deliverances and exits, she brings a new character to light. From Surin, she learns the whole vocabulary of *mystics,* at the same time, no doubt, that she intuits its meaning. She gives advice. She receives company. The pious or the affluent tourists are not lacking, as attested by the *Relation d'une visite faite par D. pendant huit jours, sur l'invitation de la duchesse d'Aiguillon, aux possédées de Loudun, et des visites faites aux mêmes possédées par la Duchesse elle-même, par Mademoiselle de Rambouillet, les marquis de Brézé et de Sablé, Monsieur de Voiture,* and so on.[27]

A Suspect Spirituality

Surin is treading a path, the steps of which he has not finished descending. But he perseveres in his task, now standing, now on the ground. He sees more people. He writes, a lot, but his work is for later, when Job will get back up, more than twenty years hence, worn of body but made peaceful by the trial he has gone through, having found the sun at the bottom of the well, and discovering in a late-coming autumn the secret of being "like a child in the bosom of Our Lord, having as little care as at the age of eight."

Around him, a kind of spiritual school forms, a "mystical" group, through which many visitors pass who will not soon forget him. But he is all the more suspect for that. In Rome, Father Vitelleschi, the superior general of the Jesuits, preoccupied with putting an end to the Loudun activity of his religious, also receives denunciations and accusations of the ailing father. On August 28, 1636, he writes to Surin's provincial superior:

> On Father Surin, whom Your Reverence praises much, I receive from our fathers numerous memoirs. They say that for some time he has believed himself possessed by the Word Incarnate as much as by the demon; that consequently he holds the Word to be at the origin of his speech and gestures, just as he holds the evil spirit to be the source of his obsessional movements. . . . They also added that he was not very submissive to the superiors and not very obedient. I await Your Reverence's advice.[28]

In October 1636 he is withdrawn from Loudun. He will return from June to November 1637. In Loudun, after having reproached him greatly for "giving himself over to spiritual inventions" and not knowing the trade, "the other exorcists also adopt his method."[29] Disappearing, he leaves a trace.

~ 14 ~

The Triumph of Jeanne des Anges

After many others, a "marvel" again occurs on February 7, 1637. Sick from the after-effects of an ill-advised exorcism imposed by the hot-headed Father Ressès, given up on by the physicians, reduced "to a state of extremity" following a pulmonary congestion, Jeanne des Anges lies in agony in the convent.

The Handsome Angel

> Then [she relates] I had the view of a great cloud that surrounded the bed where I lay. On the right side I saw my good angel who was of rare beauty, having the form of a young man of about eighteen. He had a head of long, shiny blond hair, that covered the right side of the shoulder of my confessor [Father Ressès].

Jeanne forgets a detail that Surin naively reports:

> She retained the idea [the image] of the face of Saint Joseph, which she later had painted, and, the duc de Beaufort having come a few days later to see the exorcism, she told me that the angel had a wig like the prince's.[1]

The young François de Vendôme, duc de Beaufort, the son of Gabrielle d'Estrées, is eighteen at the time. The amorous conquests of this fair-haired young dandy, who would later be called *le roi des Halles,* were as famous as his duels. One might wonder whether his visit to Loudun might have occurred before February 7. Jeanne will relate the fact much later to Surin, and she has an intelligent memory.

I also saw Saint Joseph in the form and feature of a man, having a face more brightly shining than the sun, with a great head of hair. His beard was chestnut brown. He appeared to me with a majesty far more than human; he placed his hand on my right side where my great pain had always been. It seems to me he applied an unction on that part, after which I felt my external senses return and found myself entirely cured. I said to the father and the religious women who were in my room: "It doesn't hurt anymore. I am healed by the grace of God." I asked for my clothes and got up immediately. . . . Two days later, I remembered that I had only wiped the unction with which I was cured with my chemise. I called the mother sub-prioress and asked her to come to my room to examine the spot where unction had been performed. Having done so, we both smelled an admirable odor. I took off that chemise. They cut it at the waist. We found five rather large drops of this divine balm that gave forth an excellent odor . . . This marvel being known, it is incredible how great the devotion of the people for that sacred unction was, and how many miracles God wrought through it.[2]

"They" do everything for that. The *Guérison miraculeuse de soeur Jeanne des Anges* . . . soon appears in Saumur, with a warm recommendation from the bishop of Poitiers. The account will, moreover, be further embellished. Seven years later, after having repeated it so many times, the prioress will send Father Saint-Jure the perfected and official version, the "vulgate" of the miracle.[3]

The Miraculate Woman

A beautiful career begins for the five "marvelous" drops, the sacred chemise, the bits of paper and cotton that had absorbed some of the unguent. So much for the decor of the miraculate woman. Her very body is illustrated with the names IOSEPH and MARIA, which they found traced out on her hand at the time of the last exits of devils. There remains a last demon, Behemoth. On March 19, 1637, he demands the honor of being driven out by Father Surin.

After much resistance and violence, he answered that it did not depend on him [to exit], and that God wanted Father Surin to help drive him out.[4]

The prioress herself wrote that to Laubardemont. All the characters of the story must surround the chariot of the delivered one. Her demon also requires a trip to Annecy, for a pilgrimage to the grave of François de Sales. The projects grow, piety becomes publicity, and it seems that the Jesuit exorcists, those "learned masters" called by Laubardemont, commit themselves completely to the enterprise. To the incredulity on the other side, there corresponds total credulity on this side. Their superior general becomes concerned on July 9, 1637, though he does agree to the provisional return of the exhausted man from whom so many now expect the closure of an affair that has dragged on too long. From Rome, he writes the rector of Poitiers:

> Though we do this truly with regret, but not without reasons, we have reached the decision to send Fathers Anginot and Surin to Loudun. It is our most fervent wish that our people should disengage themselves as soon as possible from this affair, and we will bring them all necessary help to this end . . .
>
> They say that the fathers of Loudun give the hand of the prioress to be kissed by everyone because of the blessed names said to be sculpted upon it by the Devil; that they have cotton, paper, and similar objects touch an unguent attributed to Saint Joseph; that despite the contrary advice of competent persons, they distribute them as authentic relics; that they spread word among the public, by their own authority, of the miracles accomplished by these relics, which we however hear are the source of many evils. . . .

Putting the Credulous on Notice

> I beg Your Reverence to bring remedy to so many aberrant deeds with sufficient efficacy so that we may not ultimately be forced to withdraw our people from these exorcisms. Let them accomplish their task, no longer in public, but within the house, as I recently wrote to Your Reverence; let them interrogate the demon only on the necessary points, for the purpose of his expulsion; let them not prolong eternally an occupation that has lasted all too long. So many of our apostolic workers could be more usefully employed elsewhere.
>
> At first they said, on the faith of a revelation, that the demon was to be driven out at Annecy; now they say, based on another revelation by the same woman, that he will not be, if Father Surin does not return to Loudun. Here we have statements that are manifestly at cross purposes. And after having acquiesced to almost all our fathers' demands, we learn of some

new project, while being assailed daily with new complaints about the imprudence of our exorcists. Whether it be by yourself, by the rector of Poitiers, or by some other father who is not too credulous and naive, Your Reverence should seriously maintain them in the strictest obedience.[5]

Surin, on his return, is "most ill." Jeanne des Anges, under his direction, spends days in retreat according to Saint Ignatius of Loyola's *Spiritual Exercises*, but, as she will say later to Guy Lanier, the abbot of Vaux, grand vicar of the bishop of Angers:

In the last Exercises the good Father had me perform, he gave me no subject. He wanted me to present myself before God in simplicity to receive or suffer whatever he pleased . . . I found great freedom of spirit in that way of proceeding.[6]

The Deliverance

It is in the course of this retreat that "the mother was entirely delivered by the expulsion of the last demon, Behemoth." On October 15, the day of Saint Theresa, "Surin celebrates mass," though very listless.

[At the moment that] he brings the communion to the mother at the little window of the grille, holding the holy host in his hand, without his having given any order to the devil, as he was saying *"Corpus Domini nostri Jesu Christi,"* the mother . . . went into a furious contortion, bending backward, having a face rendered horrifying by the presence of the devil, raising her left hand, turning the palm upward. The father saw manifestly, above the names Mary and Joseph formed in beautiful vermilion, bleeding letters, the name Jesus, as clearly as he ever saw anything. But as her hand was turned in such a way that the thumb was toward the inside where the religious women were, and the bottom of the hand toward the outside where the father was, said father did not see the forming of the name FRANÇOIS DE SALES. Suddenly, the mother came out of her contortion, the devil having left her, and having returned to her kneeling posture, back to her usual self, she received the body of our Lord, which took the demon's place. And since then, for the rest of her life, she has felt none of the devils' ordinary operations.[7]

Jeanne's devil having won out, the pilgrimage was decided upon. Surin is part of the luggage.

> My soul [he will say, speaking of this period] was like a palace,
> all the doors of which had been shut, with locks and chains
> everywhere, leaving only the janitor's room.[8]

He is treated as a "madman," and indeed, he also writes,

> he fell into that mishap in such an authentic manner that it
> would almost be an affront to common sense to say it was not
> so, because of the strange things that happened to him. . . .
> He can confess that he did not fear this title much, because
> a long while earlier he had offered himself to God for that, and
> to have this lovely feather in his hat, that no one would wish to
> have.[9]

Stricken with temporary aphasia, he leaves with Father Thomas, but,
on the order of the superiors, by a different route than Jeanne. He will
join her in Lyons, going through the Massif Central. The prioress put
Paris on her program.

A Triumphant Tour

During that crisis, probably more benign or intermittent than Surin says,
the famous trip to Savoy was organized. For Jeanne des Anges, who left
Loudun on April 26, it was a triumphant five-month tour: Tours, Paris,
Moulins, Nevers, Lyons, Grenoble, Annecy, and so on. Parliament members, high-ranking gentry, bishops, the Condés, Richelieu, Queen Anne
of Austria, King Louis XIII came successively, as did the crowds who
squeezed into the parlors and hotels where the prioress stopped, to do
homage to the hand "sculpted by the devil" and to the chemise marked
by the unguent of Saint Joseph. In her story of a forlorn little girl who
becomes a walking miracle, insatiable for successes that never reassure
her, she puts her princes, her archbishops, her palaces and coaches on
parade, their seductiveness just slightly veiled by the edifying phrases
she casts over that brilliant equipage.

When the prioress arrived in Tours with M. de Morans and Sister Gabrielle de Colombiers, the sub-prioress, Msgr. the Archbishop Bertrand
de Chaux

> sent already that evening one of his officers to invite me to come
> and visit him. The next day, he sent us one of his chaplains with
> his coach, to take me to the archbishop's palace. . . . He received
> us with extraordinary kindness. . . . Several persons of quality
> were in the room, and, among others, monseigneur the bishop

of Boulogne, the nephew of said archbishop. Msgr. President Cothereau, who had been one of the judges who condemned Grandier, was also there. They all admire the names imprinted on my hand. . . .

The rumor of the impression of these names having spread throughout the town, the people crowded in haste to see them, so much so that four or five thousand a day came to behold them.

On Tuesday, April 30, in the parlor of the Ursulines, three physicians "looked attentively at the form and beauty of the characters so well marked on the skin of my hand."

On May 5, a flattering visit by Gaston d'Orléans, the king's brother.

On Thursday, May the sixth, we set out from Tours. A dame of quality, the wife of a councilor of parliament, named Mme du Tronchet, took her seat in the coach with us and led the conversation along the way.[10]

At Amboise, "the parlor had to be kept open until eleven o'clock in the evening" to satisfy the crowds and "let them see my hand." Similarly in Blois, in Orléans where Laubardemont comes to join her, and finally in Paris, where they arrive together on May 11.

The Conquest of Paris

In Paris, Jeanne is lodged at the baron's residence:

councilors of State, *maîtres des requêtes,* coctors at the Sorbonne, religious of all orders . . . the cuc de Chevreuse, the prince of Guéménée, and several other persons of quality often came to see me.

They "come rushing to see me," they "admire my hand," they "consider what has happened to my body as a result of the demons": that tireless litany of the *Autobiographie* punctuates the procession of the body miraculate. At the heart of the monstrance, in the middle of the crowd, there is the sacred hand.

After the visit to the archbishop of Paris, who, still according to Jeanne, says loudly: "what is for the glory of God must not be hidden," the holy sacrament is exposed to the public:

The people came rushing to see me again, so much so that they had to expose me to the public from four in the morning till ten at night, with torches.

They put me in a low room in which there was a window at a man's height that opened onto a courtyard of the house. I was seated, my arm on a pillow, and my hand was extended out the window, to be seen by the people. Persons of the first quality could not enter that room because the ways leading to it were blocked by the populace. I wasn't given time to hear mass or take my meals.

Then comes the meeting with Richelieu, in Rueil.

M. de Laubardemont took us there . . . monseigneur the cardinal having been bled that day, all the doors of the castle of Rueil were closed, even to the bishops and marshals of France; however, we were brought into his antechamber even though he was in bed. He ordered a gentleman and his physician to welcome us and give us his greeting.

"Now This Is Admirable"

We were led at his order into a room where dinner stood prepared. It was magnificent, and we were served by his pages. Toward the end of the dinner, monseigneur the cardinal had M. de Laubardemont called and asked him whether there was any impropriety in his greeting us being in bed, fearing that that might hurt us. He assured him it was not so. He came to get us for him.

We approached his bed; we kneeled down to receive his benediction. I remained in that posture to speak to him. He didn't want me to, assuring me he would not allow it. The contest of politeness on his part and humility on ours lasted rather a long time, but finally I was obliged to obey. He had an armchair brought in and bade me sit in it.

Monseigneur the cardinal began the conversation by telling me that I had very great obligations toward God for having chosen me in this unfortunate century to serve his glory, the honor of the Church, the conversion of several souls, and the confounding of the wicked. He added that it was my great good fortune to have suffered for this reason the blame, ignominy, reproofs, accusations, calumny, and generally all the operations of the demons in the course of several years. . . .

Monseigneur the cardinal had me approach him to see my
hand more closely: having looked at it with great attention, he
spoke these words: "Now this is admirable. . . ."

Then, I humbly beseeched his eminence to continue his
protection and favors in support of our community, assuring
him that we would continue our vows and prayers to bring Heav-
en's blessings upon him.

Monseigneur the cardinal told me that he would have liked
to have seen Father Surin.

Msgr. de Laubardemont intervened and spoke of the unction that Saint Joseph had performed on me, and that had cured
me. He was shown the piece of chemise on which said unction
had been performed; seeing it, he was touched with respect and
expressed great feeling of piety, for, before taking it into his
hands, although he was sick, he uncovered his head and smelled
it and kissed it twice, saying: "That smells perfectly good." He
touched a reliquary, which he had at his bedside, to it. While
holding that chemise with respect and admiration, I told him
the story of how I had been cured.

After Richelieu's welcome in Rueil, that of the queen in Saint-Ger-
main-en-Laye is no less flattering. After a lengthy discourse on the dire
straits of the Loudun community, "the queen desired to see my hand
marked with the sacred names. I showed it to her. She took it and held
it more than an hour, admiring the thing that had never been seen since
the beginning of the Church."

The princesse de Condé, who is present, is absolutely ecstatic. The
king comes and, with "joy on his face," says in a loud voice: "My belief
is strengthened." He calls and disabuses some unbelievers, whose names
the prioress, "by principle of charity," withholds.

A Monstrance

We must stop, because Paris, Melun, Montargis, Nevers, Lyons, Grenoble, Chambéry, Annecy all spell out the same epiphany.[11] The sacred
hand is borne by that immobile prose as if by a reliquary, which it shares
with the precious unguent and the odoriferous chemise. There is no
longer any account, or journey, or story. It is just a mirror. Grandier,
here and there, is just one of the precious stones mounted in the *sun*
in which so many eyes, like pearls, gaze upon the beautiful object offered
for devotion. The hand of which Jeanne is but the guardian or the custo-

dial has replaced the "sacred finger" of which the exorcists were after all the mere carriers. As the texts say, the finger of God is there. In reality, *this* is the finger of God. Loudun is transformed henceforth into a caricature of the great baroque retables organized around the host.

In the middle, the monstrance: the prioress. But gradually she will also become, thanks to her "angel," the receptacle of a knowledge of the afterlife, the prophetess of the future of souls, the depository of counsels from heaven, the organizer of a pilgrimage and of a Central Office of good works, the head of a whole network of spiritual associations. In Bordeaux, Surin will only worry when he hears that she has come to the point of "maintaining a kind of shop, a bureau for finding out what should be done concerning marriages, trials, and the like."

In one corner of this tableau, Grandier and the demons, monsters now changed into caryatids and Atlases, have ceased being threats to become the foil, the *repoussoir* necessary to the overall decoration. As such, they participate in a rhetoric of images and a pious commerce.

The possession henceforth resembles the marks engraved on Jeanne's hand. One day in 1645 M. Balthasar de Monconys, on his way through Loudun, will flip a letter off these sacred words: "With the tip of my fingernail, with a light touch I removed the leg of the *M* [of the word MARIA], which surprised her greatly. . . . I was satisfied with that and took my leave of her."[12]

Yesterday's drama also falls away—a film and a scar on the surface of history. But we cannot take our leave of the prioress without wondering who she is.

A Fairy Tale

The Reverend Mother Jeanne des Anges came into the world on the second day of February of the year 1605. Her parents were of illustrious birth. Her father's name was Louis de Belcier, baron of Cozes, and her mother Charlotte de Gourmard, heir to the illustrious house of Chilles, both issued from or allied to the most considerable houses of Gascony. M. de Cozes had a brother and a sister from different beds; his brother's name was Louis de Barbézieux, lord of Nogeret, and his sister, Catherine de Belcier, was married to M. du Boudet, captain of the King's Guards under Henri IV. Madame her mother also had two brothers from two beds, one of whom was named M. de Saint-Donac Saint-Martin(?), and the other Msgr. Octave de Bellegarde, the archbishop of Sens.

M. and Mme de Cozes had nineteen children, fifteen of whom were seen to be living all together in their house, every one of whom was the best bred, rich in mind, and adorned with very advantageous natural talents. Their house was one of the most considerable of Saintonge, as much in nobility as in wealth. The income, which was twenty or thirty thousand *livres* of rent, was scarcely sufficient for the expenses that were ordinarily incurred, in such splendor did they live.[13]

Thus begins, like a fairy tale, the long, the sad, the strange story of "the venerable Mother Jeanne des Anges," as related by the Visitandine nuns of Rennes at the end of the seventeenth century, in a *Vie* [Life] replete with faithfully transcribed documents, but much less reliable in the interpretation of the "marvels," for which we are prepared by the idyllic tableau embroidered by these pious copyists, of children so well born, so rich, and so full of talents.

A Little Girl Disgraced

"Still very little," but "precocious, with a sweet and lively eye," of light brown complexion and ash-blond hair, Jeanne experienced a "disgrace" that left her scarred irremediably:

She found herself in danger of falling and wounding herself badly. She made such a violent effort to hold herself back that she dislocated her shoulder and twisted the small of her back, so that ever after her body was somewhat twisted, with one shoulder higher than the other. God used that disgrace to cause her father and mother to resolve more easily to give her to God in holy religion.[14]

A pious euphemism, it seems, for the mother resolved to "hide that daughter under a veil."

At the age of four or five, the child was sent to her aunt, at the Royal Abbey of Saintes. There she acquired a sound knowledge of Latin, and "the whole time she stayed at the abbey, she was always much loved; her sweet, lively, and playful temperament, her nature, which was obliging and pleasing to all who approached her, won her the esteem and affection of all, old and young alike." But after the death of her aunt, in 1611, another relative, also a Benedictine at Saintes, was much more severe with that child of an "inquiring" mind, "who wanted to conceive the most impenetrable things," and who stood out in the convent, not only for her exceptional affability, but already for her "fainting spells" and visions. Such strictness made the young girl disgusted with the Benedictine life, and she received permission to return to Cozes.

The Humiliated Father

Her father is joyful at seeing her again, for he had a "special predilection for his dear daughter" and "he had her read holy texts, particularly in the evening, to get her to go to sleep, he would say, in good thoughts." The baroness's reception was less warm. "Madame her mother was a very uncompromising person"; she "had a great inclination to keep her daughter hidden . . . because of the defect in her figure. . . . While she showed off her sisters," she "kept her very simply attired in order to deprive her of the means to show herself in public," which Jeanne "could not bear without great sorrow." So the girl turned to her father, taking "the liberty of telling him of her desire to meet with society, at least when they came to the house." When a suitor appeared for the young lady, "M. de Cozes immediately gave his consent; his wife did not, making the plans she had for her daughter clear," but the latter "hoped her father would at last be the master." Things did not turn out that way. The handsome beau departed, withdrawing to the Jesuit noviciate. Jeanne, impressed, decided to become a religious, despite a new admirer who presented himself (this one accepted by her mother) and, in a sudden decision, chose above all others the order in which Saint Augustine's rule was followed, that saint whose *Confessions* she had so often read to her father.

The Means to Show Herself

In 1622 she enters the Poitiers Ursulines. Her noviciate is marked by a few excesses of behavior, quite understandable but already spectacular, and too consciously connected with an awareness of the public: she devotes herself to the most repulsive patients, to whom she demands to be assigned for the greater edification of her sisters, or, at the other extreme, "before all the assembled religious" she declares one day that she wants to revert to "her secular clothing" and leave the convent. She makes her profession on September 7, 1623. Intelligent and flexible, skillful and zealous, she makes herself indispensable; she is charged with, or charges herself with, a thousand and one occupations, which distract her. She will say as much in her *Autobiographie*, written on the model of Saint Teresa's *Life* or Saint Augustine's *Confessions*, those two works she read so frequently:

I spent these three years [in Poitiers, September 1623–July 1627] in great libertinage, in such a manner as to have no application to the presence of God. There was no time that I found so long as that which the rule obliges us to spend in prayer; which is why, when I found some pretext to exempt myself from it, I embraced it with affection, without going to the trouble of making it up. I applied myself to the reading of all sorts of books, but it was not from a desire for my advancement, but only to make myself appear to be a clever girl, accomplished at conversation, and to make myself capable of surpassing the others in all sorts of company.[15]

She does not seek entertainment; nothing distracts her from herself or truly interests her; neither her readings nor her conversations captivate her. No affection, none but that of the little girl who dreamed of "showing herself," and of the nun who wants to "appear . . . in all sorts of company." It is hardly surprising that, later, she confesses on several occasions, but as if it were merely the effect of the "possession," to "an inconceivable hardness of heart": it is the obverse of her "tenderness toward [her-] self."

The Little Dodges

On August 31, 1625, Msgr. de La Rocheposay, the bishop of Poitiers, authorizes the creation of a new Ursuline convent in Loudun. The first women will not move in until July 22, 1627. In the meantime, Jeanne asks "with great insistence" to be one of them:

They made some objections. I did not give in to any of them. On the contrary, I employed all kinds of stratagems to achieve my plan. I succeeded, and was one of the number who came to set up the establishment. I had convinced myself that, in changing residences, I would be able to change myself more easily in a small house, with few people, than in a large one, where I found my rest. But alas, I was quite deluded, for instead of working toward the mortification of my passions and the practice of my rules, I applied myself to recognizing the moods of the people of the region, to have much commerce with several. . . . I took care to make myself necessary to my superiors, and, since there were few of us religious, the superior was obliged to call on me for all the offices of the community. It is not that she would not have liked to do without me, having other religious more capable and better than me, but I fooled her by a thousand and one little dodges. . . . I was so adept at accommodating myself to her mood and winning her over that she found nothing well done unless it were I who did it, and she even thought me good and virtuous. That so swelled my heart that I had no trouble performing many acts that appeared worthy of esteem. I knew how to dissimulate; I used hypocrisy in order that my superior should keep the good feelings she had for me, and that she should favor my inclinations and wishes.[16]

Jeanne des Anges portrays her whole self in that confession of shortcomings that are, in themselves, all too common. Her work spins the web in which she catches herself. With these "little dodges," she will continue to "pretend," to "adroitly do what [she] can to avoid her director," to "dissimulate," and so on, offering this mobile mask that protects her and allows her not to "uncover the state of her conscience." "*Little* dodges," she says: the adjective punctuates the entire *Autobiographie;* it disculpates the penitent halfway, but the gesture of humility it describes betrays, in that *little* woman, what are really her dreams of greatness and her feelings: "little attractiveness," "little despair," "little apprehensions," "little changes," "little stratagems," and so on. The word that minimizes the affirmation is already a flight, at the same time as being the wink of someone who is never really there. Thus the effort made "to recognize the moods of the people of the region" will not cease fixing itself upon other objects: after the superior, and, earlier, the abbess of Saintes, it will be her exorcist, Father Surin: "I resolved to study the mood of him to whom I would be given." How many visitors and, more fearsome, how many women will be studied in this way by the docile look that seeks to please, and fill their expectations in advance!

Changing

Is it bad faith, duplicity? It is not so simple. Jeanne will have the desire, ever more sincere, almost pathetic, to *change* in "changing residences." Later, she will change personas: she will be the new Teresa of Avila after having been the new Madeleine de Demandolx, the "mystic" after having been the "possessed"; she will drop one mask for another. She is the beneficiary of the role suggested to her by the circumstances, and by which she is not entirely duped, fragile, and cornered, as it were, into defending herself in these little ways and by these "little dodges." Yet she is never identical with her personas even though they may assure her of a vengeance or a triumph over a more powerful environment.

She aspires to become authentic, but imagines the conversion in the form of another place or another episode that replaces the preceding: it will be yet another face foreign to her own, formed for, and by, others.

After her "conversion" in June 1635, her visions, and her vow "of the most perfect" or "of the greatest glory of God (1636), approved by Father Jacquinot, the Provincial of Aquitaine," give her the situation of another Teresa of Avila. She has the marks, the successes, and the reputation of a great thaumaturge: the names IESUS, MARIA, JOSEPH, F. D. SALLES are mysteriously traced out on her left hand (1635–37); Saint Joseph, in appearing to her, "miraculously" cures her in February 1637 and in December 1639; she goes on her triumphant tour through France in 1638. She exercises the superiorship almost her whole life, being indefinitely reelected in Loudun (except for the period 1657–60) and sought after by other convents; she affirms that she communicates with her angel; and from Brittany, Paris, Guyenne, and Anjou, requests are made for her spiritual directives and the oracles of the "holy angel"; her "revelations" are recopied, circulated, and quickly printed.

So Many Ruses

When Surin treats her as "the only person" with whom he "feels the confidence to say . . . [his] deepest thoughts"; when, old and declining, he rejoices at thus still having the means of "sharing the morsel that God gives [him]," and states that "with her [he] has almost no reservations in saying [his] feeling and any intentions and operations or good dispositions of grace whatsoever": perhaps such confidence is understandable on the part of the apostle who paid with his health and his honor for the salvation of a poor girl confided to his care by chance. At any rate, the error on his part is inseparable from his affection for her. Nevertheless, these "communications" do not dull the intransigent clarity that makes him write one day to his confidante:

> I beg of you to put the foundation of the true spiritual life in sincerity of the heart. I hear so much said about you, and that there are in your conduct so many subtleties and ruses that it is difficult to find within you a spirit of truth, so many contradictions in the supernatural revelations and communications that one is hard put to found a good judgment on it and get a foothold on some good thing.[17]

Figures of the Other

The possession has no "true" historical explanation, since it is never possible to know who is "possessed" and by whom. The problem stems precisely from the fact that possession, or "alienation" as we would say, *is,* but *indeterminately,* and that the attempt to free oneself from it consists in transposing it, repressing it, or transferring it elsewhere: from a collectivity to an individual, from the Devil to reasons of State, from the demonic to devotion. The process of this necessary labor is unending.

The historian himself would be fooling himself if he believed he was rid of that strangeness internal to history by placing it somewhere on the outside, far from us, in a past closed with the last "aberrations" of yesteryear, as if "possession" were over with the possession at Loudun.

True, he too has received from society an exorcist's task. He is asked to eliminate the danger of the *other.* He belongs to those societies (ours is among them) that Lévi-Strauss characterizes by *anthropemy* (from *emein,* "to vomit"), contrasting them with the *anthropophagic* societies: the latter, he says "regard the absorption of certain individuals possessing dangerous powers as the only means of neutralizing those powers and even of turning them to advantage." On the contrary, our societies "have chosen the opposite solution, which consists in ejecting those dangerous individuals from the social body, and keeping them temporarily or permanently isolated . . . in establishments intended for that purpose."[1] Historiography can be placed among these "establishments," to the degree that it would be required to prove that menacing alterity, glimpsed in Loudun, is only a legend or a past, an eliminated reality.

In its historical form, this is true. The time of the possessions is dead. From this point of view, historiographical exorcism works. But the mechanisms brought into play by the uncertainty of epistemological and social criteria, in Loudun, and the necessity of establishing some, is taking place today with respect to other "sorcerers": excluding them still gives a group the means of defining and asserting itself. In the seventeenth century the phenomenon can be observed in a thousand and one forms, doubtless less visible than on the Loudun "stage," but that much more effective. Once the poison of the other no longer presents itself directly in religious language, social therapeutics and repression just take other forms.

Bound to a historical moment—that is, to the passage from religious criteria to political ones, from a cosmological and celestial anthropology to a scientific organization of natural objects ordered by the scrutiny of man—the possession of Loudun opens out also onto the strangeness of history, the reflexes triggered by its alterations, and the question that arises the moment there loom before us—different from the deviltries of former times but no less troubling—the new social figures of the other.

∼ Primary Sources and Bibliography ∼

The literature on Loudun is as enormous as it is uneven. This is especially true of the primary sources. There can be no question of presenting them here, given that, in this book, many of the important dossiers have had to be abridged, mentioned only in passing, or simply omitted. It was impossible to impose upon the readers either the mass of information gathered in the course of infernal travels in the archives, or the analysis of the metamorphoses of the possession through its bibliography.

Hence it will suffice to refer readers, on the one hand, to studies that offer good overviews of the primary sources or the bibliography, and, on the other hand, to a few fundamental books on the subject. Additional bibliographical references are given in the notes.

1. *The primary sources and the bibliography* are presented in the following works: C. Barbier, "Inventaire des pièces manuscrites relatives au procès d'U. Grandier, conservées à la bibliothèque de Poitiers," *Bulletin de la Société des Antiquaires de l'Ouest* (3rd trimester 1877): 153–54. L. Michel, "Les possédées de Loudun," MS of the Archives of the Society of Jesus of Toulouse (22, rue des Fleurs), analyzing a considerable quantity of documentation, though very apologetic. E. Jouin and V. Descreux, *Bibliographie occultiste et maçonnique. Répertoire d'ouvrages imprimés et mss relatifs à la Franc-maçonnerie, la Magie . . . jusqu'en 1717* (Paris, 1930). J. Texier, "Le procès d'Urbain Grandier" (thesis of the Faculty of Law of Poitiers, 1953). R. H. Robbins, *Encyclopedia of Witchcraft and Demonology* (New York, 1959), pp. 558–71. H. C. Erik Midelfort, "Recent Witch-Hunting Research," *Papers of the Bibliographical Society of America* 62 (1968). M. de Certeau, in J.-J. Surin, *Correspondance*, ed. M. de Certeau (Paris, 1966), pp. 91–99 and passim. R. Mandrou, *Magistrats et sorciers en France au XVIIe siècle* (Paris, 1968), pp. 18–59 (see M. de Certeau, *L'Absent de l'histoire* [n.p.: Mame, 1973], pp. 13–39 ["La Magistrature devant la sorcellerie du XVIIe siècle"]). Finally, we must mention, on the literary destiny of the subject, the "Bibliographie succincte de l'affaire U. Grandier," presented by J. Pré and others in *La Gazette du Loudunais* 48–50 (October–December 1969).

2. A few *scholarly works.* Besides a few essential works on sorcery (those of Francis Bavoux, Christian Pfister, P. Villette, and especially Etienne Delcambre), we must mention at least the following: J. Michelet, *La Sorcière* (Paris, 1862), pp. 269–91) or the 1966 reprint (pp. 195–207), a work of genius that must still be read. G. Legué (with whom the Loudun affair truly enters history, though in a very polemical perspective), *Urbain Grandier et les possédées de Loudun. Documents inédits de M. Charles Barbier* (Paris, 1880; 2nd, expanded ed., 1884). (His *Documents pour servir à l'histoire médicale des possédées de Loudun* [Paris, 1874], supplies a collection of rare texts, but the textual editing is unreliable.) G. Legué and Gilles de la Tourette, *Soeur Jeanne des Anges . . . Autobiographie d'une hystérique possédéee* (Paris, 1886). A. Huxley, *The Devils of Loudun* (London, 1952): with very deficient historical data, very penetrating views. J. Texier, "Le procès d'Urbain Grandier" (thesis of the Faculty of Law of Poitiers, 1953). M. Foucault, *Folie et déraison. Histoire de la folie à l'âge classique* (Paris, 1961) (translated as *Madness and Civilization: A History of Insanity in the Age of Reason* [New York: Pantheon, 1965]), fundamental for an understanding of the epistemological problem that is at the center of the Loudun affair. J. Viard, "Le procès d'Urbain Grandier. Note critique sur la procédure et sur la culpabilité," in J. Imbert, *Quelques procès criminels des XVIIe et XVIIIe siècles* (Paris, 1964), pp. 45–75. J.-J. Surin, *Correspondance,* ed. M. de Certeau (Paris, 1966), pp. 241–430. R. Mandrou, *Magistrats et sorciers en France au XVIIe siècle* (Paris, 1968), pp. 197–368: this is the fundamental book for the subject as a whole. E. W. Monter, *European Witchcraft* (New York, 1969), gives an excellent presentation of important texts.

On psychoanalytic interpretation, see S. Freud, "A Seventeenth-century Demonological Neurosis," in *The Standard Edition of the Complete Psychological Works of Sigmund Freud,* vol. 19, ed. J. Strachey (London: Hogarth Press, 1961), pp. 69–105; and M. de Certeau, *The Writing of History,* trans. T. Conley (New York: Columbia University Press, 1988), pp. 287–307 ("What Freud Makes of History") and, on the problem of enunciation, pp. 244–68 ("Language Altered: *The Sorcerer's Speech*").

～ Notes ～

History Is Never Sure

1. Wilhelm E. Mühlmann, *Messianismes révolutionnaires du tiers-monde* (Paris: Gallimard, 1968), p. 183.

2. Lucien Febvre, in *Annales* 13 (1958): 639.

3. Alfred Jarry, *L'Amour absolu* (Paris: Éditions du Mercure de France, 1964), p. 81.

4. See Detlef Heikamp, "L'Architecture de la métamorphose," *L'oeil* 114 (June 1964): 2–9.

5. Henri Lefebvre, *Introduction à la modernité* (Paris: Éditions de Minuit, 1962), pp. 63–71.

6. This is the title of the work on Urbain Grandier by Thomas Bensa, published in Paris in 1899 by the Société d'Éditions Littéraires.

7. The list may be found in Jean-Joseph Surin, *Correspondance*, ed. Michel de Certeau (Paris: Desclée De Brouwer, Collection Bibliothèque Européenne, 1966), pp. 92–99; and in the additional information given by Robert Mandrou in the general introduction to his *Magistrats et sorciers en France au XVIIe siècle* (Paris: Plon, 1968), pp. 18–70.

8. See Michel de Certeau, "Une Mutation culturelle et religieuse. Les magistrats devant les sorciers du XVIIe siècle," *Revue d'histoire de l'Église de France* 55 (1969): 300–319; reprinted in Michel de Certeau, *L'Absent de l'histoire* (Paris: Mame, 1973), pp. 13–39.

9. See Henri-Jean Martin, *Livre, pouvoirs et société à Paris au XVIIe siècle* (Geneva: Droz, 1969), pp. 164–89, 253–75.

10. [Father Joseph (1577–1638), a Capuchin, also known as the "éminence grise," was the counselor and personal agent of Richelieu. His full name was François Joseph Le Clerc du Tremblay.—Trans.]

11. *Mercure françois*, vol. 20 (1634) (Paris: E. Richer, 1637), pp. 746–80.

Chapter One

1. See Pierre Delaroche, *Une Épidémie de peste à Loudun en 1632* (Bordeaux: Delmas, 1936), p. 40.

2. Philippe Tamizey de Larroque, *Instructions sur la peste par le cardinal d'Armagnac,* offprint from *Les Annales du Midi* (Toulouse, 1892), p. 6.

3. *Advis et remedes souverains pour se garder de peste* . . . by Cardinal d'Armagnac (Toulouse, 1558), in *Instructions* . . ., ed. Tamizey de Larroque, pp. 10–12.

4. See Robert Favreau, "Epidémies à Poitiers et dans le Centre Ouest à la fin du Moyen ?a028?ge," in *Bibliothèque de l'École des Chartes* 125 (1967 [1968]): 349–98.

5. Delaroche, *Une Épidémie de peste à Loudun en 1632,* pp. 70–73.

6. Pierre Deyon, "Mentalités populaires. Un sondage au XVIIe siècle," *Annales* E.S.C. 17 (1962): 455.

7. Minutes of 7 and 11 October; Paris, Bibliothèque Nationale (BN), Fonds français 7619, fols. 6–9.

8. [Here and elsewhere, I have provided English translations of passages left in Latin in the French edition.—Trans.]

9. BN, Fonds français 7619, fols. 6–7.

10. Commission as intendant of justice for the nobleman d'Argenson to serve under Monsieur le Prince, in *Origines de l'institution des intendants des provinces,* ed. Gabriel Hanotaux (Paris, 1884), p. 316ff.

11. BN, Fonds français 7619, fol. 9.

12. On the Huguenot physician, information can be found in Dumontier de la Fond, *Essai sur l'histoire de Loudun* (Poitiers, 1778), part 1, p. 132; part 2, pp. 113, 120, 123, 129. But the information differs from that given in the Minutes.

13. Minutes of October 13 and the following days, BN, Fonds français 7619, fol. 12v, s.v.

14. BN, Fonds français 7619, fol. 35.

15. *Histoire admirable de la possession* . . ., part 1 (Paris: Chastellain, 1613), p. 3.

16. BN, Fonds français 7619, fol. 9. [Louis Gaufridy, or Gauffridi, was a Provençal priest who had been tried in Aix in 1610 and burned alive for bewitching and debauching Ursulines in Marseilles.—Trans.]

Chapter Two

1. Louis Trincant, "Abrégé des Antiquités de Loudun" (manuscript), quoted in Gabriel Legué, *Urbain Grandier et les possédées de Loudun* (Paris, 1880), p. 3n.

2. Edited in Élie Benoit, *Histoire de l'Édit de Nantes,* vol. 2: *Preuves* (Delft, 1693), pp. 90–91.

3. See Alfred Barbier, "Jean II d'Argmagnac, gouverneur de Loudun, et Urbain Grandier (1617–1635)," *Mémoires de la Société des Antiquaires de l'Ouest,* 2d ser., 8 (1885): 183–380.

4. Quoted in G. Hanotaux and duc de la Force, *Histoire du cardinal de Richelieu,* vol. 4 (Paris: Plon, 1935), p. 243.

5. *Véritable relation des justes procédures observées au fait de la possession des Ursulines de Loudun et au procès de Grandier,* by the Reverend Father Tr[anquille]. R.C. (Paris: J. Martin, 1634), fols. 310–32.

6. C. Menestrier, *Des Ballets anciens et modernes* (Paris, 1682), preface.

7. Sister Jeanne des Anges, *Autobiographie*, ed. G. Legué and Gilles de la Tourette (Paris, 1866), pp. 76–79; text checked against the manuscript of Tours, Biblothèque Municipale, MS 1197.

8. Paris, Bibliothèque de l'Arsenal, MS 4824, fol. 39v.

9. The account of Abbot D.; Paris, Bibliothèque de l'Arsenal, MS 5554, fol. 109; see BN, Fonds français 12801, fol. 3.

10. D'Aubignac, *Pratique du théâtre* (1657); see Jean Rousset, *L'Intérieur et l'extérieur, Essais sur la poésie et sur le théâtre au XVIIe siècle* (Paris: J. Corti, 1968), pp. 169–76.

11. Montaigne, *Essais,* I, 55; édition La Pléiade (Paris: Gallimard, 1962), pp. 301–2. [I have used John Florio's (1603) translation, as published in *The Essayes of Montaigne* (New York: Modern Library, [1933]), p. 272.—Trans.]

12. P. Zacchias, *Quaestiones medico-legales,* 5th ed. (Avignon: J. Piot, 1557), II, 61.

Chapter Three

1. Text published as early as 1693 in (Aubin), *Histoire des diables de Loudun* (Amsterdam, 1693), pp. 91–93.

2. Toulouse, Archives of the Society of Jesus, Fonds Carrère, "Vie de Jeanne des Anges."

3. J. Le Breton, *La deffense de la vérité touchant la possession des Religieuses de Louviers,* in-quarto (Evreux, 1643), 27 pp. See Robert-Léon Wagner, *"Sorcier" et "Magicien"* (Geneva: Droz, 1939), p. 196.

4. BN, Fonds français 7619, fol. 10v.

5. Exorcism of November 24, 1632; BN, Fonds français 7619, fols. 30–34.

6. Ibid., fols. 31–32.

7. Exorcism of November 25, 1632; BN, Fonds français 7619, fol. 39.

8. [There is a grammatical mistake in Jeanne des Anges's (or the devil's) response to Barré. The verb form *volo* (first person) should be *vult* (third person). This mistake is alluded to by Barré, who commands the devil to answer *congrument,* that is, in a grammatically correct manner.—Trans.]

9. Exorcism of November 25, 1632; BN, Fonds français 7619, fol. 39.

10. Exorcism of May 10, 1634: BN Fonds français 7618, fol. 9.

11. [I use the term *mystics* here, as in Michel de Certeau's *Mystic Fable,* vol. 1 (Chicago: University of Chicago Press, 1992), to render *la mystique,* as distinguished from *le mystique.* A fuller rationale for this coinage may be found in *La Fable Mystique,* ix–x.—Trans.]

12. J.-B. Van Helmont, *Confessio authoris,* 2, in *Ortus medicinae* (Amsterdam, 1652). See M. de Certeau, "Cultures et spiritualités," *Concilium* 19 (1966): 11–16.

13. Exorcism of October 13, 1632; BN, Fonds français 7619, fol. 11.

14. Exorcism of November 24, 1632; BN, Fonds français 7619, fol. 32.

15. BN, Fonds français 7618, fol. 10.

16. Exorcism of November 24, 1632; BN, Fonds français 7619, fol. 33.

17. Exorcism of November 25, 1632; BN, Fonds français 7619, fol. 36.

18. Ibid., fol. 35.

19. BN, Fonds français 12047, fol. 2.

20. BN, Fonds français 7619, fol. 28.

21. Ed. Gabriel Legué, *Documents pour servir à l'histoire médicale des possédées de Loudun* (Paris, 1874), pp. 61–62, corrected according to the MS.

Chapter Four

1. Jules Michelet, *La Sorcière* (1862; rpt., Paris: Garnier-Flammarion, 1966), p. 198.

2. [Aubin], *Histoire des diables de Loudun*, pp. 7–8.

3. Carpentras, Bibliothèque Municipale, MS 1810, fol. 50; Tamizey de Larroque, ed., in *Le cabinet historique*, ser. 2, 3 (1879): 4.

4. The parish records of Bouère do not go back further than 1604. Hence Urbain Grandier's precise date of birth cannot be established.

5. The signature of Urbain Grandier appears for the first time on a certificate of baptism on August 4, 1617, and for the last time on July 5, 1633.

6. BN, Fonds français 23064, fol. 79.

7. *Oraison funèbre de Scevole de Sainte-Marthe. . .* (1629), "Péroraison"; see Legué, *Documents pour servir à l'histoire médicale des possédées de Loudun*, p. 27.

8. Thirty-eight authentic letters from Grandier's hand to the governor, and two to the governor's wife, remain. See Barbier, "Jean II d'Armagnac, gouverneur de Loudun, et Urbain Grandier (1617–1635)."

9. Legué, *Documents pour servir à l'histoire médicale des possédées de Loudun*, p. 73.

10. BN, Collection Dupuy 645, item 151, fol. 175.

11. [In canon law, the *official* is an ecclesiastic judge to whom a bishop has delegated the right to judge in his place.—Trans.]

12. *Extraits des registres de la commission ordonnée par le Roi pour le jugement du procès criminel fait à l'encontre du Maître Urbain Grandier et ses complices* (Poitiers: J. Thoreau, 1634); BN, Lb. 36.3018; Paris, Bibliothèque Mazarine, Rés., 37297.

13. Ibid. [A letter of monition was a letter addressed by a judge of the Catholic Church to the flock, ordering them on pain of ecclesiastic prosecution to turn over any pertinent information to a secular judge in a criminal proceeding. The term *aggravation* was a technical term, originally referring to the second warning leading to excommunication.—Trans.]

14. Barbier, "Jean II d'Armagnac, gouverneur de Loudun, et Urbain Grandier (1617–1635)."

15. *Extraits des registres de la commission.*

16. [That is, a member of a regular order, which Grandier was not.—Trans.]

17. There are several copies of Grandier's *Traicté* from the period: BN, Collection Dupuy, 571, fols. 66ff.; Paris, private collection of M. Lambert, and so forth. The excerpts given here are from this last, as being the most reliable. There were editions beginning in 1634 (see BN, Lb. 36.3029, 42–51). The Robert Luzarche edition (Paris: Pincebourde, 1866), in the Petite Bibliothèque des Curieux, is based on a 1774 copy; it is adorned with additions and paraphrases more useful to the history of those nineteenth-century *curieux* than to the history of Grandier.

18. ["If your amiable spirit takes well to this lore / By your conscience your rest will be troubled no more."—Trans.]

19. *Mercure françois,* vol. 20 ("continuation de l'an 1634"), pp. 779–80.

Chapter Five

1. BN, Fonds français 7618.

2. Text edited in Legué, *Urbain Grandier et les possédées de Loudun,* p. 170. Phelipeaux is secretary of state.

3. Louis Charbonneau-Lassay, "Le château de Loudun sous Louis XIII," *Mémoires de la Société des Antiquaires de l'Ouest* (1915): 409ff.

4. M. de Morgues, *Charitable remontrance de Caton chrétien* (1631), p. 4. On M. de Morgues, the queen's chaplain and confessor, a merciless critic, as vigorous as he was well informed, see Maximin Deloche, *La maison du cardinal de Richelieu* (Paris: H. Champion, 1912), pp. 32–50.

5. Barbier, "Jean II d'Armagnac, gouverneur de Loudun, et Urbain Grandier," p. 104.

6. Compare the "rehabilitation" of Mesmin by Edmond Mémin, *René Mesmin de Silly, adversaire d'Urbain Grandier* (Saumur: Godet, 1916).

7. Ed. Barbier, "Jean II d'Armagnac, gouverneur de Loudun, et Urbain Grandier." This letter, the last in date of the Barbier MSS of the correspondence from the governor to Grandier, also seems to be the last he wrote to him.

8. Ed. Legué, *Urbain Grandier et les possédées de Loudun,* p. 174.

9. Paris, Affaires Étrangères, MS France 1627, fols. 119–36.

10. Ed. Legué, *Urbain Grandier et les possédées de Loudun,* p. 182.

11. *Extraits des registres de la commission;* BN, Fonds français 7618, fol. 25.

12. Richelieu, *Mémoires,* book XXIV, in Michaud and Poujoulat, eds., *Nouvelle collection des Mémoires relatifs à l'histoire de France,* vol. 22 (1881), pp. 568–69.

13. G. Hanotaux and duc de la Force, *Histoire du cardinal de Richelieu,* vol. 3 (Paris: Plon, 1935), p. 278.

14. BN, Fonds français 24163; edited in *Bulletin du Bibliophile* (1907): 502.

15. On Laubardemont, who seems to have been erased from history and to have become a prisoner of legend, see the following: in Paris, BN, Pièces Originales, 1873 (les Martin); BN, Fonds français 17368 and 17370–73 (letters); Archive Saint-Sulpice, MSS R. 438.3 and R. 438.4 (letters); in Bordeaux, Departmental Archives, 1 B 21–23, 1 B 25, 8 J 583 (family); at the Grand Fougeray, Archives de la Visitation, MS F I, 1–142 (letters); and so forth. A few notices in *Archives historiques du département de la Gironde* 30 (1895): 155 and 44 (1909): 287; Louis Lesourd, *Notice historique sur Martin de Laubardemont* (Paris: René, 1847); R. Mousnier, *Lettres et mémoires adressés au chancelier Séguier* (Paris: Presses Universitaires de France, 1964), especially p. 1207; Pinthereau, *Le progrès du jansénisme. . .* (Avignon, 1655), especially the "Information de la doctrine de Saint-Cyran"; Surin, *Correspondance,* ed. Certeau, pp. 277–80 and index.

16. Letter of May 21, 1636, to Séguier, in Mousnier, *Lettres et mémoires adressés au chancelier Séguier,* p. 291.

17. Marc Duncan, *Discours sur la possession des Religieuses de Loudun* (Saumur, 1634), BN, 16 Lb. 36.3961.

18. Letter of May 15, 1636, in Mousnier, *Lettres et mémoires adressés au chancelier Séguier*, p. 290.

19. This is what he declares to Vincent de Paul. See J. Orcibal, *Origines du Jansénisme*, vol. 2 (Paris: J. Vrin, 1947) p. 580.

20. ["You whom the King commits and gives / To condemn in his stead / The demons, and to crush them / Like a second Michael the Archangel"], BN, Fonds français 7619, fol. 125.

Chapter Six

1. *Extraits des registres de la commission;* BN, Fonds français 7618, fol. 25.

2. See the sources in note 1 above and Paris, Biblothèque Mazarine, Rés. 37297.

3. [Jeanne Estièvre writes *caneçons* (instead of *caleçons*) following the popular pronunciation.—Trans.]

4. Illegible, due to a hole in the page.

5. Ed. Legué, *Urbain Grandier et les possédées de Loudun*, p. 194, and corrected according to the MS.

6. Ibid., pp. 195–97, and corrected according to the MS.

7. *Extraits des registres de la commission.*

8. Ed. Legué, *Urbain Grandier et les possédées de Loudun*, p. 200.

9. Ibid., pp. 198–99.

10. *Extraits des registres de la commission.*

11. Ibid.

12. Letter from Father du Mont to M. Hubert, Paris, Bibliothèque de l'Arsenal, MS 4824, fol. 23.

13. See Poitiers, Bibliothèque municipale, MS, edited in Legué, *Urbain Grandier et les possédées de Loudun*, p. 203.

Chapter Seven

1. [A theologal is a lecturer on theology and scripture attached to a cathedral or collegiate church.—Trans.]

2. BN, Fonds français n.a. 6761, fol. 9.

3. Letter of the English writer Killigrew; London, Bodleian Library, Ashmole, N.S., 21. The text was edited in *European Magazine* 43 (February 1801): 102. On Thomas Killigrew (1612–83), R. Flecknoe published *The Life of Tomaso the Wanderer* in 1667 (republished in London, 1925). [I have translated Certeau's French version of the text.—Trans.]

4. Ibid. [I have reproduced this excerpt from the version edited in the *European Magazine*, pp. 104–5.—Trans.]

5. Pierre de Lancre, *L'incrédulité et Mescréance du sortilège plainement convaincue* . . . (Paris, 1622), p. 41.

6. *La gloire de Sainte Ursule*, by a Father of the Company of Jesus (Valenciennes, 1656), dedication page, not numbered.

7. See Marie de Chantal Gueudré, *Histoire de l'Ordre des Ursulines en France* (Ed. Saint-Paul, 1957), vol. 1, pp. 201–16.

8. In Paris: BN, Coll. Dupuy, vol. 776, fol. 254; BN, Fonds français 6764, fol. 7; Arch. Affaires Étrangères, France, vol. 1696, fol. 109; Archives Nationales, K 114, pièce 22. Dijon, Bibliothèque Municipale, Fonds Baudot, MS 144, pp. 1–7. To this must be added the "list" placed at the end of *La Démonommanie de Loudun, qui montre la véritable possession des religieuses ursulines et autres séculières, avec la liste des religieuses et séculières possédées* . . . (La Flèche: Griveau, 1634) (BN, octavo, Lb. 36.3024).

9. Dijon, Bibliothèque Municipale, Fonds Baudot, MS français 144, p. 1.

10. Letter of July 26, 1634; Paris, Bibliothèque de l'Arsenal, MS 4824, fol. 17.

11. Poitiers, Bibliothèque Municipale, MS 303, document 26.

12. BN, Fonds français 7618, fol. 45. Autograph by Laubardemont.

13. The MS was in the Archives of Poitiers, from which it has disappeared. M. Collin de Plancy published a facsimile of it in the second edition of his *Dictionnaire infernal* (Paris: Mongie, 1826). Jules Garinet translated it in his *Histoire de la Magie en France* . . . (Paris: Foulon, 1818), p. 327.

14. BN, Fonds français 7619, fol. 83; it was published (with some inaccuracies) by Legué, *Documents pour servir à l'histoire des possédées de Loudun,* p. 23.

15. Quoted by René Pintard, *Le libertinage érudit dans la première moitié du XVIIe siècle* (Paris, 1943), pp. 28–29.

16. See ibid., pp. 29–30.

17. *La Science expérimentale* . . ., book II, chap. 1; BN, Fonds français 14596, fol. 39.

18. Jeanne des Anges, *Autobiographie,* pp. 71–72.

19. Ibid.

20. Yves de Paris, *Théologie naturelle,* 3d ed. (Paris, 1641), vol. 4, pp. 393ff.

21. See, e.g., Mühlmann, *Messianismes révolutionnaires,* p. 251; or Joost Meerlo, in *Journal of the American Psychiatric Association* (July 1963).

22. BN, Fonds français, n.a. 24.383.

23. Jeanne des Anges, *Autobiographie,* pp. 67–68.

24. BN, Fonds français 7618, fol. 2.

25. ["On se tutoie . . .": they use the familiar *tu* form among themselves, which is a sign of intimacy.— Trans.]

26. See Géza Roheim, "Die Wilde Jagd," *Imago* 12 (1926): 467ff.

27. BN, Fonds français 7618, fol. 8.

28. See Michel de Certeau, "Ce que Freud fait de l'histoire," *Annales: Economies, sociétés, civilisations* 25 (1970): 654–67. [Also in Michel de Certeau, *The Writing of History* (New York: Columbia University Press, 1988), chap. 8.—Trans.]

29. Psalms 90:13 (translated from the Vulgate).

30. BN, Fonds français 7618, fols. 50–51.

31. Joachim du Bellay, *Regrets,* Sonnet 79. See Auguste Viatte, "Du Bellay et les démoniaques," *Revue d'histoire littéraire de la France* 51 (1951): 456–60. ["Dolcin, sometimes when I see these poor girls who have, or seem to have, the devil in them, move their bodies and their heads horribly, and do what those old sibyls are said to do; when I see the strongest powerless, trying in vain to constrain their diabolic power, and when I see even those who are esteemed most skilled in your art lose all their lore; when I hear them cry out frightfully, and when I see them roll back the whites of their eyes, all my skin horripulates, and I no longer know what to say. But when I see a monk with his Latin feeling their bellies and dugs up and down, that fright subsides and I am forced to laugh."]

Chapter Eight

1. An initial synthesis of these reports is presented by Alfred Barbier, "Rapports des médecins et chirurgiens appelés au cours du procès d'Urbain Grandier," *Gazette médicale de Nantes,* August 9–November 9, 1887.

2. *Factum pour Maître Urbain Grandier, prêtre, curé de l'église de Saint-Pierre du Marché de Loudun* . . . (1634), in-quarto, 12 pp.; BN, Lb. 36.3016. See BN, Coll. Dupuy, vol. 641, fols. 220–24; 500 Colbert, vol. 619, fol. 138; Recueil Thoisy anthology, vol. 92, p. 337; Paris, Bibliothèque de l'Arsenal, 5554 and 4824; and so forth.

3. *Préceptes particuliers . . .,* ed. René Pintard, in *La Mothe le Vayer, Gassendi, Guy Patin* (Paris: Boivin, n.d.), p. 67.

4. BN, Fonds français, n.a 24.380, fol. 145.

5. Ibid., fol. 156.

6. Ibid., fol. 147.

7. BN, Fonds français 12047, fol. 2.

8. *Préceptes particuliers,* ed. Pintard, p. 69.

9. Gui Patin, *Lettres,* ed. J.-H. Reveillé-Parise, vol. 1 (Paris, 1846), p. 302.

10. P. Yvelin, *Apologie pour l'autheur de l'examen de la possession des Religieuses de Louviers* . . . (Paris, 1643), p. 17. See Robert Mandrou, *Magistrats et sorciers,* pp. 288–89.

11. Such is Pilet de la Mesnardière's criticism of it, *Traité de la mélancholie* (La Flèche, 1635), pp. 48–49.

12. The letter, addressed to M. Quentin, in Paris, and dated October 14, 1634, was published in the *Mercure françois* (1634), vol. 20 (Paris: E. Richer, 1637), pp. 772–80, despite the concluding request (imposed by the literary genre) of Dr. Seguin: "I beg you to communicate it to no one but our friends."

Chapter Nine

1. BN, Fonds français 7618, fol. 8.

2. *Discours de la Méthode,* 3; in *oeuvres de Descartes,* ed. Ch. Adam and P. Tannery (Paris, 1897–1910), vol. 6, pp. 24–25.

3. Pilet de la Mesnardière, *Traité de la Mélancholie . . .* (La Flèche, 1635), p. 51.

4. Ed. Frédéric Lachèvre, *Les oeuvres libertines de Cyrano de Bergerac,* vol. 2 (Paris: Champion, 1922), p. 213.

5. MS from the library of M. Lambert, "Dialogue spirituel," part 2, pp. 4–5.

6. Le Grand Fougeray, Archives de la Visitation, MS, "Extraits de la Vie de Jeanne des Anges," p. 59.

7. BN, Fonds français, n.a. 24.380, fols. 180–81.

8. Pilet de la Mesnardière, *Traité de la Mélancholie,* p. 23.

9. BN, Fonds français 7618, fol. 30 (May 23, 1634).

10. Le Grand Fougeray, Archives de la Visitation, MS, "Vie de la Mère Jeanne des Anges," pp. 71–72.

11. BN, Fonds français, n.a. 24.380. On these drugs, see Nicolas Lémery, *Pharmacopée universelle contenant toutes les compositions de Pharmacie . . .* (Paris: L. d'Houry, 1697).

12. *Discours de la possession des Religieuses de Lodun* (Saumur, 1634), p. 64. See BN, Lb. 36.3029, Rés., pp. 2–20: an early copy.

13. On the *Satire,* see Pintard, *Le libertinage érudit,* pp. 221–23. Quillet's *Relation*

is in BN, Fonds français 12801, fols. 1–10. The minutes of the exorcism of May 20, 1634, in which Quillet participated, are preserved in BN, Fonds français 7618, fols. 25–26.

14. *Attestatio Chesnati Medici Coenomanensis* (1635); BN, Lb. 36. 3029, Rés., pp. 148–54.

15. *In actiones Juliodunensium virginum, Francisci Pidoux doctoris medici Pictaviensis exercitatio medica, ad D. Duncan, doct. medic.* (Poitiers: J. Thoreau, 1635), in-octavo; two editions, one with 77 pp., the other with 160 pp. (BN, in-octavo, Td. 86.15 and in-octavo Td. 86.15 A). *Deffensio exercitationum Francisci Pidoux* (Poitiers: J. Thoreau, 1636), in-octavo.

16. Pilet de la Mesnardière, *Traité de la Mélancholie*, p. 3.

17. See Pietro Pomponazzi, *Les causes des merveilles de la nature . . .*, trans. and introduced by Henry Busson (Paris: Rieder, 1930).

18. Pilet de la Mesnardière, *Traité de la mélancholie*, pp. 44–45.

19. Ibid., pp. 57–58.

20. Ibid., dedication.

21. Ibid.

22. Ibid., pp. 119–20.

23. See Pintard, *Le libertinage érudit*, p. 222, citing a later letter from Naudé to Guy Patin.

24. *Discours sur la possession . . .* (1634), duodecimo, 64 pp.; BN, Recueil Thoisy, vol. 92, fols. 292–330; BN, Lb. 36.3023.

25. See Pomponazzi, *Les causes des merveilles de la nature*, ed. H. Busson (1930), pp. 62–86.

26. "Portfolio" of Vallant, ed. P.-E. Le Maguet, in *Le Monde médical parisien sous le grand roi* (Paris: Maloine, 1899), p. 540.

27. See Martin, *Livre, pouvoirs et société à Paris*, pp. 527–29.

28. *Factum pour Maître Urbain Grandier.*

29. *Lettre au Roy du sieur Grandier accusé de magie* (1634); BN, Fonds français 7619, fols. 84–89; Fonds français, n.a. 6764, fols. 115–17; Paris, Bibliothèque de l'Arsenal, MS 5423, pp. 1209–18; and so forth.

30. BN, Fonds français, n.a. 6764, fols. 81–82.

31. BN, Fonds français, 7618, f. 30.

32. Ibid., fol. 25.

33. Ibid., fol. 32.

34. Ibid., fol. 30.

35. Paris, Archives Nationales, Minutier Central, Étude 64, liasse 92, Testament, fol. 7.

36. BN, Fonds français, n.a. 6764, fol. 145.

37. BN, Fonds français, 20973, fol. 241.

38. See Michel de Certeau, "L'illettré éclairé. L'histoire de la lettre de Surin sur le jeune homme du coche (1630)," *Revue d'Ascétique et de Mystique* 44 (1968): 369–412. [See also Certeau, *The Mystic Fable* (Chicago: University of Chicago Press, 1992), chap. 7.—Trans.]

39. *La Science expérimentale*, I, 1 (first version); BN, Fonds français, 14596, fol. 8.

40. *De l'immortalité de l'âme*, 1,056 pp., in-quarto (Paris: Bilaine, 1634), p. 3.

41. Letter to Gassendi (September 7, 1634); Carpentras, Bibliothèque Inguimbertine, MS 1810, fol. 48; edited in *Le Cabinet historique* 25 (1879): 6–12.

42. Ibid.

43. *Remarques et considérations servant à la justification du curé de Loudun, autres que celles contenues en son Factum,* in-quarto (1634), 8 pp.: BN, Lb. 36.3017; BN, Coll. Dupuy, vol. 641, fol. 214; BN, Fonds français 24163, pp. 1–8; BN, Fonds français 12047, fol. 3; BN, 500 Colbert, vol. 219, fol. 144; Paris, Bibliothèque de l'Arsenal, MS 4824, fols. 8–11; and so forth.

44. S. Birette, *Réfutation . . .,* 219 pp., duodecimo (Rouen: J. Besongne, 1618).

45. St. Thomas Aquinas, *Summa theologica,* IIa–IIae, quaest. 9, art. 2.

46. Blaise Pascal, *Pensées,* ed. Lafuma (Paris, 1960), frag. 44 (82).

47. J.-J. Surin, *La Science expérimentale,* I, chap. 5; BN, Fonds français 14596, fol. 22.

48. Several editions: La Flèche: Griveau, 1634; Poitiers, 1634; Paris: J. Martin, 1634 (BN, in-octavo, Lb. 36.3019); and a manuscript (BN, Fonds français, n.a. 13192, fols. 27ff.). The first edition appeared at the beginning of August 1634.

49. Quoted by Hanotaux and duc de la Force, *Histoire du cardinal de Richelieu,* vol. 4, p. 246.

50. *Véritable relation des justes procédures.*

Chapter Ten

1. *Extraits des registres de la Commission,* pp. 22–23.

2. See Marion, *Dictionnaire des institutions de la France, aux XVIIe et XVIIIe siècles* (Paris, 1923), pp. 449–51; Babinet, "Le présidial de Poitiers," *Mémoires de la Société des Antiquaires de l'Ouest* (1885).

3. Legué, *Urbain Grandier et les possédées de Loudun,* p. 232.

4. Etienne Delcambre, "Les Procès de sorcellerie en Lorraine. Psychologie des juges," *Revue d'histoire du droit* 21 (1953): 408.

5. BN, Fonds français 7619, fol. 103.

6. Tours, Bibliothèque Municipale, MS 1197, first part, p. 61.

7. Letter of Father Du Pont to M. Hubert; Paris, Bibliothèque dd l'Arsenal, MS 4824, fol. 25.

8. Ibid. fol. 19.

9. Ed. Legué, *Urbain Grandier et les possédées de Loudun,* pp. 233–34.

10. *Véritable relation des just procédures,* opening; BN, Fonds français 7619, fols. 104–5.

11. See chap. 8, note 2, above.

12. *Remarques et considérations;* BN, Lb. 36.3017; BN, Fonds français 12047, fol. 3; BN, Fonds français 24163, pp. 1–8; Coll. Dupuy, vol. 641, fol. 214; BN, 500 Colbert, vol. 219, fol. 144; Paris, Bibliothèque de l'Arsenal, MS 4824, fols. 8–11; and so forth.

13. *Conclusions . . .;* BN, Fonds français 6764, fols. 116–23; BN, Fonds français, n.a. 24.380, fols. 203–10; and so forth.

14. BN, Fonds français 7619, fol. 108.

15. Ibid., fols. 104–6.

16. Ibid., fols. 82ff,; BN, Fonds français 6764, fol. 80.

17. See chap. 9, note 29, above.

18. BN, Fonds français 7619, fol. 129.

19. Ibid., fol. 109.

20. See especially J. Texier, *Le procès d'Urbain Grandier,* typed document (Poi-

tiers, 1953), p. 140; and also M. Foucault, *Les procès de sorcellerie dans l'ancienne France devant les juridictions séculières* (Paris: Bonvalot-Jouve, 1907).

21. Pierre de Lancre, *Tableau de l'inconstance des mauvais anges . . .* (Paris: N. Buon, 1612), book VI, pp. 487–89.

22. Texier, *Le Procès d'Urbain Grandier,* p. 107.

23. See BN, Fonds français 24163, doc. 11.

24. BN, Fonds français 24163, fols. 29–34 and 129–37 (two identical texts); BN, Fonds français 6764, fols. 103–9; BN, Fonds français, n.a. 24.382, fols. 92–99. The text was published (with a few errors) and commented upon by (Aubin), *Histoire des diables de Loudun* (Amsterdam, 1752), pp. 171–97.

25. Unless otherwise indicated, the following texts are from the *Extrait des preuves.*

26. J. d'Autun, *L'incrédulité . . .* (Lyons, 1671), pp. 541ff.

27. De Lancre, *Tableau de l'inconstance,* p. 189.

28. J. Fontaine, *Discours des marques des sorciers* (Lyons: Larjot, 1611): Lyons, Bibliothèque Municipale, 363842/363868.

29. D'Autun, *L'incrédulité,* p. 541.

30. See Legué, *Urbain Grandier et les possédées de Loudun,* p. 212.

31. BN, Fonds français 24163, fol. 113.

32. See Oscar de Vallée, *De l'éloquence judiciaire au XVII siècle* (Paris, 1856), pp. 277–79.

33. M. Del Rio, *Les Controverses . . .,* in Texier, *Le Procès d'Urbain Grandier,* 91.

34. *L'Arrest de condamnation,* immediately printed in Paris by Estienne Habert and Jacques Poullard (1634, in-octavo), is found, handwritten or printed, in several miscellanies: BN, Coll. Thoisy, vol. 92, fol. 385; BN, Fonds français 24163, fol. 113; Paris, Archives Nationales, K. 114; and so forth.

Chapter Eleven

1. Paris, Bibliothèque de l'Arsenal, MS 4824, fol. 25 (Father Du Pont); BN, Fonds français 24163, fol. 113 (Father Archange).

2. *Mesmoire de ce qui s'est passé à l'exécution de l'arrest contre M. Urbain Grandier, prestre, . . . exécuté le vendredy 18 aoust 1634,* BN, Fonds français, n.a. 24.383.

3. BN, Fonds français 7619, fol. 111.

4. See Delcambre, "Les Procès de sorcellerie en Lorraine. Psychologie des juges," pp. 414–15.

5. BN, Fonds français 7619, fol. 111.

6. Paris, Bibliothèque de l'Arsenal, MS 4824, fol. 28.

7. See Texier, *Le Procès d'Urbain Grandier,* pp. 204–5.

8. BN, Fonds français 7619, fol. 112.

9. Ibid.

10. Luke 23:43.

11. *Relation véritable de ce qui s'est passé en la mort du curé de Loudun . . .,* BN, Fonds français 6764, fols. 124–30; ed. F. Danjou, *Archives curieuses de l'histoire de France,* 2d ser., 5 (1838): 278–79.

12. Paris, Bibliothèque de l'Arsenal, MS 4824, fol. 27.

13. See reproduction of MS in Legué, *Urbain Grandier et les possédées de Loudun,* p. 266.

14. Ibid., p. 264.

15. A. Pericaud, *Notes et documents pour servir à l'histoire de la ville de Lyon,* part 2 (1594–1643), pp. 270–72.

16. Letter from I. Boulliau to Gassendi; see chap. 9, note 41, above.

Chapter Twelve

1. Edited in (Aubin), *Histoire des diables de Loudun,* p. 380.

2. Ibid., p. 379.

3. *Géographie Blaviane,* vol. 7 (Amsterdam, 1667), p. 403.

4. *Mercure françois,* vol. 20 (1634), p. 772.

5. Martin, *Livre, pouvoirs et société à Paris au XVIIe siècle,* pp. 356–57.

6. *Mercure françois,* vol. 20 (1634), p. 780.

7. Paris, Bibliothèque de l'Arsenal, MS 4824, fol. 13.

8. BN, Lb. 36.3023; and so on.

9. Letter to Laubardemont, in Surin, *Correspondance,* ed. Certeau, p. 280.

10. BN, Lb. 36.3018. See chap. 4, note 12, above. For the first four works, the references are given above.

11. BN, Fonds français 24163, pp. 129–37; 6764, fols. 103–9; and so on.

12. BN, Coll. Thoisy, vol. 92, fol. 385; and so on.

13. BN, Fonds français 7619, fol. 112; 6764, fol. 124; and so on.

14. BN, Cabinet des Estampes, Qb1 1634.

15. Ex Poitiers, Bibliothèque Municipale, MS 303; edited in Legué, *Urbain Grandier et les possédées de Loudun,* p. 259.

16. BN, Fonds français 6764, fol. 127; Carpentras, Bibliothèque Municipale, Papiers Peiresc, Reg. X, fol. 517; and so forth.

17. Paris, Bibliothèque de l'Arsenal, MS 4824, fol. 27.

18. BN, Lb. 36.3021.

19. BN, Lb. 36.3022. See BN, Fonds français 7619, fols. 114–16; 6764, fol. 149.

20. Published in *Cabinet historique* 2, part 1 (1856): 61–63; and by Tamizey de Larroque, *Documents relatifs à Urbain Grandier* (Paris, 1879).

21. BN, Fonds français 6764, fols. 138, 147, 149.

22. BN, Lb. 36.3023; Carpentras, Bibliothèque Municipale, Papiers Peiresc, Reg. X, vol. 10, fol. 524.

23. BN, Lb. 36.3590.

24. BN, Fonds français 24163, fols. 113–15.

25. Ibid., fols. 117–28.

26. Later published at the end of the *Traité de la Mélancholie* (1635).

27. *Mercure françois,* vol. 20 (1634), pp. 772–83.

28. BN, Lb. 36.3961. On the publisher, see Pasquier, *Imprimeurs et libraires de l'Anjou* (Angers, 1932), p. 270.

29. BN, Lb. 36.3020; Fonds français 23064, fols. 79–82.

30. BN, Lb. 36.3019; BN, Fonds français 7619, fols. 104–6; and so forth. See Pasquier, *Imprimeurs et libraires de l'Anjou,* p. 317.

31. BN, Lb. 36.3024.

32. BN, Fonds français 6764, fols. 124–30.

33. Incomplete document, without beginning or end; BN, Fonds français, n.a. 24.380, fols. 246–57.

34. Ex Poitiers, Coll. Barbier, cart. III, no. 71.

35. Ex Poitiers, Bibliothèque Municipale, MS 303, no. 21.

36. Ibid., no. 20.

37. Ibid., no. 26.

38. *Relation véritable des justes procédures.*

39. These lights are connected with the legend of Castor and Pollux.

40. See Martin d'Arles, *Tractatus de superstitionibus,* (Lyons, 1544), and, on the subject of these lights, the eighteenth-century documents cited by A. Van Gennep, *Manuel de folklore français,* I, IV, pp. 1817–28.

41. Autograph, Coll. Feuillet de Conches; edited in Michaud, *Biographie universelle,* vol. 23, p. 334.

42. Letter, ed. E. Griselle, *Bulletin du bibliophile* (1907): 495.

43. See his letter to Richelieu in 1637, ed. E. Chavaray, *Revue des documents historiques* 4 (1877): 91.

44. Letter of September 20, 1634, to des Roches, p. 496.

45. Letter of November 28, 1634, MS from the Morrisson Collection, published in *Bulletin du bibliophile* (1907): 498.

46. See Grand Fougeray, Archives de la Visitation, MS, "Lettres spirituelles de Loudun," vol. 1, pp. 1–143.

47. See ibid., vol. 1, pp. 73–88. This *Journal,* still attested by M. de la Menardaye (*Examen et discussion critique des diables de Loudun* [1747], preface, p. xiv), has since disappeared.

48. Ed. E. Chavaray, in *Revue des documents historiques* 4 (1877): 91.

49. *Le grand miracle arrivé en la ville de Loudun en la personne . . .;* BN, Lb. 36.3022.

50. Poitiers, Archives Départementales, MS 7.

51. [See chap. 3, note 11, above.—Trans.]

Chapter Thirteen

1. Surin, *La Science expérimentale,* I, chap. 1; BN, Fonds français 14596, fol. 5.

2. Ibid., fols. 5–6. See Surin, *Correspondance,* ed. Certeau, pp. 246–47.

3. Ibid., Letter 85, pp. 339–40.

4. *La Science expérimentale,* I, chap. 1; BN, Fonds français 14596, fol. 6.

5. Ibid., fols. 7–8.

6. J.-J. Surin, *Triomphe de l'amour divin,* chap. 2; Chantilly, Archives S.J., MS 231 *bis,* fols. 20–22.

7. Ibid., fol. 24.

8. Ibid., fols. 39–42.

9. *La Science expérimentale,* I, chap. 1; BN, Fonds français 14596, fol. 7.

10. MS from the Barbier coll., edited in Legué, *Urbain Grandier et les possédées de Loudun,* p. 280.

11. Paris, Affaires Étrangères, France, vol. 1696, fols. 105–14.

12. *La Science expérimentale;* BN, Fonds français 14596, fol. 7.

13. Paris, Affaires Étrangères, France, vol. 1696, fol. 113.

14. Ibid.

15. Jeanne des Anges, *Autobiographie,* pp. 58, 87, 88.

16. *La Science expérimentale;* BN, Fonds français 14596, fols. 9, 18–19.

17. Ibid.

18. Grand Fougeray, Archives de la Visitation, MS, "Lettres spirituelles," vol. 1, p. 1.

19. Surin, *Correspondance,* ed. Certeau, pp. 263–65.

20. P. Marin Mersenne, *Correspondance,* ed. Mme. P. Tannery and C. De Waard, vol. 5, p. 271.

21. Ibid., p. 320.

22. Nicolas-Claude Fabri de Peiresc, *Correspondance,* ed. Tamizey de Larroque, vol. 3, p. 347; see Surin, *Correspondance,* ed. Certeau, pp. 267–68.

23. *Relation véritable de ce qui s'est passé . . .* (Paris: J. Martin, 1635), p. 27.

24. Letter of October 23, 1635, *Correspondance,* ed. Certeau, p. 286.

25. Letter of July 22, 1635, ibid., pp. 279–80.

26. On these various editions, see *Correspondance,* ed. Certeau, pp. 294, 290ff., 359, 301ff., 417, and so on.

27. Paris, Bibliothèque de l'Arsenal, MS 555, pp. 108–47; BN, Fonds français 12801, fols. 1–10.

28. Rome, Archivo Romano Soc. Jesu, Aquit. vol. 2, fol. 458.

29. See *La Science expérimentale,* IV, chap. 8; BN, Fonds français 14596, fols. 58–59.

Chapter Fourteen

1. *La Science expérimentale,* I, chap. 11; Paris, BN, Fonds français 14596, fol. 38.

2. Jeanne des Anges, *Autobiographie,* pp. 196–99.

3. Letter of February 6, 1644; Grand Fougeray, Archives de la Visitation, MS, "Lettres spirituelles," vol. 1, pp. 220–24.

4. Ibid., p. 10.

5. Rome, Archivio Romano Soc. Jesu, Aquit., vol. 2, fols. 477–78.

6. Letter of July 6, 1639; Paris, Bibliothèque Mazarine, MS 1209, n.p.

7. Surin, *Triomphe de l'amour,* pp. 258–59.

8. Letter of 25 August, 1660; see *Correspondance,* ed. Certeau, p. 983.

9. *La Science expérimentale,* II, chap. 4.

10. Jeanne des Anges's account of her trip is in her *Autobiographie,* pp. 208–54.

11. Ibid.

12. *Journal des voyages de Monsieur Monconys, conseiller du Roy en ses conseils d'Estat et privé et lieutenant criminel au siège présidial de Lyon,* vol. 1, pp. 8–9.

13. Grand Fougeray, Archives de la Visitation, MS, *Vie de Jeanne des Anges,* p. 1. See *Autobiographie,* p. 200.

14. Grand Fougeray, Archives de la Visitation, MS, *Vie de Jeanne des Anges,* p. 3.

15. *Autobiographie,* pp. 55–56.

16. Ibid., pp. 57–59.

17. Surin, *Correspondance,* ed. Certeau, p. 1205.

Figures of the Other

1. Claude Lévi-Strauss, *Tristes Tropiques* (Paris: Plon, 1955), p. 418; English translation, *Tristes Tropiques,* trans. J. and D. Weightman (New York: Penguin, 1992), p. 388 [translation slightly modified—Trans.].

∼ Index of Proper Names ∼

This index does not include place names or names of edifices. Names of demons and titles of works are given in italics and stigmata in small capital letters.

Achaos, 91
Adam, M. René, 20
Adam, Pierre, 109, 111
Admirable History of the Possession, The, 21
Agal, 91
Agnès, Sister, 31, 97, 107, 127
Agrippa, Cornelius, 165
Allain, 109, 112
Allumette d'impureté, 91
Aman, 90
Anatomy Lesson of Doctor Tulp, The, 109
Angélique de Saint-François, 92
Anginot, Father, 215
Anne de Saint-Augustin, 92
Anne de Sainte-Agnès, 85, 91
Anne d'Escoubleau de Sourdis, 92
Anne of Austria, Queen, 217
Antoine de la Charité, 19
Antonin de la Charité, 14
Aquinas, Saint Thomas, 34, 148
Archange, Father, 168, 171
Archer, Séraphique, 85
Argenson, René d', 143
Aristotle, 139
Armagnac, Sieur Jean II d', 25, 26, 55, 57–58, 66–68
Asaph, 91
Asmodaeus, 91, 107, 166, 167
Astaroth, 92, 107
Astarte, 15
Atheismus triumphatus, 101

Atheomachie, 101
Atheomastix, 101
Aubignac, d', 32, 33
Aubin, Guillaume, Sieur de la Grange, 77
Aubin, Paul, 74
Aubry, Nicole, 4
Aubry, Paul, 21, 49
Auffray, Catherine de la Présentation, née, 91, 107
Auger, Charles, 21, 109
Augustine, Saint, 223
Autobiographie (Jeanne des Anges), 218, 223, 225
Autun, Jacques d', 100, 167

Bachelerie, Father, 200, 204
Balam, 90
Baradat, M. de, 69
Barbézieux, Louis de, 221
Bardin, 118
Barot, widow, 85
Barre, de la, 106
Barré, Pierre, 14, 15, 40, 41, 42, 43, 47, 65, 70, 79, 86, 152, 166
Baruch, 92
Basile, 36
Beaugé, 57
Beaulieu, Marie, 93
Beëlzebub, 92, 120
Behemoth, 92, 93, 214, 216

Béhérit, 143. *See also Berith*
Belciel, Mother Jeanne de, 115, 139,
  140
Belcier, Catherine de, 221
Belcier, Louis de, baron of Cozes, 221
Béliard, Madeleine, 93
Bellegarde, Msgr. Octave de, 221
Benjamine, Léonne, 114
Bergerac, Cyrano de, 123
Berith, 91, 92. *See also Béhérit*
Bermond, Françoise de, 89
Bernier, René, 7
Bertrand, 82
Bignon, 57
Bion, 128
Birette, Frère Sanson, 148
Bishop of Poitiers, 80
Blake, William, 6
Blanchard, "Isabelle or Elisabeth," 92,
  107, 108, 113, 114, 196, 197
Bodin, Jean, 164
Boguet, 4
Bohyre, Father Arnault, 199
Boinet, Madeleine, 146
Boisguérin, 25
Bonnereau, Prégent, 12
Bontemps, Sergent, 83
Boucher, Pierre, 83
Boudet, M. de, 221
Bouguereau, 111
Bouilliau, Ismaël, 53, 135, 147, 179
Bourbon, Prince Louis, 69
Bourgneuf, 77, 79
Brazavole, 138
Brézé, la maréchale de, 135
Brézé, M. le maréchal de, 106, 115
Briault, 160
*Briefve Intelligence de l'opinion de trois
  docteurs de Sorbonne, et du livre . . . ,*
  150
Brion, François, 21, 49, 106, 109, 110,
  113, 114
Brognoli de Bergame, Candido, 149
Brossier, Marthe, 4
Brou, Madeleine de, 59, 160, 194.
Brou, René de, 58
Buffétison, 92
Bullion, Claude de, 205
Buontalenti, Bernardo, 6

Caleph, 91, 92
Calixte de Saint-Nicholas, 14
Callipaedia, 135

Caph, 91
Capuchins, 14, 25, 42, 70, 104, 171, 205
Carion (pseudonym of J. Nägelin), 63
Carmelites, 14, 15, 47, 48, 86, 155, 165,
  168, 205
Carmelites, Discalced, 25
Caron, 91
Carré, François, 109, 114, 128
Castorin, 91
Catherine de la Nativité, 92
Catherine de la Présentation, née Auffray,
  85, 91
Caudacanis or *Queue de chien*, 92
Cédon, 91, 93
Celse, 91
Censure (against Tranquille's booklet),
  160, 161
Cerberus, 91, 92
Cerisay, Guillaume de, lord of La Gué-
  rinière, 20, 58, 65, 160
Champion, 58, 104
Charbon d'impureté, 92
Charlemagne, 161
Charpentier, 69
Charton, Jacques, 141
Charvet, 65
Chauvet, Charles, 20, 49, 65, 153, 160
Chauvet, Louis, 20, 49, 194
Chaux, Archbishop Bertrand de, 217
Chavigny, Bouthillier de, 71
Chevalier, Sieur de Tessec, 152, 154
Chirurgie (Pigray), 138
Chroniques (of Carion and Jerome of
  Prague), 63
Chrysostom, St. John, 148
Claire de Saint-Jean, Sister. *See* Sazilly
Cohon, Anthyme, Msgr., 204, 205
commedia dell'arte, 3
Commentaire (Brasavole), 138
Concupiscence, 91
Condé, prince de, 24
Condé, princesse de, 220
Condés, the, 217
Confessions (Augustine), 223
*Conquête du Char de la Gloire par le grand
  Théandre*, 28
Constant, Sieur, 153
Contre les sorciers, 123
Cordeliers, 14, 25, 177
Cosnier, Alphonse, 21, 109, 110, 114, 128
Cothereau, M. le président, 121, 152, 218
Coustier, Dr. Gabriel, 49, 109
Cozes, M. de, 222, 223

Cozes, Mme de, 222
Cursay, M. de, 168

Dampierre, Mademoiselle de, 92
Daria, 91
d'Armagnac, 190
d'Artagnan, 198
Daughters of the Calvary, 25
de Burges, 152
de La Barre. *See* La Barre
de Lancre, 4, 102
De l'immortalité de l'âme (Silhon), 147
*De naturalium effectuum (admirandorum)
   causis, sive de incantationibus,* 130
De Nyau, 154
de Sazilly, Claire. *See* Sazilly
De Vanitate scientiarum (Agrippa), 165
Deffensio (Pidoux), 129
del Rio, Martin, 164
Deliard, 179
Demandolx, Madeleine de, 225
Démonomanie des sorciers (Bodin), 164
des Roches. *See* Roches
Descartes, 2, 122
Desloix, Jean, 164
Devils of Loudun, The (Penderecki), 6
Discours contre l'athéisme, 101
Discours contre les athées et libertins, 101
*Discours de la possession des religieuses de Lou-
   dun,* 129, 135
Discours des esprits, 22
Discours des marques des sorciers, (Fontaine),
   167
Discourse on Method, 122
Disquisitionum magicarum libri sex (del
   Rio), 164
Domptius, François, 21
Doni d'Attichy, Father, 207, 209
Doulcin, Remi, 108
Dreux, 106, 152, 154, 164
Drouin, Daniel, 49
du Bellay, Joachim, 108
Du Bois-Daufin, Sieur, 129–30
Du Chesne, 129
Du Chesne, Dr., 127
du Pin, Sieur, 205
Du Pont, Father, 31, 84, 94, 108, 155,
   171, 173, 178, 183
Du Puy, Father Mersenne, 101, 184, 209
Du Puy, Peiresc, 184, 196, 209
Duclos, François, 109, 113, 114, 128
Dugrès, M., 21
Dumas, Alexandre, 6

Duncan, Dr. Marc, 118, 129, 135, 137,
Dupont, Urbain, 21
Dupuy brothers, 54. *See* Du Puy
Duval, André, 141, 151

Easas or *Easar,* 91
Eléazar, Father, 194
Elijah, 180
Elimy, 91, 92
Elisabeth de la Croix, née Bastad, 85, 91
Elisée, Father, 105, 165
Elisée de Chinon, 14
Eloi de Saint-Pierre, 14
Eminence Grise. *See* Joseph, Father
Ennemi de la Vierge, 91
Esron, 93
Estièvre, Jeanne, 157
Estièvre, Jeanne Renée (Grandier's
   mother) 54, 77–79, 81, 82, 84
Estièvre, Sieur, 57
Estonnements (Remarques et considérations), 161
Estrées, (François-Annibal), maréchal d', 134
Estrées, Gabrielle d', 213
Eudemus, 119
Eulalius. *See* Duval, André
Eusèbe de Saint-Michel, 14, 15, 19
Extrait (of proofs), 164, 167, 168
Eynatten, Maximilien de, 149

Fabri, Claude, 11
Factum pour Mâitre Urbain Grandier, 110, 161
Fanton, Mattieu, 21, 50, 109
Febvre, Lucien, 3
Féry, Jeanne, 4
Fillastreau, Françoise, 92, 114
Fillastreau, Léonce, 93
Fontaine, Jacques, 167
Forge, Sieur de la, 126
Fornication, 92
Fos, Vincent de, 20, 50, 109
Fouquet, Jean, 11
Fourneau, François, 11, 169
Fournier, Pierre, 79, 83, 106, 153
FRANÇOIS DE SALES, 216
Fresnaye, M. de la, 58
Freud, 106

Gabrielle de Colombiers, Sister, 217
Gabrielle de l'Incarnation, 92
Galen, 139
galerie des femmes fortes, La, 104
Gassendi, 53, 135, 179
Gaufridy, 4, 22

Gault, Father, 105
Gayet, F., 172
Genebaut, Dorothée, 59
Genesis, 61
Girard, 49
Goulard, Simon, 138
Grandier, François, 54, 81
Grandier, Jean, 54
Grandier, Pierre, 54
Grandier, René, 54, 57, 59, 194, 195
Grandier, Urbain, 3, 7, 8, 12, 14, 19, 21, 22,
    31, 35, 49, 52, 54, 55, 57, 63, 67–74, 77,
    79, 81, 83–85, 98, 104, 106–8, 135, 148,
    155, 156, 158, 159, 161–63, 165–77,
    179–81, 187, 190, 195, 218, 220, 221
Grémian, Guillaume, 12
Gresil, 21
Grillau, Father François, 7, 14, 177
Grisard, 169
Grolleau, Jean-François, 106, 109, 110,
    113, 128
Grouard, M. Paul, 20
Guérison miraculeuse de soeur Jeanne des
    Anges, 214
Guilloteau, 86

Hagar, 92
Hammon, Catherine, 69, 70
Hammon, Suzanne, 93
Henri IV, 221
Henriciados, 124
Hercules, 182
Hervé, Sieur René *(lieutenant criminel)*, 20,
    49, 57, 68, 160, 161
Hippocrates, 116
Histoire (Michaelis), 138
Histoire admirable de la possession et conver-
    sion d'une pénitante, 4
Histoire généalogique de la maison de Savon-
    nières en Anjou, 58
Histoires admirables (Goulard), 138
Houmain, 152, 154, 155
Hubert, M., 31, 183
Huguenots, 20, 24, 25, 26, 69, 160, 179,
    204
Huss, John, 63
Huxley, Aldous, 6

IESUS, MARIA, JOSEPH, F. D. SALLES, 226
Ignatius of Loyola, Saint, 216
Imitation of Jesus Christ, 45
In actiones Juliodunensium virginum . . . , 129
Isabelle. *See* Blanchard

Isacaron, 90, 92
Isambert, Nicolas, 141
IV Livres des spectres ou apparitions et visions
    d'espirts, anges et démons, 130

Jabel, 92
Jacquet, Antoine, 106, 109, 110, 128
Jacquinot, Father, 226
Jarry, Alfred, 5
Jeanne des Anges, 7, 8, 14, 29, 37, 38, 41,
    45, 59, 85, 90, 96, 103, 105, 125, 146,
    167, 195, 197, 198, 200, 202, 204, 205,
    206, 213, 216–18, 220–25
Jeanne du Saint-Esprit, 85, 91
Jerome of Prague, 63
Jesuits, 25
Joan of Arc, 182
Joseph, Father, the "Eminence grise," 9,
    70, 71
Joseph, Saint, 214, 215, 226
Joubert, Gaspard, 20, 50, 109
Joubert, Laurent, 11
Juvenal, 124

Killigrew, Thomas, 87

La Barre, Sieur de Brisé, 152, 154
la gazette des sots, 183
La Grange, 169
La Ménardière, (Hippolite) Pilet de, 124,
    127, 129, 130, 132, 133, 134
La Picherie, 152
La Rocheposay, Msgr. Henri de Chas-
    teignier de, 35, 36, 56, 72, 84, 86, 94,
    95, 106, 139, 142, 155, 156, 224
La Tremoille, Madame de, 143
Lactance, Father (Capuchin), 86, 114
Lactance, Father Gabriel (Recollect exor-
    cist), 30, 86, 103, 104, 105, 106, 127,
    142, 165, 174, 176, 193, 194
Lancre, Pierre de, 89, 167
Lanier, Guy, 216
L'Anti-Anglois, ou responses aux prétextes dont
    les Anglois veulent . . . , 58
Laubardemont, Jean Martin, baron de, 9,
    26, 57, 65–68, 70–78, 81–83, 85, 95,
    104–7, 112, 151, 152, 154–57, 160, 163,
    164, 166, 169, 172–75, 178, 181, 190,
    192–95, 198, 202, 204, 205, 207, 210,
    214, 215, 218–20
Launay Razilly, M. de, 120
Le grand miracle arrivé en la ville de Loudun
    en la personne d'Elizabeth Blanchard, 197

Le Loyer, Pierre, 130, 137
Le Masle, Michel (Prior des Roches), 68, 193
Le Pelletier, Marthe, 58
Le Tourneur, Sieur Léon, 126
Le Verrier, 8
Lefebvre, Henri, 6
Lemaistre, Maître, 168
lettre à ses amis ("N"), 184
Lettre au Roi du sieur Grandier accusé de magie, 161
Lettre de la cordonnière de la reine-mère à M. de Baradas, 69
Lettre de la Motte Le Voyer, à Paris, 145
Léviathan, 90, 96, 97
Lévi-Strauss, Claude, 227
Lezear, 93
Life (Teresa), 223
Liguel, Sieur de. *See* Brou, René de
L'imposture des diables (Uvier), 138
L'incrédulité savante et la crédulité ignorante (J. d'Autun), 167
Lion d'Enfer, 92
Loches, Father Gilles de, 209
Louis XIII, 9, 24–26, 67, 72, 161, 217
Louis, Henry, 162
Louise de Jésus, Sister, 17, 18, 85, 91
Lucas, Sieur Michel, 66, 67, 71, 85
Lucien, 93
Luther, 93

Manuale exorcismorum (Maximilien de Eynatten), 149
Manuale exorcistarum ac parochorum (Brognoli de Bergame), 149
Marescot, 36
Maria mater gratiae, 105
Marie Archer, 92
Marie de la Visitation, 92
Marie de Saint-Gabriel, 92
Marie du Saint-Sacrement, 92
Maron, 92
Marthe de Sainte-Monique, 91
Marthe de Sainte-Monique, Sister, 13, 15, 16
Martin, Antoine, 141
Martin, Mathieu (Laubardemont's father), 74
Maunoury, René, 11, 20, 49, 109, 112, 167, 194
Maurat, Canon, 85
Maynié, Jaquette de, 89
Mechanics (Aristotle), 139
Médicis, Queen Marie de, 24, 69

memento salutis, 105
Mémoires (of Richelieu), 72
Ménage, 70
Menestrier, Father Claude, 28
Menuau, 77, 79, 80, 161
Mercure françois, 9, 64, 183, 184
Mersenne. *See* Du Puy, Father Mersenne
Mesmin, 77
Mesmoire de ce qui s'est passé à l'exécution de l'arrest contre M. Urbain Grandier, 172
Michaelis, Father Sébastien, 4, 22, 138
Michelet, Jules, 6, 53
Micolon, Antoinette, 89
Mignon, Jean, 14, 15, 22, 49, 86
Milon, Françoise, 201
Mils, 36
Mizault, Antoine, 11
Moloch, 147
Monconys, M. Balthasar de, 221
Monique de Sainte-Marthe, 85
Montaigne, 33
Morans, Sieur René de, 36, 83, 194, 205, 217
Moreau, Jean, 159
Morgues, Mathieu, 67
Morin, Pierre, 179
Moussault, M. Louis, 20
Moussaut, Prior Nicolas, 13, 52, 85, 104
Moustier de Bourgneuf, Auguste du, 153
Mühlmann, W., 2

N (unknown author), 184
Nägelin, J., 63
Naples, Trucardo de, 139
Naudé, 135, 183
Nephtaly, 91
Nogaret, Jean-Louis de, duc d'Epernon, 174
Nort, Isabeau de (Laubardemont's mother), 74
Nozay, Jacques, 83
Nyau, Jacques de, 153

On the Use of the Parts (Galen), 139
Oraison funèbre de Scevole de Sainte-Marthe, 54
Orléans, Gaston d', 133, 218

Panegyric (Trajan), 124
Paris, Yves de, 102
Pascal, 148
Pasquier, Jeanne, 93
Patience, Father, 176
Patin, Guy, 111, 116, 118
Paul, Saint, 62
Penault, 91

Penderecki, 6
Pequineau, 152
Perou, 92
Petrus, 18
Phélypeaux, Louis, 66, 71, 72, 152
Philippe de Saint-Joseph, 14
Philosophie occulte (Agrippa), 165
Pidoux, François, 129
Pierre Thomas de Saint-Charles, 14, 15
Pigray, 138
Pinette de Jésus, Sister, 89
Pliny, 124
Poétique (d'Orléans), 133
Poitiers, M. de, 194
Pollution, 91
Pomponazzi, Pietro, 130, 137
Poucquet, Sieur Jean, 77
Pratique du théâtre, 32
Protais, Father, 86
Protestants. *See* Huguenots

Quaestiones medico-legales, 33
Quillet, Claude, 124, 134, 135

Raisonnements sur la nature des esprits, 133
Ranfaing, Elisabeth de, 53
Rangier, Pierre, 14
Rasilly, Mlle de, 93, 145
Refutation de l'erreur du Vulgaire touchant les responses . . . , 148
Relation de la mort du père Tranquille (Eléazar), 194
Relation de tout ce que j'ai veu à Loudun . . . , 129
Relation d'une visite faite par D. pendant huit jours . . . , 211–12
Relation véritable de ce qui s'est passé aux exorcismes . . . , 209
Remarques et considérations servant à la justification . . . , 148
Rembrandt, 109, 116
Remy, Nicolas, 4
Renaudot, Théophraste, 70
Renée de Saint-Nicolas, 92
Requête (Lettre), 161
Ressès, Father, 213
Revol, 165
Richard, 152
Richelet, 95
Richelieu, 9, 26, 36, 58, 68–72, 74, 135, 168, 174, 190, 192, 194, 195, 199, 204, 205, 217, 219, 220
Rivarin, 152

Roatin, Sieur de Jorigny, 152, 154, 173
Roches, Michel Le Masle, Prior des, 105, 193, 194, 204
Rogier, Daniel, 20, 49, 50, 109, 112, 114, 128
Rondin, Jacques, Sieur de la Hoguetière, 69–70
Roth, 93
Rousseau, Father Gilbert, 165, 194
Rousseau, Mathurin, 14
Rueil, Claude de, 83

Sablé, Marquise de, 137
Saint Vincent de Paul, 195
Saint-Cyran, 35, 195
Saint-Donac Saint-Martin ("?"), M. de, 221
Sainte-Marthe, Scévole de, 53, 59
Saint-Jure, Father, 214
Saint-Sauveur Du Puy, M. de, 209
Sales, François de, 215
Sansfin, 91
Santeul, Jean de, 137
Sazilly, Sister Claire de Saint-Jean, née de, 17, 18, 49, 85, 104, 107, 115, 139, 140, 166
Séguier, Chancellor, 71, 75
Seguin, Dr., 64, 118, 122, 183
sentence en decret (Aug. 10, 1633), 165
Séraphique, 91
Silhon, Jean de, 147
Silly, Mesmin de, 66, 68, 74, 79, 161
Sister Catherine (de la Présentation). *See* Auffray
Sister des Anges. *See* Jeanne des Anges.
Sonneillon, 21
Sourdis, the Archbishop of, 163
Sourdis, Henri d'Escoubleau de, 36, 37
Souvillon, 92
Speculum inquisitionum (Desloix), 164
Spiritual Exercises (Loyola), 216
Sully, Duc de, 35
Surin, Father Jean-Joseph, 5, 8, 101, 145, 148–50, 184, 198–205, 207, 209, 212, 213, 217, 220, 225

Teresa of Avila, Saint, 223, 225, 226
Texier, 152, 154, 155, 171
Théâtre françois, 111
Theophrastes, 119
Thèses générales touchant les diables exorcisés (Tranquille), 158
Thibault, Marthe, 93
Thibault, Pierre, 21, 49

Thomas, Father, 197, 217
Thomas, Saint, 145, 147
Thomas Aquinas, Saint, 34, 148
Thoreau, Julien, 58
Topinambou, 121
Traicté du coelibat, 83
Traité de la mélancholie, 129
Trajan, 124
Tranquille, Father, 27, 83, 86, 127, 150,
    151, 158, 160, 165, 176, 190, 191, 193,
    196
Trincant, Louis, 58
Trincant, Philippe, 58
Triomphe des dames, Le, 104

Uriel, 14
Ursulines, 11, 12, 13, 23, 25, 37, 48, 68,
    71, 72, 73, 80, 89, 99, 100, 103, 112,
    114, 139, 154, 162, 164, 169, 170, 204,
    218, 223
Uvier, 138

Vallant, Dr. 137
Van Helmont, 45
Vanini, 130
Vendôme, François, 213
Verdier, Jan, 179
*Véritable relation des justes procédures observées
    . . .* (Tranquille), 150, 158, 161
Verrine, 21, 107
Vigny, Alfred de, 6
Ville, Maître Jean de la, 85
Villeneuve, M. de, 115
Visitandine Nuns, 222
Vitelleschi, Father, 212

Wars of Religion, 13

Yvelin, Dr., 117

Zabulon, 15, 19, 91
Zacchias, Paul, 33